THE QUEST

Keys to Unlocking the Mysteries of Humanity

Dr. Cheryl Bauman

By unfolding the pages of this book, discover the supernatural truths that will unlock the mysteries of humanity.

THE QUEST

Keys to Unlocking the Mysteries of Humanity

DR. CHERYL BAUMAN

The Quest: Keys to Unlocking the Mysteries of Humanity by Dr Cheryl Bauman
Copyright © 2025 by Cheryl Bauman
All Rights Reserved.
ISBN: 978-1-59755-855-6
Published by: ADVANTAGE BOOKS™, Orlando, FL, www.advbookstore.com

All Rights Reserved. This book and parts thereof may not be reproduced in any form, stored in a retrieval system or transmitted in any form by any means (electronic, mechanical, photocopy, recording or otherwise) without prior written permission of the author, except as provided by United States of America copyright law.

Scriptures marked NIV are taken from THE HOLY BIBLE, NEW INTERNATIONAL VERSION ®. Copyright© 1973, 1978, 1984, 2011 by Biblica, Inc.™. Used by permission of Zondervan

Scriptures marked ESV are taken from the THE HOLY BIBLE, ENGLISH STANDARD VERSION ® Copyright © 2001 by Crossway, a publishing ministry of Good News Publishers. Used by permission.

Scriptures marked NKJV are taken from the NEW KING JAMES VERSION®. Copyright© 1982 by Thomas Nelson, Inc. Used by permission. All rights reserved.

Scripture quotations marked (GNB) and (GNT) are taken from the GOOD NEWS BIBLE© 1994 published by the Bible Societies/HarperCollins Publishers Ltd UK, Good News Bible© American Bible Society 1966, 1971, 1976, 1992. Used with permission.

Scripture quotations marked (NLT) are taken from the Holy Bible, New Living Translation, copyright ©1996, 2004, 2015 by Tyndale House Foundation. Used by permission of Tyndale House Publishers, Carol Stream, Illinois 60188. All rights reserved.

Scriptures marked KJV are taken from the KING JAMES VERSION, public domain.

Library of Congress Catalog Number: APPLIED FOR

Name:	Bauman, Cheryl, Author
Title:	***The Quest: Keys to Unlocking the Mysteries of Humanity***
	Dr. Cheryl Bauman
	Advantage Books, 2025
Identifiers:	Paperback: 9781597558556
	eBook: 9781597558693
Subjects: Books ›	Religion: Christian Life – Inspirational

First Printing: November 2025
25 26 27 28 29 30   10 9 8 7 6 5 4 3 2 1

Dedication

To my beautiful and magnificent daughter, Sara. You are the gift that keeps on giving. Every day is an adventure with you; your energy, your joy, your wit, and your compassion are an abundant blessing reflecting God's loving goodness. I love you to the moon and back! (xo)27 Mamma.

To the Creator of Heaven and Earth, who relentlessly pursues all of us with His loving-kindness, mercy, and grace.

Dr. Cheryl Bauman

Introduction

All of humanity in all cultures, places and times have sought out the mysteries of THE QUEST. People have done this through experience, emotionalism, experimentation, trying to add logical reasoning to it, and seeking out a higher being so these four letters...this one word...*LOVE*...bears meaning in their lives, and brings greater happiness.

Countless love stories are written in novel form and acted out on the big screen. Humans have a deep longing to quench the greatest internal desire. We want to "feel full", to "fill-up" the hollow void. You might be asking, *what will satisfy my emptiness?* It is only normal we are all questing after happiness and love, to diffuse the torment of emptiness. To seek after happiness and love is a natural inborn human desire. Unfortunately, the QUEST led some to become addicted to finding true love at all costs, and the price they paid has been dear.

If you believe in unlocking the mysteries of the QUEST and have the desire to belong and be loved unconditionally, ask yourself, *where did my search start and how do I think it will end? Is the mysterious answer found in one human being? Do I believe one person can fan the flame of true unconditional love forever and ever?* If you do, consider these facts: approximately 50 percent of marriages end in divorce, while another 10 to 15 percent of couples permanently separate leaving 7 percent to report they remain in unsatisfying unions. These disheartening statistics show only 3 in 10 couples end up happily married. What a bleak reality! As relationship experts note, if people want to make love last, they should focus less on chemistry and more on compatibility. If we choose to listen to the experts, then *what makes us compatible with another human being? Is compatibility the key to unlocking the mysteries of true unconditional love?*

Pondering the compatibility factor, I would contend I am of the same mind as the writer of the famous hit song *Lookin' for Love*.

How about you? Have you been questing for love, yet lookin' for it in all the wrong places? Do you expect one single human being to satisfy this unquenchable desire to love and be loved? Is this even a realistic expectation to place on one person? I would suggest looking for one person to fill all our "love needs" is a major factor why we see such a soaring rate of divorce in our nations. As well as broken relationships among parents, kids, grandparents, friends, and relatives. Society is feeding us false idealism as it perpetuates the belief what everyone is longing for is a true lasting love found in the union of two hearts. *Are you expecting too much from your spouse or partner? Are your dreams of true unconditional love broken because another human is not perfect, as they are incapable of meeting all your expectations? Where has this belief stemmed from, that one human being can meet all your needs in terms of love? Is it even realistic to place such an expectation on one person? Is it fair others would impose such an expectation on you?*

The pages of this book will help you to uncover the many complexities associated with unlocking the mysteries of your QUEST to discover what true lasting love is and where to find it. It will also help you to decide if you are placing too much faith in people to fill the emptiness within your soul. Many people are seeking others to fill the void and to bring them true happiness, when no one on this earth can perform such a feat. Many try, yet in our humanity, we all fail at some time or another. Even when fully committed to filling up your partner or your child's life with true unconditional love, all of us suffer from the human condition of being imperfect. None of us can meet all our loved ones' desires and needs. We are a flawed species.

Romeo and Juliet, Samson and Delilah, and King David and Bathsheba all of these were love stories, yet they were engulfed in the addictive QUEST to find true romantic love at any cost. Each one of these stories was tainted with tragedy, and the characters paid dearly for their unbridled QUEST for love. So, the questions beg to be asked: *Is finding true love worth it at any cost? What should these historical figures have been seeking after to find true, pure, unconditional love that would fill the empty void in their lives? The cost of true love is great. How many of you have paid a steep ransom like that of Samson and Delilah or King David and Bathsheba, to try unlocking the mysteries of the QUEST? Yet the results have been devastating and long-suffering!*

> *We are all questing a LOVE to complete us and to make us whole. This is part of every human being; it is how we are all designed.*

I encourage you to read through the pages of this book, stop and meditate on the content. If you do, I believe you will discover the mysteries of humanity to unlock the truth as to how, *what, where, when,* and *why* true unconditional love can be obtained in all its splendor and glory! My hope is as you read you can wave good-bye to heartache, yesterday's brokenness, and instead choose to step out in courage, finally putting to rest your QUEST to unlock the mysteries of humanity.

Please note this book will not address the symptoms of addictions in our lives. Although throughout, I will direct you to seek wise, Godly counsel, and to attend a Bible-based church. The focus of this book seeks to ensure you are aware of the importance of addressing your spiritual nature and allowing God to make you whole from the "inside" to the "outside". I believe all of us daily need to be made new as we allow God to take our hearts of stone and soften them into spirit-filled and spirit-led hearts.

> *I will give you a new heart and put a new spirit within you; I will take the heart of stone out of your flesh and give you a heart of flesh. I will put My Spirit within you and cause you to walk in My statutes, and you will keep My judgments and do them (Ezekiel 36:26-27, NKJV).*

Dr. Cheryl Bauman

Acknowledgments

I recognize I am not an island, and I am forever grateful to the many people who helped me on this journey. Your lives and your love are such an inspirational blessing to me. I am humbled by the kindness and compassion of so many.

To my beloved sister in Christ, Jill Sell. I do not even have adequate words to describe Jill's tender heart, her unwavering faith in the unseen and her God-given wisdom. I could not have completed this project without Jill's prayers and faithful friendship. Christine Lockie, who is a mom, a teacher as well as a meticulous editor. I have only mentioned a few of Christine's roles and God given talents. When I first met Christine, we clicked right away. It was not until months after our first encounter that I discovered she is a teacher, as am I. I then understood why God brought us together for such a time as this. I so appreciate Christine's editorial eyes and words of wisdom as she graciously poured over the pages of this book, providing me with sound advice and much needed correction.

To Mariola Musial, my longtime friend and wise counselor. Even though there are many kilometers that separate us in the physical realm, in the supernatural realm we are united! Mariola, you can provide a distinct perspective that sets you apart and is a welcome addition to my life. Thank you for your honesty, for your mercy, and for your love. I always know you have my best interests at heart! Mariola kindly read through the pages of this book and provided necessary edits – thank you, thank you, thank you! To Georgia and Alan, you two are a gorgeous gift in my life. Every day I thank God for both of you. Your witty sense of humor, your timely discerning messages, and your continual belief in me propped me up on occasions when situations in life have not been so kind. Thanks to the two of you for loving me, when I was "raw". Thank you for being honest with me, because I know through your wise wisdom you care for me. Thank you for being authentic and real! Every time I leave your presence I leave lighter, and better! Both Mariola and Georgia are my "sisters" from "another mother".

The acknowledgements would not be complete without thanking my parents for loving me and for pointing me in the direction as to how to obtain eternal life. Mom and dad, through the love of the Father in Heaven, you chose to spend countless hours of your time teaching and guiding me in the ways of God. I do not know where I would be now if I was not taught the word of God by the two of you. What an eternal testimony of unconditional love! To my beautiful and magnificent daughter Sara. You are the gift that keeps on giving. Every day is an adventure with you as we unwrap the surprises of God's goodness. Your life and your love are such a blessing to me. I am in awe as to the gorgeous young woman you are on the inside and the outside. You continuously radiate forth the light of God's love for all the world to see!

I am aware I had many additional cheerleaders standing strong in faith as I endured this QUEST. I am aware I have not named all of you. I want to thank everyone who poured their heart and wise advice into this book as well as into my life. I am so grateful God has been the steadfast anchor in all these relationships, as we are united by His unconditional love.

I love all of you with the love of our Lord and Savior Jesus Christ,

Cheryl (xo)27.

Table of Contents

DEDICATION 5

INTRODUCTION 7

ACKNOWLEDGMENTS 11

TABLE OF CONTENTS 13

#1: I AM LOVABLE 15
Key 1: The Great Pretenders.. 17
Key 2: Just Believe 21
Key 3: The Journey To Lovableness 25
Key 4: Breakout Of Old Thought Patterns 28
Key 5: What Does The Bible Say About You Being Lovable?........................ 33
Unlocking Mystery #1: I Am Lovable! 36

#2: I AM LOVABLE JUST AS I AM 37
Key 6: Body Image Starts In The Mind, Not In The Mirror 39
Key 7: Searching For Mr. Or Mrs. Right... 42
Key 8: Lookin' For Love In All The Wrong Places 46
Key 9: Wise Navigation: Detecting Obstacles And Jumping Over Hurdles 48
Key 10: What Does The Bible Say About Loving Yourself Just As You Are? 51
Unlocking Mystery #2: I Am Lovable Just As I Am 55

#3: I BELONG 57
Key 11: The Power Of 1 and The Power Of 3.. 59
Key 12: Trust Is Paramount.. 63
Key 13: Love Actually 66
Key 14: The Greek Love Language.. 68
Key 15: What Does The Bible Say About Belonging To The Family Of God?....... 88
Unlocking Mystery #3: I Belong 91

#4: TRUE LOVE DOES NOT DEPEND ON FEELINGS 93
Key 16: He Loves Me, He Loves Me Not; She Loves Me, She Loves Me Not 95
Key 17: Is Love A Feel-Good Potion?.. 97
Key 18: Three Phases Of Love.. 99
Key 19: Have You Lost That *Lovin'* Feeling? 103
Key 20: What Does The Bible Say About Basing Relationships On That "Lovin Feeling"? 106
Unlocking Mystery #4: True Love Does Not Depend On Feelings 111

#5: I CAN BELIEVE IN THE IMPOSSIBLE 113
Key 21: Private Pain.. 115
Key 22: Heart-To-Heart... 117

Key 23: Peace In Times Of Trouble 121
Key 24: Don't Underestimate The Power Of The Impossible 126
Key 25: What Does The Bible Say About How You Can Believe In The Impossible? 132
Unlocking Mystery #5: I Can Believe In The Impossible 136

#6: PERFECT LOVE CASTS OUT CONFUSION 137
Key 26: Do Your Words Really Mean What I Think They Do? 139
Key 27: Time Spent At Home Versus Time Spent Elsewhere 143
Key 28: Can Anything Be Done About This Couple Crisis? 145
Key 29: Suffering From Confusion? 149
Key 30: What Does The Bible Say About Confusing Lust With Love? 156
Unlocking Mystery #6: Perfect Love Casts Out Confusion 164

#7: BETRAYAL IS A REFLECTION OF THEIR CHARACTER, NOT YOURS 165
Key 31: Just In Time 167
Key 32: Betrayal Takes On Many Forms 172
Key 33: Do You Believe In God's Rescue Plan? 175
Key 34: The Giant Of Pride Keeps You From God's Perfect Plan 178
Key 35: What Does The Bible Say About Betrayal And Loving Those Who Betray You? .. 184
Unlocking Mystery #7: Betrayal Is A Reflection Of Their Character, Not Yours 190

#8: FREEDOM IS FOUND IN FORGIVENESS 195
Key 36: Stuck In The Moment 197
Key 37: Must I Love My Enemies? 203
Key 38: Final Surrender 209
Key 39: Unlovely, Loving 213
Key 40: What Does The Bible Say About The Importance Of Forgiveness And Freedom? 219
Unlocking Mystery #8: Freedom Is Found In Forgiveness 224
The Lord's Prayer 225

#9: GOD IS LOVE 227
Key 41: Never-Ending Love Story 229
Key 42: God's Relentless Pursuit Of You 231
Key 43: Do You Believe In The Goodness Of God's Love? 236
Key 44: God Is The Lover Of Your Soul 241
Key 45: The Bible Says Your Quest Can Be Over 243
Unlocking Mystery #9: God Is Love 246

AFTERWORD 249

BIBLIOGRAPHY 251

#1

I Am Lovable

Accept and fall in love with self. Smile and let others know that they are accepted. It's contagious acceptance - Georgia Morissette.

Dr. Cheryl Bauman

Key 1

The Great Pretenders

Kyle always looked so picture-perfect. He was impeccably dressed, and his hair was immaculately styled. In public places, he spoke with such eloquence and kindness. He would laugh often and freely compliment others. Kyle was perfect, or so it seemed. The perfect employee, the perfect friend, the perfect boyfriend and eventually the perfect husband. Yet, the more I got to know Kyle, he began to reveal the cracks in his *perfectness*. Unfortunately, he had anger boiling just below the surface. It was often unleashed in a passive aggressive way. Kyle's anger was set ablaze intentionally on those with whom he knew he had power over, particularly in personal relationships. Every day, as he prepared to go to work, he would hide his true self by placing on a mask. This well-crafted mask successfully covered up the scars that were the results of deep wounds proceeding from years of mistreatment by others.

Regrettably, Kyle was unable to find intimacy and a sense of belonging in a one-partner relationship due to the childhood abuse suffered at the hands of those who should have been his safety net. His parents saw relationships as objects, and he quickly learned to mimic them. Kyle was taught to view a spouse as the enemy, as disposable. Strife was a constant part of his childhood home, and so this strife stuck around and clouded his adult relationships and marriages. Kyle did not know anything different; this was a normal way of functioning for him. He went from one relationship to the next, unsatisfied. He married a few times, but always had extramarital affairs, hoping to finally find relief and completeness in the perfect woman. If he was honest with himself, he really did not know what he was questing after. Kyle thought his QUEST would end once he found Mrs. Right. Hopping in and out of unsatisfying relationships, he would leave a wake of devastation behind. As the bomb would go off in the backdrop of his life, Kyle would carefully place his mask back on, continuing his QUEST. A spouse or partner to him was easily tossed aside.

The meticulously sculpted disguise worn by this man only hid the outside world from his pain and suffering. Partners with whom he desired to find true, lasting, unconditional love, confusingly discovered he was incapable of surrendering and being open to the vulnerability a marriage relationship needs. Due to pride, Kyle never wanted to take off the mask, because behind it was brokenness and pain. His QUEST was for an intimate loving relationship with another person, yet it was the QUEST for love and intimacy that kept forcing the mask to be pried off, exposing his weaknesses. This raw vulnerability was too overwhelming for him, as he believed he could just "stuff down" the past, as it was too painful to admit. Kyle never wanted anyone to see his flaws, as his mind tricked him into believing he needed to always appear perfect.

The pictures he posted on social media showed his relationships as fun loving. Sadly, this image of his life was an intentional and well-constructed lie. Living in proximity with a spouse unveiled his less than perfect self. Kyle's partners saw his flaws, such as addictions to pornography, continual extramarital affairs, lying, deception and gaslighting. Instead of humbling himself and dealing with his private pain, pride helped him craftily cloak his flaws by flaunting those of his partners'. He would often exaggerate, or make-up lies about his partners' faults, just to escape confessing and taking accountability for his own shortcomings. Kyle would go to great lengths to condemn his partners and slander them to others around him. Even with his own family members who abused him, he would join them by feasting on the juicy morsels of gossip, heaped with extra helpings of slander. His family loved to gossip and mock others; it was all they knew. Kyle's family bonded by bullying others, by putting others down, so they felt better about themselves. *Hurt people hurt others.*

Kyle received great negative strength and power by condemning the person who should have been his confidant and his soul mate. Playing the victim, by covering up his lies, garnered Kyle with support from those around him. People would rally with him, believing the untruths Kyle told, as his relationships dissolved one after the other. In the beginning it was easy to believe this man, as he presented himself as picture-perfect. It was easy to believe he was the victim being wronged by women. In the beginning it was easy for others to blame the women in his life, as he continued to masquerade falsities. Kyle acted out his life on an unrealistic stage of cover-up and condemnation. However, as the years progressed and Kyle was unable to deal with the deep pain and hurt from an abusive childhood, his broken life started to unravel and expose him for who he really was. The mask was dissolving, uncovering deep despair, isolation, and loneliness.

Unfortunately, Kyle's story is an all too familiar story in today's world.

There are people on this earth today who are just like Kyle, walking around with masks on, disguising private pain. They are actors and actresses on the stage of a fantasy existence, flying about on a magic carpet ride, never wanting to land. For landing would ground them back into a painful reality. So instead, they pretend to be someone they are not, skillfully fooling unsuspecting people just long enough to enter a relationship or a marriage union. Yet once united with another person, their partners are intentionally abused by them. The mask is only able to cover certain aspects of their lives. Living with these pretenders, day in and day out, inevitably exposes their painful blemishes.

The pretenders are stifled by intimacy, as they are incapable of loving themselves let alone loving another human. At times the pretenders can fake being loving and kind, through manipulation and deceit. Unfortunately, though, their endgame is to get what they want and need at any cost. At other times this well-crafted mask falls off, exposing the naked truth, the abusive pain from the past that haunts and grips them. It is the fear of intimacy, of being real and of exposing their less than perfectness that upholds their pretense. Pain and love are so closely associated, when faced with developing an intimate relationship with another person, they are incapable of doing so. Failure is not perfection, and so the pretender must cover up the failure, as they believe the only way to keep control is to wear the flawless mask of perfection out in public. The truth is unconditional love and belonging are what the pretenders are questing, they just don't know it, or where to find it.

Kyle's story is tragic, yet it is an unfortunate reality for some people in today's world. Some of you reading this book may resonate with Kyle's story as you have a version of love that has been rooted in suffering caused by many broken, unsatisfying relationships. You may be continually trying to unearth true love through multiple pleasurable experiences, or addictive behaviors that often start out as enjoyable. However, at the end of it all, you find yourself mired in mud, empty and lost, seeking out the next, and the next, and the next, pleasurable experience. You may be suffering from the pain caused by a parent who throughout your childhood continually belittled you. You may be suffering from a broken heart due to the betrayal of an unfaithful partner. While others of you may be suffering from the pain of watching your parents argue and fight as addictive behaviors controlled them. Addictive behaviors such as over-eating, not eating, alcoholism, gambling, drugs, adultery, or pornography, lead to a lonely and dead-end life. These addictive behaviors often have negative repercussions on the lives of those near the addict.

Throughout this book I will continually direct you to seek wise Godly counsel, and to attend a Bible-based church. However, the message as you journey to unlock the mysteries of your QUEST, is to delve into the importance of getting fixed at the "foundation" of your life. It is not about "fixing" the symptoms. This book is about acknowledging, accepting and adjusting to the root of the problems and ridding your life of them! The expected outcome of this book is to help you develop a "new heart". Jesus came to this earth to give all of us a "new heart". He came to take our hearts of stone and to make them soft and pliable. Having a new heart is only possible through allowing impartation of love by the Great Physician.

Whatever your past or present situation is, know the entire human race is on a QUEST for the keys to unlock the mysteries of humanity and to discover it at any cost; many of us just do not know it! We were all created out of love, to love, and to be loved. While seeking it, some of us settle and accept the love we think we deserve. We do this because we feel unworthy, and possibly many of us are unaware as to why we are making the wrong choices in relation to love. Yet something deep down inside is saying, *you are worthy of much more.* This *still small voice* is declaring you deserve to be loved unconditionally. It is telling you not to settle for anything less. So, as mysterious as it may be, I encourage you to continue your QUEST.

In the past, you may have compromised because you did not believe you deserved genuine love. Right now, you might be fumbling around in the dark, desperately trying to unlock the truth, in hopes of ending your QUEST. You may think true love is impossible to have here on earth. Doubt crowds your mind, causing you to lock the door to love and throw away the key. Your heart is hardened by hurtful memories, and you want nothing at all to do with love. Loneliness, bitterness, and rage have become your new best friends. You are hanging out in cold, dark, damp places, afraid to ever risk getting close to the warmth and security true love offers. Rejection rules. Yet emptiness is so difficult to bear, life has become nothing more than day-to-day drudgery.

What will the turning point be for you to finally accept the love you were created to have?

Key 2

Just Believe

Do you believe you are lovable? Do you believe you are worthy of being loved? Do you believe you can find true unconditional love on your own? If you believe you can fill the void, you might be filling the emptiness through addictive behaviors to alcohol, drugs, gambling, over working, excessive eating, under eating, pornography, adultery, abusive relationships, co-dependent relationships, or overindulgent spending. All of us want the world to think we are okay, even if we are not. So, we frantically try hiding our problems, and the results of our stress may manifest through behaviors such as overdrinking, overspending, or overeating, hoping the pain will be numbed, and the void will be filled. The sad reality is that our addictions only make the void larger, deeper and darker. Unfortunately, if we choose addictions to try to fill the void, we can become increasingly lost in hopelessness. The truth is, the agonizing pain of covering up our issues is exasperated by our addictions, not solved by them.

The desire to love and be loved may be so intense that you try to intellectualize love in your head. You do this as you do not believe true love is even available to you because you do not believe you are lovable. Especially if you suffer from addictions, whether you admit it or not, these addictions are "masking up" the real issue which is an unquenchable QUEST to be lovable and to be loved. Maybe your confidence has hit rock bottom as the addictions overtake you. *Are you struggling with intimacy, and relying on an addiction to fill the void? If so, are you able to admit it, or are you still into justifying and covering up your actions? Like Kyle, are you able to hide your addictions most of the time by putting on a fake mask to coverup the pain caused by drugs, alcohol, gambling, adultery, pornography, overworking or overeating? Are "cracks" starting to appear on your self-constructed mask?*

You may not believe you are lovable because of thought patterns tricking you into believing it is necessary to take part in addictive behaviors, so you are lovable and worthy of love.

Excuses are easy, but lethal. Accountability and honesty are difficult, but healthy.

I encourage you to ask yourself the following questions, *what will it take for me to be free from the pain and suffering created by dysfunctional patterns of thoughts? How can I rid myself of my past hurts that have been caused by destructive acts and words? Can I admit my thoughts are flawed and imperfect? How can I finally be set free from all the pain and negative thought patterns and false beliefs I have about myself which led to unhealthy addictions?*

Right at this moment as you are reading these words, my hope is they resonate within your innermost being, making you aware they are speaking truth into your life. Just believing these negative thoughts and the people who damaged you and caused you to believe you are unlovable are wrong. You are created in the image of God and loved by God. All good things come from God, and you came from God. God designed you with abilities, skills, a purpose, and a destiny to fulfill on this earth. God's plans for you are to prosper you and not to destroy you. I encourage you to seek out the truth found in God's word and the truth will set you free!

I encourage you to challenge these negative thoughts about yourself you believed. Possibly you believed falsities about yourself for many years, thus these negative thought patterns are well-engrained in your brain. Know and admit these thoughts are false. Replace these condemning thoughts with truth. The truth is you are created with a purpose and a destiny only you can fulfill. You have been given a special assignment for this time in history. God chose you to be born for such as time as this! Believe the only lasting truth is found in the word of God, which is the Bible. You may have hidden talents that still need to be uncovered and discovered. The world is waiting for you to blossom; your destiny awaits you!

Reflect on the following:

- Is it worth carrying awful memories around in your thought-life, as added baggage, listening to the play-by-play in your mind day-after-day, year- after-year?

- Are you filling the void and trying to forget these painful memories through addictive behaviors such as drugs, alcohol, overspending, overeating, pornography, or gambling?

- Have negative thought patterns become so engrained into your mind they are now the essence of your very being, speaking lies and telling you that you are not lovable?

- What good are these lies to you? Have they ever helped you out for one minute, or have they just been a heavyweight you are carrying around?

- Do you believe it would be wonderful to be free from the weight of the emotional baggage holding you back from loving yourself and others?

- It is possible to live the life you were created to live, filled with hope and promise. You might be asking, how is this possible?

First, you must believe you are lovable before you can know, understand, and experience what true unconditional love is.

Studies show people often genuinely care for others more than they care for themselves. Caring for self is self-love. Self-love is believing you are worth it because you are. Self-love is not selfish; it is valuing you and the person you are designed to be. So do not feel guilty when you take care of you! It is important to your health and well-being. Treat yourself as if you are important and you care for you! Monitor how you value others you love and care for. *How can you treat yourself as you treat others you love and care for? What can you do to change these thought patterns around and believe you are worth it and you are worthy of love and to be loved?*

Studies prove when a mother takes her child to the doctor and is prescribed medicine, in most cases, the mother ensures the medication is properly administered, and the child takes all of it. However, when a mother is not feeling well, she will often not take the time to go to the doctor. Or if she does go to the doctor and the doctor prescribes medication, she will only administer the proper dosages to 50% the required amount. Many of us do not practice self-love and take care of our essential needs linked to our own health and well-being. If we are not physically, emotionally and spiritually healthy, it is impossible to take care of others around us. If this is you, *what changes do you need to make so you can genuinely care for you, like you genuinely care for others?* You are worth it! You are lovable!

Dr. Cheryl Bauman

God's word instructs us in new commandments found in Matthew 22:31 (NIV), *"The second (commandment) is this: 'Love your neighbor as yourself'. There is no commandment greater than these."* We are to love others like we love ourselves. *However, if we do not love ourselves, how are we able to love others?*

Key 3

The Journey to Lovableness

You may wonder if it is ever possible for you to develop new ways of thinking about yourself. It is important you do so that you take care of you, to care for and love others. You need to believe you are lovable. Dr. Caroline Leaf shares with us very good news in her bestselling book *Switch on Your Brain*. Dr. Leaf suggests we can train our brain to rewire itself. Your brain does not just absorb information; it also rewires itself in response to certain repeated activities and experiences. This is known as neuroplasticity. If you suffered abuse because of a relationship or relationships in your life, you may allow negative thought patterns to connect love and pain together. The result being your brain has selectively transformed itself to respond negatively to love. Your negative response to love may be without your awareness, as your brain wired itself to default to these engrained patterns of thinking and behaving due to the abuse and rejection you suffered. Not being truly loved or having a real sense of belonging may have left you insecure. Yet, amid much confusion and pain, you are still questing true, unconditional love, as something deep within you is "knowing" it is possible. You feel relentless tugging to aim for true love.

Due to the neuroplasticity of your brain, it is vitally important to understand the monumental effects as to the choices you make. Especially in connection with what you feed your mind, body, and spirit as to what you believe to be truth. These beliefs, which are thought patterns, affect your entire being – mind, body, and spirit. Your thoughts develop the information highways in your brain. As a result of repeated activities, your brain selectively transforms itself in response to certain experiences, be they negative or positive. If you are continually being treated unkindly by others, you will start to form thought patterns and beliefs you are not lovable. If your thoughts associate pain and love together, due to confusing messages by ill meaning people, your brain reorganizes. It builds structures and connections to respond in this negative manner by telling you that you are not lovable. And that love is painful! Within the brains of many who have experienced years of abuse and rejection are manufactured neural pathways feeding your thoughts to believe love, rejection, and pain are related.

As a result of these entrenched thought patterns, you may be consciously or unconsciously dismissing any notion of love or how to love. This is because what you thought was love has hurt you deeply. Due to these false ways of thinking, you may be at a point in your life you are unable to believe you are lovable. And as a result, you cannot love yourself or others the way God created you to love. I challenge you to honestly reflect on what voices you are listening to – both inside your head as well as the voices of others. If you believe in lies you are not lovable, know this is not the truth, you are lovable. You were created by God to love and to be loved. *If you believe these lies, how then can you arrive at a point where you can believe you are lovable?*

If you desire to rid yourself of painful and hurtful thoughts haunting you and instead believe and say *I Am Lovable*, then I challenge you to continue the QUEST to wholeness and health. Do this by developing new thought patterns about yourself with the help of God. Seeking to be healthy and whole will require you to accept and accept you are lovable. It will require of you to "retrain your brain" into thinking and believing you are lovable. It will require you to "take down the walls of protection" you have built up around yourself to guard against hurt. You might be afraid to "tear down the walls". For when these walls come down, you may think you will be more vulnerable. But this is not true. Instead, with God's help, if you develop healthy patterns of thinking, and healthy relationships, you will be able to interact with people on a spiritual, social and emotional level you were originally created for.

Possibly you have been so hurt by the church, or some people in the church, you are unable to step through the doors of one. If this is you, I challenge you to begin reading the word of God every day in the confines of your own space. Search out scriptures that talk about God's love towards you. Talk to God out loud just like you are talking to a friend or speak to Him quietly in your thoughts. He is only a thought or a word away. You need not travel far to find God. He is right there with you all the time; He never leaves you. Even if you do not believe it, I challenge you for the next 21 days to speak to God every single day. Ask God to show you His love and to help reveal to you the negative patterns of thinking holding you captive. I promise you He will show you truth if you are willing to listen. I encourage you to seek out a journey with God by your side. If you commit to this 21-day renewal process your mind will transform.

Do not conform any longer to the pattern of this world but be transformed by renewing of your mind. Then you will be able to test and approve what God's will is--his good, pleasing, and perfect will (Romans 12:2 NIV).

What does this verse mean to transform your mind? Ask yourself, *are you living your best life?* If the answer to this question is no, then shifting your thought patterns and focus can change your life. That is what Romans 12:2 is all about. It calls you to renew your mind. Renewing your mind can be accomplished by changing the way you think about yourself and others with the end goal of creating a better life for yourself, a life that honors God. Always remember, as enticing as it may seem, the world wants you to conform to their patterns of thinking. These patterns are anti-God, and they will lead to a broken life.

In the process of renewing your mind, I also challenge you to choose to meditate on the word of God (found in the Bible), day and night for 21 days. I promise if you allow the word of God to penetrate through you, it will drive out fear. The word of God will also drive out misconceptions you set in in your brain feeding you lies. Change the lies and rid yourself of the toxicity taking up space in your mind. Replace these thoughts with the truth found in the word of God. You do not have to spend the rest of your life with where your life began or where it is now. If you choose to meditate on the word of God, continually marinating your spirit, body, and mind with the spirit of truth, you will finish your days on this earth as a victor not a victim.

Lastly, find a Christian counselor, whose beliefs and values are solely based on the true living word of God, to work with you on your journey from pain to receiving the promises of God. God's promises are enveloped in perfect love. Reach out and receive them. They are there for you. You are lovable, and you were created to be blessed with the promises of God. Seek out people who can help you know and believe you are lovable. Surround yourself with only positive influences within your inner circle. As Dr. Leaf contests through solid evidence, you can train your brain to think good and loving thoughts about yourself. But none of us can do this on our own.

Seek support. Find support. Engage support.

Key 4

Breakout of Old Thought Patterns

Researchers have found the frequency of small positive thoughts and actions matter most in terms of changing your way of thinking and being. Repetition and habit-forming behaviors on a frequent basis are what will change the voices you are choosing to listen to. Occasional big positive experiences do have an influence, but they do not make the necessary impact on your brain to override the tilt to negativity. It takes frequent small positive experiences to tip the scales towards belief in yourself and towards happier, healthier thoughts, which lead to overall positive wellbeing. It is intentionally developing positive thoughts about yourself, regardless of the circumstances. It is valuing and believing in you! It is placing importance on loving you and caring for you. This is not selfish behavior; this is essential behavior. Before you can genuinely love others, you need to love and value yourself. If changing your view of yourself is important to you, then I encourage you to start to develop self-regulatory behaviors that recognize and remove negative thoughts and to replace them with positive, uplifting, truthful thoughts. It is important to train your mind to tilt towards positivity, not negativity. Ask yourself the following:

- What other choices do you have? Well one choice is you can remain stuck forever in a cycle of thinking and believing you are not lovable.
- How have these negative thought patterns worked out for you so far?
- Is this what you want for the rest of your life, to remain in the mire of believing you are unloved and not lovable?
- What steps do you need to take on the road to recovery to believe you are lovable and you are loved?

Doubt or feeling unworthy may be gripping you and keeping your unhealthy thought patterns cemented in your mind. These ways of thinking negatively about yourself are all you know. Your current ways of thinking are normal for you and to change will mean admitting there is a problem, and to adjust by changing the way you are currently thinking. Fear and feelings of unworthiness can really seize you when you are trying to change. I challenge you to step out from the hold that fear and failure have on you, as this is a false comfort zone. I encourage you to listen to the VOICE of truth saying, "*Do not be afraid, do not be discouraged*" (Deuteronomy 31:8 NIV).

I encourage you to name the GIANTS in your life that are speaking lies to you. As I would bet some of the GIANTS' names are shame, guilt, abuse, adulterer, alcoholic, gambler, drug addict, over-spender, over-eater, workaholic, or gossiper. These GIANTS only speak lies; they do not know how to speak truth. *What lies are these GIANTS telling you? Are they mocking you? Are they reminding you of the times you failed, and lying to you by suggesting you will never be whole and victorious?* Remember Satan does not know how to tell the truth, he only knows how to tempt, deceive, manipulate, and accuse.

Listen to the song "The Voice of Truth" recorded by Casting Crowns (written by Mark Hall and Steven Curtis Chapman). It really sums this up.

Joel Osteen's ministry has greatly impacted my life. Joel is always encouraging people to listen to the words we are speaking and to choose to speak words of God's blessings over our lives and the lives of others. If you do not want to continue believing the lies you tell yourself whispered to you by the GIANTS in your life, I challenge you to say out loud 21 times a day for 21 days:

- I am lovable.
- I am loved by God.
- I love all people, and I am loved by all people.
- I am a victor not a victim.

I also recommend you take this list, print it out and post it around your house in common places where you can regularly see it. This list will act as a reminder to declare these powerful truths over your life. I also encourage you to add to this list, the "I Am's" meaningful to you.

You might wonder, *how can I live a victorious life?* It can only be carried out by believing it is possible, developing the habit of intentionally declaring truths over your life, as you walk with God by faith and not by sight. I encourage you to:

- Speak your truth. Resist speaking negatively about yourself.
- Speak to those future dreams and goals as if they are already here.
- Envision yourself happy, healthy, and whole.
- Stop allowing the GIANTS in your life to use your mind, body, and spirit as a garbage dump.
- Stop meditating and focusing on the negative things the GIANTS try to offer to you.

I also encourage you to visualize yourself as:

- Being a winner.
- Being lovable.
- Being worthwhile.
- Being worthy of being cared for.

Visualization is an important step in this process of knowing you are lovable. It helps you "see" yourself as lovable and as worthy. According to the Cambridge Dictionary, visualization is "the act of visualizing something or someone" or "forming a picture of it in your mind". It is like looking through a particular lens, your imagination, and seeing your life unfold within your inner eye. Your mind is powerful. Once you allow God to direct your thoughts through guidance by the Holy Spirit, God provides you with the true image of who He created you to be. Know you are beautifully and wonderfully made. You are LOVEABLE. Muhammad Ali's famous quote, *"If my mind can conceive it and my heart can believe it – then I can achieve it"* shows he believed in the power of visualization to help him achieve his goals.

Make a conscious choice to do away with parts of the old you that held you back from believing you are lovable. Visualize yourself as lovable and believe it with all your heart! Decide today to be of strong mind, and to be of good courage and to be continually talking and listening to the Lord. It is essential to build up a strong mind and to have strong faith. In essence you need to develop spiritual muscles that are powerfully supernatural. You cannot do this alone, you need to rely on God's supernatural power and on others around you who are rooted and grounded in the true faith of God, based on Biblical principles. If you do not have others around you who are rooted and grounded in faith, pray to meet people who are. Find a good Bible-based church. Speak with the pastor and counselors at the church. They will be able to guide you and support you. As well, it is vitally important you daily read the word of God, reflect, and be motivated by what the Holy Spirit is speaking to you through the truth found in scriptures. The word of God will transform your mind. Replace old thought patterns with scriptures from the Bible.

You might not have a Bible. If you have a cell phone, which most people do nowadays, you can download the Bible App free of charge. Just "google", Bible App, and it will bring you to the Bible App. If you do not have a phone to download the free Bible App and you would like a Bible, I encourage you to contact a local church and ask them for a Bible.

My people are destroyed from lack of knowledge (Hosea 4:6 NIV).

These tasks may be more difficult for some of you, as the GIANTS in your life may appear to be large and unmovable. But if you want freedom from negative thought patterns and negative voices, you need to develop new neural pathways in your brain. Override the old patterns, speak new truths, visualize new truths, listen to the new VOICE of God. I also suggest you listen to Christian music and watch Christian shows on the television and the internet. As it is vital as to what you are "listening" to. You need to "feed your mind with healthy, spiritual food". If you start out on a course to change for the better, the good news is, the neuroplasticity of your brain will develop new information highways, setting you in the direction of believing in yourself. The new neural pathways can be set to direct new thoughts in your brain you are lovable, you are loved by others and most importantly you are loved by God. Start a new recording in your mind, start a new VOICE in your head. Believe the VOICE of TRUTH telling you, *I Am Lovable! What are your alternatives?* You could remain in the chains you currently find yourself bound up in, chains of heartache, unbelief, and pain. You can choose to continue to listen to the voices lying to you! This is your choice to remain stuck in misery.

If you are ready to step out and listen to a new VOICE, you need to be set free. This can be accomplished by putting off the old you and replacing it with the new you. Pray to God, cry out to Him. God is always holding you, even when you think you cannot hold on anymore. Ask Him to change your ways of thinking and the voices you are currently listening to. Ask Him to renew your mind with the goodness and wholeness that only comes from Him. Ask Him to break the old patterns that held you as a captive, as a slave to untruths. Ask God to slay the Giants in your life. Ask Him for the words to speak to the Giants in your life so they scatter in 1,000 different directions! Tell God you want to be set free, to love and to trust without any fear of rejection or of being hurt. Honestly cry out to God, and He will answer you. You must listen to the VOICE of TRUTH, it is the only way to discover true unconditional love.

I guarantee you the solutions I proposed do work, as my mind has been renewed. This is the result of practicing and choosing to resist negative thought patterns and to replace them with positive ones. And all the while meditating on the word of God, and by listening to Christian music, radio, television and podcasts. However, some of you reading this book may need to go a step further and seek support in changing your beliefs about yourself, so you can know you are lovable. If this is you, I encourage you to find a good Bible-based Christian counsellor who will support you along this journey. If you do not know of a counsellor, then I encourage you to find a Bible-based church, and they will direct you to one. I will repeat the scripture verse that was quoted earlier on in the chapter. To achieve a new mind-set, it is imperative that you believe it and practice it!

> *Do not conform any longer to the pattern of this world but be transformed by renewing of your mind. Then you will be able to test and approve what God's will is--his good, pleasing, and perfect will (Romans 12:2 NIV).*

Key 5

What Does the Bible Say About You Being Lovable?

In the book of Romans, the Apostle Paul encourages us not to conform to the patterns of this world - meaning the negative things people are claiming about us or falsely trying to teach us. In today's world there is so much slander and toxicity occurring on social media sites and in day-to-day interactions with people. We must be weary of these ungodly ways and negative influences. Do not get caught up in a war of words on the internet or face-to-face. With the help of God, you can be daily transformed by renewing your mind. "Do not conform to the pattern of this world but be transformed by the renewing of your mind. Then you will be able to test and approve what God's will is—his good, pleasing and perfect will" (Romans 12:2 NIV). In essence this means we must be discerning and wise, to query our thoughts, and sift through all that is said and done to us. We are not created to be mere sponges, soaking up everything that is tossed our way. Instead, we must critically question what is being slung at us by others and train ourselves to reject untruths. *How do we know what untrue is?* Plain and simple, study the word of God, as the Bible is all truth. Anything that is negative and cruel is untrue.

We all need to develop an awareness of the impact negative voices and thoughts are having on us. We need to intentionally develop behaviors that help us to stand strong and firm, and to not believe lies or untruths. We need to arrive at a point where we can deflect the negative by allowing negative words to roll from us like water off a duck's back (an old cliché).

Believe and know you are created with a keen mind, to be wise and to question what you are being told. Only accept truths founded on Biblical principles and rid yourself of all untruths. If you commit to doing this, you are on the road to being free, healthy, and whole. By ridding yourself of a toxic lifestyle you will instead live the life you were designed to live. Your life has been divinely designed by the Creator of the Universe. You may be experiencing false beliefs from unkind words and actions still haunting you. You need to ask God if you accepted untruths from the way your family said things or did things (even if intentions were good, or if they were unaware of the harm they caused). We are not to take on the thoughts and beliefs of people who do not live by the truths found in the Bible. Instead, we are to ensure, *"We demolish arguments and every pretension that sets itself up against the knowledge of God, and we take captive every thought to make it obedient to Christ"* (2 Corinthians 10:5 NIV).

God teaches us all throughout the Bible He created each one of us to prosper and to not be harmed (Jeremiah 29:11). If you suffered harm, it is not because God's word instructed people to harm you. Be discerning as it may be someone intentionally tried to discipline you, however, possibly it was not done in the love of God. Some correction and discipline would not have been meant to harm you, but you might have also misinterpreted the intentions of the person. Seek godly counsel to decipher what was good and godly discipline, and possibly when you might not have listened and instead acted in rebellion. Be wise, be discerning. Ask God for help and direction in this area. Seek out believers who will help you to be set free from patterns of behavior and beliefs that are harmful. Know what was meant for harm, and know what was meant in discipline. You need discernment to be able to distinguish between the two.

And we know in all things God works for the good of those who love him, who have been called according to His purpose (Romans 8:28 NIV). You are called by God. The question is, *do you accept this calling?* God does not force Himself on anyone (1 John 4:18). The Bible speaks only truth, and it states that perfect love drives out all fear (1 John 4:18). The Bible teaches us God's ways are perfect (Psalm 18:30; 2 Samuel 22:31), and they are higher than our ways (Isaiah 55:9). It also teaches us God so loved the world He gave His only son to die for our sins so we might have life in all its abundance, both now and forever more (John 3:16). That is a lot of love, and that love is for you! God loves you, so believe you are lovable, as God is unable to lie, He only speaks the truth!

Below are some Biblical affirmations to state over your life every single day. I encourage you to develop a pattern where you declare these truths at least three times a day for the rest of your life!

- *I praise you because I am fearfully and wonderfully made; your works are wonderful, I know that full well* (Psalm 139:14 NIV).

- *The one who gets wisdom loves life; the one who cherishes understanding will soon prosper* (Proverbs 19:8 NIV).

- *See what great love the Father has lavished on us, that we should be called children of God! And that is what we are! The reason the world does not know us is that it did not know him* (1 John 3:1 NIV).

- *We love because he first loved us* (1 John 4:19 NIV).

- *Therefore, if anyone is in Christ, the new creation has come: The old has gone, the new is here!* (2 Corinthians 5:17 NIV).

- *Teach me your way, O LORD, that I may walk in your truth; unite my heart to fear your name* (Psalm 86:11 ESV).

Unlocking Mystery #1

I Am Lovable!

> **Reflect:** Being completely honest, can you look at yourself in the mirror every morning, telling yourself you are lovable and deserve being loved? Can you visualize what being lovable looks like?
>
> **Relate:** Is it easy for you to tell yourself you are lovable and beautiful? If it is easy for you to tell yourself you are lovable and deserve to be loved, why do you think it is so easy for you to do? If it is a struggle, what is holding you back?
>
> **Respond:** I challenge you to wake up every morning and look at yourself in the mirror and declare, "I Am Lovable". If you are not at the point in your QUEST to be able to say and do this every morning, I challenge you to work towards this truth. Work towards this daily goal, step-by-step. For it is truth. If you cannot speak this truth every day, I challenge you to try to at least one day per week. Look at your beautiful self in the mirror and Just Say It! "I Am Lovable".
>
> *Speak the Truth.*
>
> *Just Say It! I Am Lovable.*

#2

I Am Lovable Just As I Am

My brokenness is a better bridge for people than my pretend wholeness ever was –
Sheila Walsh.

Dr. Cheryl Bauman

Key 6

Body Image Starts in the Mind, Not in the Mirror

The biggest obstacle many of us face is to believe we are lovable just as we are. Many of us are caught up in body image. Body image starts in the mind, not in the mirror. *Do you remember the supermodel Bo Derek, and how her body was rated a perfect 10? How about Arnold Schwarzenegger and his very fit body?* As a result of some of us living in that era, we may have set the bar too high in terms of our physicality and wanting to be a perfect 10 yet never getting it. Thus, for some of us we believed we were not quite lovable enough until we became that perfect 10 - which for most of us is virtually impossible!

Body image and how we view ourselves are highly important in today's world. Our society is setting impossible benchmarks for children, adolescents, women, and men to obtain, and many of us have terrible views of who we are as a result. We often judge ourselves and others based on physical appearance, instead of inward appearance. Some people developed eating disorders because of never feeling as if they measured up. When some of us women glanced at the images of Bo Derek, and her rating as a perfect 10, we knew we would never acquire her shapely body. Some of us might have falsely tried to achieve a perfect 10, striving, and striving and striving. Unfortunately, research has shown how we think about ourselves in our minds changes the way we understand who we are and whether we value ourselves enough to believe we are lovable. A healthy body image plays a significant role in our overall well-being.

Body image is mental, emotional, social, and spiritual. It is both the mental picture you have of your body and the way you feel about your body when you look in the mirror that is important. Some of you reading this book are not even able to look at yourself in the mirror. My prayer is by the time you finish this book you will have a healthy body of image of yourself, as you understand and accept who you are in Christ. My hope is you accept the truth you are beautifully and wonderfully made just as you are (Psalm 139:14). A healthy body image is more than just simply tolerating what you look like.

It is difficult for us to love others and to believe God loves us if we do not first like and love ourselves. A healthy body image is connected to you truly accepting, liking, and loving you! You need to get to the point of liking the way you look at this very moment. You will know if you like the way you look right now if you aren't trying to change your body to fit the way you think it should look. This is a good check-in time. *Can you honestly say you like everything about you and how you look? Are you able to recognize the individual qualities and strengths that make you who you are beyond your weight, shape, or appearance? Are you honestly able to resist the pressure to strive for the myth of the "perfect 10 body" you see in the media and on-line?*

How you value and respect yourself as a person, which is the opinion you have of yourself inside and out - will impact how you take care of yourself, emotionally, physically, mentally, and spiritually. What you believe you will achieve. *What are you saying to yourself and to others in terms of how you value yourself?* Listen to the words that come out of your mouth as you talk about yourself. Moreover, the image you have of yourself doesn't have to be in the form of a verbal expression. It can be the way you dress, the way you walk, your tone of voice, what you think, or what you eat. *What messages are you portraying to yourself and to others around you? Are you messaging that you value yourself, and you are valuable? Or are you sending messages to others you are not worthy, and you are a mistake? Can you celebrate your strengths and abilities without focusing on your weaknesses?*

Do you take good care of your body? Can you honestly say "yes" to the following: I eat right, I look good, I feel good, and I weigh what God wants me to weigh (1 Corinthians 9:27; 1 Timothy 4:8). If you cannot honestly say "yes" to these statements, then it is vitally important for your health and well-being you do take good care of yourself. By doing this you might need to seek help from a doctor, a trainer, or a nutritionist. However, keep in mind you need to be realistic in relation to your view of your own uniquely designed body.

God is the great designer of you. He crafted and molded you in His image. He created you for greatness. It is the untruths you are bombarded with in this world that whisper lies telling you that you do not measure up. The power of God's love holds you closer than you can ever imagine. God created you to soar like an eagle. God created you in His perfect image. Sin brought about imperfection. If you continue to develop a close relationship with God, by talking with Him and reading the Bible, He will show you through His faithful love the perfect plans He has for your life. These plans include prosperity spiritually, physically, financially, socially, mentally, and emotionally. He created you for greatness and purpose, beyond what you can imagine. God will help you to recognize through the power of His love you are lovable just as you are! Stick close to God and He will help you to celebrate your strengths without putting yourself down for the way you look. God will repair you from the inside out so you can stand tall and believe you are lovable just as you are! I guarantee if you allow God to do a great work in your life, you will be able to peer at yourself in a mirror and declare you are beautifully and wonderfully made!

> *For you created my inmost being, you knit me together in my mother's womb. I praise you because I am fearfully and wonderfully made; your works are wonderful; I know that full well (Psalm 139:13-14 NIV).*

Dr. Cheryl Bauman

Key 7

Searching for Mr. or Mrs. Right

Lauren was a 58-year-old woman I met at a conference. She told me after she graduated from university, she moved across the United States from the east coast to the west coast to build a very successful career in marketing. Lauren dated, took up hobbies, regularly attended church and developed a loving circle of friends. For most of her life she assumed Mr. Right would eventually show up. She now thinks there has been a detour. *Does this sound like you, or someone you know?*

Never making a home with Mr. Right or Mrs. Right has left many single people without a partner for years and years, that eventually turned into decades. We talk about singles a lot, but we do not talk about what it is like to be single. In the United States and in Canada, approximately 51% of people who are of the age to be eligible for marriage are single. This is a stark contrast to the 1960's when 28% of the population, who were of the age to be married, were single. For these people, the recognition of finding kindred has not happened or at least not yet.

Some of you may have a false belief, often perpetuated by our culture if you are a single person and have not found Mr. Right or Mrs. Right, you are flawed. You may believe there is something terribly wrong with you. This is a false belief system that is reinforced by popular teachings in our society. Many single people who believe in marriage and have been raised in homes where their parents loved each other and doted on them. Yet they were unable to find a person with whom to marry. Therefore, they continue to remain single. There are also singles who are very happy and content with being single.

What about that cousin, sibling, neighbor, or co-worker who always seems to be on their own? You might not give much thought in relation to them being on their own, because perhaps it is easier not to. With nearly half of the marriages in Canada and the United

States ending in divorce and many others reporting staying married yet are unhappy, in these modern times, the institution of marriage is in crisis. Rationally we all know life has so many struggles, regardless of our relationship status. Many of us do marry on the belief it will add something fundamentally good to our lives. I believe many who are married would concede it does. Research does agree that people who are married live longer than people who are single. *Yet, how do we discover the happily ever after if it is not found in a human being?*

This QUEST for true love is the hope for a constant companion who will bear intimate witness to our lives, who will help to write the chapters of our book. Our hope is this partner will heighten our joy and ease our suffering. They will be our designated collaborator and caretaker, sparing us the effort of constantly fending for ourselves. Hollywood promises us there is a lid for every pot, someone for everyone. King Solomon acknowledges, *two are better than one, because they have a good return for their labor; If either of them falls, one can help the other up* (Ecclesiastes 4:9-10a NIV). King Solomon's wise words are in support of us not being alone in life, as he is emphasizing the institution of togetherness in community. Even if you are currently single and not married, it is still not good to be alone, you need companionship and fellowship with others. Community and belonging are vital. The whole notion we are not an island on this earth, is reinforced in these verses found in Ecclesiastes, that we belong and need to find belonging with others. We are hardwired this way; it is part of who we are as humans. It is our fundamental nature to want to belong and to be loved.

The Bible offers advice for both the married and the single, as it establishes some people on this earth will be single, and others will be married. The Bible continually reinforces everyone is destined with purposes to be fulfilled throughout their lifetime. Some of these purposes last for seasons, others are gradually and continually developed and expanded on (Ecclesiastics 3:1-8). As people walk in relationship and in obedience with God, these purposes will continue to grow and develop into greater purposes, if one proves to be responsible and accountable for what they have been given. These purposes are tied to our relationship status with God and are ordained by God for seasons of our lives. If God can trust us in little, He will then trust us with increased responsibility either as a married person, or as a single person (Luke 16:10). God's trust factor does not correlate as to whether a person is united with another, or not.

Dr. Cheryl Bauman

In 1 Corinthians 7, the Apostle Paul instructs us on the matter of marriage and of being single. Paul acknowledges a person does well not to marry, yet he concedes due to immoral issues and lack of self-control, it is better for a person to marry. However, later in Chapter 7 he states he would prefer all were like him (It seemed as if Paul was single during his ministry. Although there is not a definitive answer.). However, he realizes God created some of us to remain single, while others of us will marry.

Being single in your adult life may be for a season, or it may remain throughout your life span here on this earth, the same applies to marriage. Some people are married for a season, and due to unfortunate circumstances, such as divorce or death, they find themselves single. Good news is if you are obedient, surrendering to God's will, reading and meditating on the Bible, you will be in a steadfast place to use the talents and gifts God bestowed on you. This is regardless of your relationship status. Fulfilling your purpose on this earth is not reliant as to whether you are a married person or a single person. You are lovable, created and designed for greatness just as you are! If you are surrendering to God's will for your relationship status and understanding God works all things for your good (Romans 8:28), then you will be fully at peace and content with being single or married.

Currently too many married people are complaining and wanting to be single, and too many single people are complaining and wanting to be married. We must be content with the purposes and the will of God for our lives, regardless of our relationship status. We must stop complaining or God will never be able to fully work in our lives. If we do not stop murmuring and complaining, we will keep going around in circles just like the children of Israel did in the desert for 40 years. They were never satisfied, always being stuck, and never getting out of the rut!

For you to fully move into your destiny and carry out all you were created to accomplish, you need to believe you are lovable just as you are. Being lovable is not dependent on your relationship status with a significant other. Instead, I encourage you to give thanks and praise for the many forms of healthy relationships you have. I urge you to stop looking at others and focusing on what they have and what you do not have. Quit zeroing in on your flaws and instead work towards seeing yourself as lovable. Understand God can work through you, regardless of whether you are single or married as He continues to refine you for your ultimate purposes here on this earth. Trust God, surrender your life to Him. Do your best and God will do the rest!

Just as we seek God as to what our roles and responsibilities are to be on this earth, we also need to seek God as to whether He wants us to marry or remain single. Every individual's answer will be different according to God's ultimate plan for their lives. The Bible provides examples of people who are single, married, divorced, and widowed. Be careful not to compare your answer to others', as your answer is unique, and it is perfectly designed for you. God's plans are to prosper you and to bring you hope, they are not to harm you (Jeremiah 29:11). They are to give you a future filled with overflowing abundance in more ways than you could even imagine or hope for. Being single or being married may only be for a certain time and it may change according to the will, and the direction God leads and guides you. Stay close to God and you will remain in perfect peace in being single or being married.

Know and believe you are lovable, regardless of whether you are single or married.

Being single is not less than being married, just as being married is not more than being single, it is all part of your destiny. God recognizes some people will marry, and others will remain single, this is His perfect plan. Being single does not equate to being unlovable and not being worthy of true unconditional love. God's ultimate message to all of us, regardless of relationship status, is we know we are loved, we are lovable, and we deserve His unconditional love. As I have spoken with countless people over the years on the topic of love, the resounding truth is we all seem to want and are seeking true unconditional love. Yet, if we are all honest, it cannot be provided to us in human form. *So how do we find it, and how do we know when we found it?*

Key 8

Lookin' for Love in All the Wrong Places

Never knowing what true unconditional love is and how to find it, has left many feeling empty, unfulfilled, seeking desperately to be made whole. We do not have to look very far to realize this stark reality. Our society declares this through the many songs, novels, movies, and television shows that this long search and eventual discovery of a beloved is significant and monumental. Without it, we are made to believe we are less than. Our society hinges on the belief of true, romantic love. The phrase we heard repeatedly, *happily ever after*, implies a singular outcome: two lives made better by virtue of their union. This, however, is a false notion, a false belief system one single human being is going to be our *happily ever after*. People will always disappoint, even if this is not their intent, as we are all flawed by the human condition of imperfection.

You need to first love yourself and believe you are worthy of love before you can love others! Next, you need to love yourself just as you are. *Can you honestly say you love yourself right at this moment, regardless of your status in life or how you look? Do you believe you are worthwhile enough to be loved unconditionally even without the perfect job, the perfect mate, the perfect outfit, the perfect child or the perfect body?* You need to accept perfection can never be reached, only God and His love are perfect (1 John 4:18). This is the whole truth, and nothing but the truth.

Know and believe your life is worth being loved and cared for regardless of your current relationship status. You are worth it! You are lovable! Learning to love yourself just as you are, may be a difficult task for some of you reading this book, as you do not believe in yourself or your worth. You think you must earn love, or you need someone else to fully complete you. I challenge you to begin today and to stop the negative thinking about yourself and to believe you are lovable just as you are, regardless of your status.

You cannot earn a love that is a pure, unconditional love as it is only found in God. God's love is free for all.

I encourage you to begin new patterns of thinking and acting. *What other choice do you have?* I suppose you could remain in the rut of self-doubt and continue to try to attain unconditional love by climbing to new heights to prove you are lovable. If you are tired of never measuring up to perfection. If you are tired of always feeling unlovable, and you are ready to throw away self-doubt and the unlovable thoughts, then I encourage you to start each day off by giving thanks for your life. I encourage you to love yourself as you are. I encourage you to begin each day by declaring such as the following I AM statements:

- I am lovable.
- I am lovely.
- I am a winner.
- I am favored by people.
- I am loved by people.
- I am a believer not a doubter.

Create healthy habits of speaking healthy and prosperous words over your life. With the above I AM statements, try to go one step further and visualize yourself using these statements. Then visualize God saying these statements to you. Declaring truths over your life may not come naturally. In the beginning it may seem contrived and forced. It is probably something you cannot do instantaneously without thinking about saying and doing it. You may have to work very hard at beginning new patterns of behavior in relation to how you talk to yourself and how you think about yourself. I encourage you to not look to the past, always look ahead as there is a new day on the horizon. Looking back on past mistakes will only keep you stuck. View life in the here and now, looking straight ahead, believing in a clear path. Stay motivated to change your belief and thinking systems about yourself. Do not ever give up or let negative thoughts continue to control who you are. Do not believe you need to gain a certain status to be lovable. This is a lie. You are lovable just as you are!

Dr. Cheryl Bauman

Key 9

Wise Navigation: Detecting Obstacles and Jumping Over Hurdles

We need to love the sinner, not the sin. Many of us are too caught up in what we have done wrong, we think we are not lovable just as we are. As we explored in the first chapter, there are ways of thinking and behaving that can be changed to help us recognize our worth. It is important to hold onto the belief we are uniquely created by God to fulfill an assignment on planet earth that is specifically our own personal mission. The purposes we are to accomplish can only be carried out by us. You and I are lovely just as we are, created in the image of God. *Yet why do many of us have a difficult time accepting and knowing our unique personalities and character traits were perfectly designed by God to complete our purposes here on this earth? Why do some of us try to change to become someone we are not to please ourselves or others? Why do we not love who we are at this very moment?* The reason is many of us have false thoughts clouding our minds telling us we are not good enough, and we will never measure up. We believe untruths that demand us to alter our God-given talents and abilities in hopes of becoming loveable. We think we need to be someone who we are not so we can love ourselves and be loveable. This is false thinking. The problem of not believing we are loveable begins in our minds and becomes a wrong way of thinking about ourselves. These untruths about who we are take over and rule our thought lives and eventually take command over our lives. Our thoughts become our words, and our words become our actions. *How do we break these destructive patterns of belief?*

Detecting these obstacles requires you to continuously monitor your thought life. Jumping over this hurdle requires recognition. Recognition of old patterns of thinking and then a desire to change these old patterns of thinking. Adopting the approach of continually monitoring thoughts takes discipline and perseverance. If your thoughts are not speaking truth about who you are, then according to the truth found in the Bible, you need to immediately cast these untruths and destructive thoughts out of your mind. *Casting down imaginations and every high and lofty thing that exalts itself against the knowledge of God and bringing every thought into captivity to obedience of the Christ* (2 Corinthians 10:5 KJV). For if you allow these thoughts to take hold, and form patterns within your mind, then you begin to believe these negative thought patterns about yourself. Soon these thoughts become habits, and they start to become who you are instead of who you were created to be. Our minds are powerful, and the enemy of this world tries to attack us here. If Satan can rule over our thought lives than our thoughts become habits and our habits can lead to destructive, addictive behaviors.

Our minds are not created to just accept everything being said about us, as they are created to be discerning of good and evil. *A fool finds pleasure in wicked schemes, but a person of understanding delights in wisdom* (Proverbs 10:23 NIV). *The god of this age has blinded the mind of unbelievers, so they cannot see the light of the gospel that displays the glory of Christ, who is the image of God* (2 Corinthians 4:4 NIV). Some of us have not trained our minds to be discerning and instead believed negative things said and done to us. We accepted untruths about who we are. We allowed this negativity to form and mold us into the person we are today. Instead of believing we are lovable, regardless of how much money we have. Regardless of what our job is, or our position is in life, we often falsely believe we must gain world status or be perfect to be truly lovable. We are not willing to love ourselves just as we are, the way God has uniquely and wonderfully designed us.

A large and dangerous hurdle needed to be conquered for some people is their striving for continuous status and money. This is a false belief that once riches are gained this will wipe away sadness, pain and hurt. Or you may mistakenly belief if you just find Mr. or Mrs. Right, or get a promotion at work or buy a fancy car, all your problems will disappear, and you will automatically become lovable. Gaining positional power or material wealth is not going to make you more or less lovable. These false teachings will tell you that you are only good enough after you earn worldly wealth and worldly status. However, once obtained, if you do not know the God of the universe, who is the giver of all good things, you will remain empty and unsatisfied.

Many who have been treated badly and told you are not lovable believe these lies and instead are striving for love through methods that will never quench the internal desire to be made whole and complete. In fact, these destructive thoughts have possibly turned into destructive actions leading to further emptiness and dissatisfaction. I urge you to first recognize you have been deceived into believing "things" will fulfill the emptiness and make you more lovable. I encourage you to combat these untruths feeding your mind. If this is you, it is important you form habits that will bring about a disciplined thought life. You can accomplish this by challenging the negativity being hurled at you and swirling around inside your head.

The only way to change negative thought patterns is to become closer to God. Through following three wise habits that may be missing from your life, they could help you to wisely navigate by detecting obstacles and jumping over hurdles. The first habit you may need to form is to be in continuous prayer with God, through His Holy Spirit. The Holy Spirit will help to guide you by gently pointing out the areas in your thought life that need cleaning up. Secondly, seek God's truth in the Bible daily. Decide on a study plan, read the word of God and reflect on the learning. You may be thinking you do not have time to do this. However, I would challenge you to reflect on how much time is currently being taken up in your thought life as it feeds on negative garbage. Lastly, worship God in Spirit and in Truth. Worshiping God is essential to enter a realm of praise and thanksgiving for all He has given to you. With worship comes appreciation. With appreciation comes satisfaction with who you are, and who God created you to be. If you choose to discipline yourself and to form these three daily habits, you are making the choice to become more discerning as to what you are allowing to "stick" in your mind. As what you believe, think, and say about yourself is what you will eventually become!

Key 10

What does the Bible Say About Loving Yourself Just as You Are?

On your QUEST to find the keys that unlock the mysteries of humanity, you need to first believe you are lovable, and true unconditional love is available to you. Secondly, you need to believe you are loved no matter if you are single or married. Thirdly, you need to believe you are loveable just as you are. Marriage adds another dimension to life, but it does not fully complete a person in terms of true unconditional love. Only God can do that. God is perfect, pure love, as He first loved us.

> *Your unfailing love, O Lord, is as vast as the heavens; your faithfulness reaches beyond the clouds. Your righteousness is like the mighty mountains, Your justice like the ocean depths. You care for people and animals alike, O Lord. How precious is Your unfailing love, O God! All humanity finds shelter in the shadow of Your wings (Psalm 36:5-7 NIV).*

As the psalmist contends, God's love is endless, it is everywhere, and it is readily available. God's promise of love abounds throughout the scriptures; it is free for us to accept. Yet it is our choice, it is not forced on us. God relentlessly pursues us, as His true unconditional love is always available. Our job is we need to accept God's love. Some of you reading this might think this is hokey. You might have been looking for an absolute answer that involved a 12-step program and once you followed it, then you would know "how to" find true unconditional love. You might even be disappointed, as you are looking to find true unconditional love with another human being on this earth. If this is you, ponder on the thought, *"have you been lookin' for love in all the wrong places?"*

If finding another human being who will never disappoint or let you down hasn't happened, then you might be open to the possibility God is the only provider of a steadfast, unchanging, and enduring love. In this verse the psalmist describes God's love for us, *give thanks to the God of heaven, for his steadfast love endures forever* (Psalm 136:26 NIV). Steadfast, steady, and enduring, this is the love God freely gives to us. All you must do is accept it. This scripture verse is a promise God's love is unchanging; you can be confident in knowing and believing this truth. God loves you more than you could ever love Him. That may seem impossible, but it is true. His love is endless, it is free, and it never changes. It is without strings attached. God is continually pursuing you with a relentless love that is just for you, if you are willing to accept it by faith.

Guess what, you are lovable just as you are! The Maker of Heaven and Earth created you, and God does not make mistakes. God is unable to mess up. Therefore, God made you lovable and He loves you with a love that pales in comparison to any other love found on this earth. You may feel as though you are damaged or have been damaged because of what others have done to you. God wants to take your life! He wants to turn it around! Turn you in a direction that will force you and others to bear witness to the fact you can confidently believe in and love yourself knowing you are lovable, because God first loved you!

> *Finding true unconditional love on this earth is not dependent on your earthly relationship status, it is dependent on your heavenly relationship status.*

True, unconditional love is found in a solid relationship with God through His Son Jesus Christ. God, through Jesus, is the only true way to find peace, joy, and love in all its purity and perfection. Jesus answered, I am the way the truth and the life. *No one comes to the father except through me* (John 14:6 NIV). Relationships are a two-way street. Your relationship status with God is dependent on you:

- Accepting Jesus Christ as your Savior and Lord (John 3:16; Acts 2:38; Romans 10:9-11; 1 Thessalonians 5:28; 1 John 1:9).

- Spending time with God daily through prayer and talking with Him on a continual basis throughout the day (Psalm 145:18; Matthew 14:23; Mark 1:35; Acts 17:11; Philippians 4:6).

- Reading the Bible daily and reflecting on the truth found in the word of God (Deuteronomy 17:18-20; Psalm 62:8; Psalm 119:9; Amos 8:11; 2 Timothy 3:14-17); and

- Worshipping with praise and thanksgiving through the continuing guidance led by the Holy Spirit (1 Chronicles 16:8-12; Job 1:20-21; Matthew 6:33; John 4:23; Philippians 4:4; Hebrews 12:28-29).

The Trinity (God, The Son, and The Holy Spirit), is always available for you, are you always making yourself available for Them?

Developing a love relationship with the Trinity does not hinge on your relationship status here on earth. It does not matter if you are single, married, divorced, or widowed. All three members of the Trinity want to develop a deep loving relationship with you. All relationships take time to develop. TIME is a key factor. You cannot expect to have a relationship with the Trinity if you do not invest in the time it takes. Making an intentional investment to spend time with them will foster a closeness and love you have never experienced before. This part of the relationship building hinges on you and your commitment.

God, the Son, and the Holy Spirit are the only beings that can offer you true unconditional love. The Trinity's love is the type of love that will never disappear, disappoint, discourage you or let you down. *If you do not believe me, ask yourself, am I fully and completely satisfied with human love? Do I have a peace that passes all understanding in everything no matter what and in every human relationship I am involved in?* If you cannot answer yes to these questions, I challenge you to start by erasing the old patterns of unbelief regarding the unlovable image you have of yourself. Also, get rid of the false belief system as to what true love consists of and how to obtain it.

Remember, as well, some of the beliefs you maintain could very well be at an unconscious level. Therefore, your awareness surrounding what they are and why you hold fast to them could possibly be quite vague. Start by intentionally forming a habit to rid yourself of confusing beliefs about love and instead replace them by believing you are lovable. This process will more than likely take time, continual prayer and building a relationship with God, the Son and the Holy Spirit who are the only givers of true unconditional love. I encourage you to stop with the false belief systems crowding your mind and occupying the precious space that needs to be filled by the only true belief system found in the word of God. The Bible's belief system states you are lovable just as you are. I encourage you to begin the journey today. Run towards God in your QUEST to find true unconditional love by removing the false patterns of thought! I guarantee you God will never disappoint you. He is right there waiting for you!

Dr. Cheryl Bauman

> *You are the people of God; He loved you and chose you for his own. So then, you must clothe yourselves with compassion, kindness, humility, gentleness, and patience (Colossians 3:12 GNB).*

Unlocking Mystery #2

I Am Lovable Just as I Am

Reflect: To be honest, how has the challenge at the end of Chapter 1 been going? Are you trying to establish the habit of waking up every morning and looking at yourself in the mirror and declaring, "I Am Lovable".

Relate: Experts say it takes 21 times of continuously repeating the same behavior to form a habit. So, keep working at forming this new habit for the next 21 days. I challenge you to work towards this truth, as well as to add new words to the end of the sentence.

Respond: Look at your beautiful self in the mirror and Just Say It!" I Am Lovable Just as I Am."

Next, visualize yourself as lovable as you are!

Repeat this challenge for at least 21 days and take note of the difference it makes in your life and in the lives of those around you.

Speak the Truth.

Just Say It! I Am Lovable Just as I Am.

Dr. Cheryl Bauman

#3

I Belong

Not everyone loves me, but I have to be okay no matter what they think of me – *Joyce Meyer.*

Dr. Cheryl Bauman

Key 11

The Power of 1 and the Power of 3

We all have an innate desire to belong. It is part of our DNA. We were created to belong. Belonging is a fundamental part of being human. We need people and this need is hardwired into our brains. God imprinted every human being born on the planet with both the need for belongingness and the need to be part of meaningful communities. A sense of belonging is crucial to our life satisfaction, happiness, mental, and physical health. Research has proven belongingness even adds to our longevity in life on this earth. Belonging to a family, and a community gives each of us a sense of purpose and meaning. Research has also pointed out loss of belonging has been associated with stress, illness, depression, and decreased well-being.

Belonging is a fundamental part of being human. We need people. Recent studies have also explained people crave interactions with others and this "craving" is associated with the same region of the brain where we "crave" food. Another study showed when people experience social isolation or exclusion, this is associated with the same region of the brain where people experience physical pain. It is physically and emotionally painful to not find belonging and to experience ostracism. Being ostracised at work, can lead to job dissatisfaction as well as health problems. Studies suggest people who have a lack of a sense of belonging there is a stronger correlation to depression than feelings of loneliness.

Jonathan Haidt, in his book *Happiness Hypothesis*, asserts belonging is vital to our happiness, and it is of critical importance to engage with others. He states it is a web of relationships and a sense of community in which people feel connected with activities, traditions as well as the group itself. When we share a sense of social identity with a group, we can lean into them, use our strengths and be authentically who we are created to be. I found this belonging in several groups I have been a member of, particularly, my church community, small Bible study groups, and small gatherings with the "special women" in my life.

However, a word of caution, is even though we may be surrounded by other people, it does not guarantee a sense of belonging. Belonging must do more with the identification as a member of a particular group, coupled with the higher quality interactions that accompany it. It is the accumulation of the interactions over time which are supportive of you and I as authentic human beings that is paramount. Belonging is much more than just about "having friends". Being a member of a group that contributes to your spiritual, physical, social, and emotional well-being is vital. Groups have value and belief systems, and when we identify with groups, this provides us with a "lens" to help us focus as to how we see the world.

It is therefore crucial to find groups that are based on biblical principles and beliefs so we can grow in our God-given assignments on this earth. To be a member of a group that encourages us in the Lord is essential to fulfilling our belongingness, as well as our overall purpose on this earth. Communities are such a powerful source of belonging because we often share a sense of identity with its' members. If you are a member of a community group that is not based on biblical principles, it may be necessary, due to work obligations, or a sporting event. Yet this is why you might be feeling a tension, as the belief systems of the organization do not align with the beliefs and values proclaimed in the Bible. This is where conflict among individuals and/or groups of individuals may arise.

Joyce Meyer suggests in her quote written at the beginning of this chapter, not everyone is going to love us. We need to be okay with not "belonging in every circle", because we can turn into a people pleaser instead of doing what God's will is for our life. This took me years to accept and understand not everyone was going to be in my corner encouraging me on my journey. I so wanted everyone to love me, until one day the light went on inside my head, and I realized this was not ever going to happen here on this earth. Instead, I accepted I needed to be grateful for the people in my life who did love and respect me. I needed to be satisfied and content with my "belonging circle"; yet to be open, wise, and discerning when the "belonging circle" was to include more people. Through Joyce Meyer's teaching and others like her, I realized I belong, and I am important regardless of what some people may think of me. As Joyce teaches the word of God, her ministry helped me to recognize the error in my thinking and as a result my life has been transformed.

#3: I Belong

I am honored and blessed to have a beautiful and talented friend by the name of Georgia. She truly knows the meaning of gathering others in positive fellowship and how to let people know they belong. Georgia is a unique individual who intentionally chooses to view her life and her relationships in a positive light. Her love for life and for making a significant difference in the lives of everyone she meets is a testimony to the love of God shining through her. Every time I am with Georgia, she energizes me with the words and gestures she uses. She makes me feel as if I belong, and I always leave better than when I arrived. Georgia speaks truth and provides very sound advice. She can inter-mix wise advice with humor and wit. Yet the way she provides counsel is founded in love. At times she does not mince words, but I know she has my best intentions at heart.

Georgia is the type of person we all need to be and the type of friend we all need to hang out with. Life is too short to waste our precious moments being with people who are continually negative and who continually bring us down by speaking words that are full of rotten, disgusting garbage. I encourage you to listen to the words others speak about you. *Are the words uplifting and kind? Or are their words filled with condemnation and corruption?* We all need to be a part of a community of people who treat us like we belong! *Are the people you socialize with telling you through their words and actions you belong or that you don't? How do you feel when you are with them? How do you feel after you leave their presence?* The answers to these questions are an indication as to how you are being treated by them.

Georgia has so many ways to tell and demonstrate to people her love and affection. She has taught me some methods to express love when I cannot verbally convey my love to those around me. One non-verbal approach Georgia shared with me is to hold up three fingers. The three fingers represent, "I love you"! So, if Georgia is across a room and I see her holding up three fingers, I know exactly what she is signalling to me. These non-verbal loving gestures are a creative way to let myself and others know they are loved, and they belong! Georgia also taught me by squeezing someone's arm or hand three times, she is signalling to them, "I love you"! When you can't speak the words out loud, "I love you", I encourage you to use Georgia's non-verbal cues to remind those who are dear to you that your love and affection is always steadfast. Expressions of love tell others, "You Belong".

Just like the *3* words, "I love you" can have a great impact on many lives, you are *1* person who possesses the power to make changes in your life and impact lives around you. You hold the power of *1*! Georgia is *1* person. However, by using non-verbal cues she lets those around her know, "I love you", by the powerful act of holding up *3* fingers, or by squeezing someone's hand *3* times. These thoughts turned into action may seem so simple, yet they can make all the difference to *1* person's life. Georgia reminds us to be intentional with what we have. God as well reminded Moses when He said to him in Exodus 4:2 (NIV), *"What is that in your hand?"* Moses replied to God, *"A staff"*. To Moses, a staff was just a staff. But to God it was so much more than that. It was an instrument to which miracles were performed, such as the parting of the Red Sea. I believe God always asks you and I, *"What is in your hand?" How will you answer? How will you put your thoughts and words into action so God can create miracles in your life and in the lives of those with whom you meet? How will you display to others they are important, and they belong?* We should never act alone. We should include God in everything we do. God is *3* in *1* - Father, Son and Holy Spirit. Always remember, the power of *1*, the power of *3*!

Key 12

Trust is Paramount

In Chapter #1 we learned our brains are designed to be able to develop new patterns of behavior, as they are hardwired this way. This is a good thing to know! If you do not feel as if you belong, or know how to develop positive, healthy connections with others, built on common beliefs and values, you can learn new ways of doing so. However, you also need to be motivated to choose to change and determined to commit to making the change, whatever it takes. If you do not have a strong bond with family due to past abuse, I challenge you to find people in your life you can trust and develop relationships with them built on trust and love. If you do not have a parental figure in your life, I encourage you to find one. An older, wiser and sincere, trusting adult who can hopefully take the place of your mother or father and act as a mentor to you. Locate a friend with whom you can develop a close bond with, so they become like your sister or brother. However, be cautious, you do not find yourself in a similar, familiar abusive relationship with the new people in your life. As if you are not careful and discerning, patterns can repeat themselves. Ask God to guide and direct you and to bring people into your life who love Him and who will genuinely care about you. Pray for discernment and use it when seeking out positive, healthy relationships with others. Trust what God is telling you. God created you to belong to Him and to belong to a community of believers. He wants you to be connected in right relationships with other people. Let Him direct your path in this area of your life. Trust and obey the voice of God.

Some people do not have close relationships with family members because of abuse and unhealthy ties. Some of you, due to broken family relationships may have looked for belonging and love in all the wrong places. If you seek to develop genuine bonds with people built on love and trust, God will honor this desire and bring people into your life who will act as a surrogate mother, father or sibling. This will happen, just seek God and let Him know that having a surrogate parent or sibling is the desire of your heart and He will bring this to pass. Believe me, it is God's desire you relate to a community of believers. He created all of us to be in community with one another. God created the family unit. Trust God, and be discerning as to who you trust here on earth. Ask God for wisdom as to who you should seek to find loving and belongingness with. Yet I also realize no human being is without flaws.

Being in unity with one another is the will of God. God created us to belong in loving relationships with others. When God created Adam, He realized Adam was lonely and needed a companion, so God created Eve. In the same way, God hears your lonely cries for right relationships here on this earth, it is not God's will you are alone. God designed you to belong. You are not an island. You might be alone for a season in your life, so you are able to heal from past hurts and to become more discerning as to who to trust and who not to trust. Take this time to allow God to refine you into the person you were created to be. Accept God as your Heavenly Father. Allow God to define belongingness for you. Learn how to love as you are guided by the greatest lover of your soul. You need to learn how to love yourself first, and then how to love God second. If you do not know how to love "you" first, it is difficult to understand God's love for you. By accepting you are worthy of love, and worthy of God's love, you can then love yourself and love others. In due season, if you seek His will, God will bring people into your life, so you are enveloped with love and belongingness. I encourage you to find a Bible-based church where you feel and know you belong, and where others accept and love you for who you are!

Some of you grew up in a home that was not very loving, where there was a lot of strife. If this is you, I encourage you to work through the hurt and pain of rejection, with the help of God, before you find yourself in the same unhealthy relationship. Patterns tend to repeat themselves if we are not fully healed from past pain. Knowing a sense of belongingness is important to your overall health and well-welling. You make ask, *"what is belongness" and how do you obtain it?* Belonging is feeling connected to a family, group or community. It is that overall sense you are a part of something. We all long for this, even if we do not realize we do. When you feel you belong, you feel attached and close to others. You feel you are thoroughly accepted by them. But belonging is more than just being a part of a group. Belonging is also tied to your social identity, which is having a set of shared beliefs and values with the people with whom you belong with. For you to feel a true sense of belonging, you need to feel unity and a common sense of character with and among the members of your family or group you belong to.

As a result of past situations, you may not have this true sense of belonging, and unity with people. Thus, some of you may have difficulty trusting others. If you seek, God will ensure He brings people into your life that will fill this void. He will fill it in a healthy, godly manner, so you are able to develop trusting relationships built on common values such as honesty and integrity. I encourage you to stick close to God! Listen to that inner voice and be discerning as to whom you develop close connections, especially if you were not raised in a family that had healthy, loving relationships, where you felt attached and closely connected. I urge you to seek out a counselor or pastor from a faith-filled church who will help to guide and direct you on this journey to spiritual, emotional, social, and physical wholeness. I also encourage you to develop a healthy understanding of one person or several people. Remember they cannot fully be everything to you all the time. People cannot meet your every need, only God can through His true unconditional love for you. Humans will always fail. That is why we need to build flexibility into our relationships, understanding everyone will let us down at some time. However, God's love never fails, it is perfect. Trust in God and He will show you the way.

Dr. Cheryl Bauman

Key 13

Love Actually

On my journey to discover this age-old QUEST of what love is and what does unconditional love between others entail, I am reminded of one of my favorite movies of all times, *Love Actually*. I would encourage you to watch this movie, as it presents love in many forms. The movie skillfully acknowledges the many flaws of humans as the characters attempt to display their love towards others by creating communities of belonging. Some characters in the movie are more capable of demonstrating and saying, "I love you", while others are not as adept at it. This is what makes *Love Actually* so appealing.

The movie is a decent attempt at portraying the messiness that can happen among our human relationships, due to the sin that entered this world. *Love Actually* represents love between a husband and wife, between newlyweds, between friends. As well as between people who are tempted to cheat on their partner, between people who do cheat, between a father and a son who have lost their wife/mom, and new love. The movie's theme centers around how love needs to play a central role in ALL our relationships if we are to find true belonging. Yet it grapples with the delicate balance of defining boundaries due to our flawed human condition. It highlights the human need and desire to belong. By the end of the movie the audience is aware every person is created to belong, to be loved and to love. The QUEST to find true love is the crux of *Love Actually*, yet it leaves the audience knowing the empty void we are all questing after is not fully satisfied by people.

Some of the characters in the movie *Love Actually*, were at times confused by love or what they thought love was. *Why are we in our modern society confusing varying forms of love that are found within our current relationships?* I decided to look more closely into the actual word, "love" to try to solve this query. English is a relatively new language being only 1600 years old. At its beginning it was purely Germanic evolving by the modifications of its grammar and vocabulary. Over time, words were added to the English language. Approximately 100 years ago, many of these words came from Norman-French. The modern English we use today is only about 600 years old. In translating the importance of distinguishing our love relationships with the various people in our lives the meaning often becomes lost. Because the English language does not have the "stock of vocabulary words" to describe the varying forms of love we experience in our many relationships. Ancient languages do have a "stockpile" of words to associate when one attempts to attach varying forms of love to the many types of human relationships, we often find ourselves involved with.

In the English-speaking world, "I love you" does not always mean what we think it does. This single word "love" is the only word in modern English we must describe many types and forms of our love relationships. We may find ourselves saying, "I love eating oranges for breakfast", but this does not hold the same meaning as saying, "I love eating breakfast with my family". The English language is limited in distinguishing our affection for objects as well as for a spouse, child, parent, grandparent, friend, neighbour or co-worker. Whereas, in the ancient Greek language there are four words to describe our love relationships with others. The Sanskrit language has ninety-six words (Ray & Dash, 2019) for love in all its forms, and the ancient Persian language has eighty.

I believe because the English language is limited to only one word for love, this is where some of the confusion spawns from. Complexity comes from in terms of loving people and things in varying forms of relationships. I believe this is why expressing our belongingness and love to others can become messy. The issues surrounding defining love still does not negate we must love ALL unconditionally. Nor does this argument excuse inappropriate and sinful behavior. However, this one descriptive word for love in the English language is restrictive and I believe this is why we are often not able to suitably express our earthly relationships where affection is concerned. To better understand how we all belong and create belongingness in our relationships, I decided to investigate the Greek language and its descriptions of love. Greek is the world's oldest recorded living language. It dates to between 1450 and 1350 B.C.! It delves deeper into the four words the ancient Greek language uses for love helped me and hopefully will help you more fully understand the true meaning of love in ALL our relationships.

Key 14

The Greek Love Language

Four Greek Words to Describe: LOVE

In the ancient Greek language, the four words for love are *Agape*, *Eros*, *Philia* and *Storge* (Liddell & Scott, 1940). Historians often had difficulty separating the meanings of these four words, however many attempts to make a distinction between them have occurred. At the time when the New Testament was written, Ancient Greek was the gold standard. However, a less complex version of the language, called Koine, was more accessible to diverse audiences. As a result, many of the authors of the New Testament choose this version of the language so the New Testament was accessible to more people. For the purposes of our discussion on the importance of the four Greek words to describe "love", we will focus on the Ancient Greek language. The four words to describe types of love that are rooted in the Ancient Greek language, will be discussed on the pages that follow. The definitions of these four ancient Greek words will be explained by connecting real life stories to their meanings. Hopefully on our journey to find true unconditional love, this will enable you to further understand how to distinguish your own relationships with others.

Agape Love

The Greek word *Agape* defines love in a spiritual sense (Liddell & Scott, 1940). Using the ancient Greek term s'agapo, which is translated, "I love you", reveals a word that provides a deeper sense of true unconditional love. This *Agape* love is selfless, as it gives and expects nothing in return. *Agape* is used in the biblical love chapter, 1 Corinthians 13. Love as described in this chapter and throughout the Old and New Testament is a sacrificial and spiritual love. Whether the love that is given is returned or not, the person continues to love. This love is without self-benefit. Christians use the word

Agape to express the unconditional love of God towards humankind and the love of humankind towards God.

Only through the grace of God can we continually love others unconditionally, although remembering none of us can be perfect and flawless on this earth. God the Father, His Son Jesus, and the Holy Spirit are the only beings that ARE pure unconditional love. The trinity - Father, Son and Holy Spirit - is love in the purest of forms. If we have the love of God within us and live with the goal of continually manifesting the fruits of the spirit, there are blessings! Such as love, joy, peace, patience, kindness, goodness, faithfulness, gentleness and self-control - (Galatians 5:22-23). Then having and demonstrating *Agape* love towards others becomes a way of wanting to conduct our daily lives, it is not something that is forced on us. Remember, God granted to each one of us free will and choice.

Agape love is so real, so perfect, yet so difficult to attain in our human ways. *Have you ever thought, why do we all want to obtain perfect Agape love? Why do we QUEST after this love when it is impossible to secure it 100% from anyone here on this earth?* I believe the reason is because when God originally created Adam and Eve, they were perfect, without sin and without flaw. God interacted with them in perfect, flawless, *Agape* love. In the beginning, the exchange of love and the connection between God and humans was perfect. God was, is and will always be perfect *Agape* love. Adam and Eve were originally filled with and were perfect, *Agape* love. Being perfect and living in *Agape* love with others is the way in which humans are designed. Yet the fall of Adam and Eve, when sin entered humanity, forever halted people from being perfect and able to completely 'be' *Agape* love. We are now a flawed species; however, we were not originally created this way. I believe this is why we all want "perfect love'", yet we fail at it on a continual basis, due to our sinful nature. Perfect love is integral in the original "blueprint" of the human species. Thus, the desire for *Agape* love is within all of us. This is why I believe many of us are perfectionists and are so hard on ourselves when we fail and let ourselves and others down, as our original programming is perfection. Sin makes us imperfect.

I know intellectually the love between a man and a woman is to be unconditional. *How many people in a marriage relationship or close relationship between family members or friends would agree we are so imperfect, even though we try very hard, we fail at perfect Agape love?* While writing this section, I began thinking of the times when I was married, I let my spouse down, or he let me down, not demonstrating the unconditional love as found in 1 Corinthians 13. I believe everyone reading this book can attest they have not always "been" *Agape* love to those you are in a close relationship with. The Apostle Paul frankly discusses this stark reality in Romans 7:15-20 (NIV), *"I do not understand what I do. For what I want to do I do not do, but what I hate I do. And if I do what I do not want to do, I agree the law is good. As it is, it is no longer I who do it, but it is sin living in me. For I know good itself does not dwell in me, that is, in my sinful nature. For I have the desire to do what is good, but I cannot carry it out. For I do not do the good I want to do, but the evil I do not want to do - this I keep on doing. Now if I do what I do not want to do, it is no longer I who do it, but it is sin living in me that does it."*

The Apostle Paul is recognizing his innate desire is to live a flawless life demonstrating and being *Agape* love. However, the sin that is a part of him (due to the fall of Adam and Eve) and in all of us, is what tempts us to do what we know is wrong. Our responsibility is to recognize the temptations that befall us! To choose to not fall into the snares of sin, but instead to run fast into the loving arms of God by seeking His strength and wisdom in all things. Sin came into this world. Through Jesus dying on the cross, sin was conquered. The only way we can overcome the sin that wages war against us is with the help of God. *"I can do all things through Christ who strengthens me"* (Philippians 4:13 NKJV). The more our sinful nature takes over, the less convicted we become, to the point we do not even recognize it as sin, instead we start to believe it is a normal way of being. The more we deny the truth that is found in the Bible the more we distance ourselves from *Agape* love by allowing our sinful nature to take over.

Agape love is a sacrificial love; it is a selfless love. Some of you reading this book may be so involved in sin, and self-centered you do not want this form of selfless love in your life. *Agape* love may be so foreign to you that you have not even allowed yourself to consider it as a way of living and interacting with others. You may want life to revolve around you and your needs. Yet let me ask you, *"are you happy, are you satisfied, or do you keep trying to fill a void with more stuff, and with more addictive behaviors? How has this selfish love worked out for you in your relationships with others? Are you joyful and happy as a human being or are you constantly cranky and filled with anger?"*

If you want to change, what can you do about it?

Saying "I love you" and practicing *Agape* love are two different things. We can say it. But when we do, we are challenged to live it out. This is when the choice of implementing unconditional love can flourish and grow into fruits of the Spirit - love, joy, peace, gentleness, kindness, patience, and self-control. It is by intentionally thinking and then the following through of selfless acts that provides the true evidence of *Agape* love. Choice is the major factor in living out *Agape* love. Choice begins in the mind and then flows out of the heart. Sometimes we do not want to demonstrate *Agape* love. It is at such times we need to deny our feelings and use the wisdom of God. We do this by being led by the Holy Spirit to do what we are called to do, even when we don't want to. *What are your thoughts towards wanting to act out Agape love to those around you? Do your actions and words back up what you are instructed by the Holy Scriptures to do?*

Several years ago, my daughter asked me to attend a particular event involving people I would rather not spend time with. My daughter felt obligated to accept the invitation due to who was organizing the event. On the other hand, I did not feel the need to attend and instead I found myself objecting. I was making statements such as, "I would rather stay home and sort my socks" or "I think I have grocery shopping to attend to". *Have you ever had one of these moments of protest where you know the event is not going to prove rewarding and so you make up a hundred excuses?* I was hoping my resistance would be heard, somehow reasoning the pain that had been wrongfully inflicted on me by these people would show through the thin veneer of protest. In all reality, it was not even close to any attempt at demonstrating *Agape* love towards my daughter, as she needed to attend the event. In fact, it was rather self-serving and fully informing of record keeping as to how these people wronged me. I knew it was an event my daughter had to attend.

Sara, instead of speaking with me about it again, texted me asking if I would take part in this function with her. Both of us knew I was going to be in the presence of my enemies. After reading the text, I was practicing the speech I was going to give my daughter when she returned home from school that evening. During my speech practicing session, God interrupted me. I heard God speak in a still small voice, "Tell your daughter you love her and that is why you will attend this gathering with her, because you want to support her". Oh, dear God, I think you are telling me to pass over my feelings and to practice *Agape* love. *Is this the unconditional love that looks out for the benefit of others above my own benefit and gain you continually declare in your word? Can I really do this?* Immediately this scripture came to mind, *I can do all things through Christ who strengthens me* (Philippians 4:13 NKJV).

I automatically conceded and allowed God to direct my steps instead of listening to my own protests - even though I was right. I so wanted to establish the order of my life as it pertained to this event. Yet God in all His wisdom intervened and provided clarity as to what I needed to do, not what I wanted to do. I still had a choice. I chose to walk in obedience with what God was telling me to do. It was not easy to take part in this get together; however, I knew God was teaching me to be selfless, not selfish. I also knew God never leaves me or forsakes me not even for one minute. God was going to be with me at the event on a continual basis, walking beside me and never leaving me. God was with me in the presence of my enemies. This He promised in Psalm 23:5 (KJV), *Thou preparest a table before me in the presence of mine enemies: thou anointest my head with oil; my cup runneth over.* The next verse is where the promise is established when we walk in obedience with God. *Surely goodness and mercy shall follow me all the days of my life and I will dwell in the house of the Lord forever* (Psalm 23:6 KJV).

The above illustrated example I believe is all too familiar in today's society. I think many of you reading this book would agree you had similar interactions and words with family members you are in close relationship with. I think in today's modern world many of us are too caught up in our own way of doing things and wanting things. We allow pride and stubbornness to seep in and take over, neglecting to demonstrate this unconditional *Agape* love for others around us. Instead, our way becomes the most important regardless of the opinion, needs or desires of others and often regardless of common sense. We must remember God's ways are always higher than our ways. God knows the beginning from the end. If we stay in close relationship with God and ask Him to guide us during these times of indecision and opposition, He will teach us to love with *Agape* love.

Sadly, I think marriages and families fall apart because we are too caught up in the *Eros* love – this feeling of physical passionate love, with sensual desire and longing, instead of selfless *Agape* love. When these romantic desires dwindle, when we have lost *this lovin' feeling* we are left with nothing. This is because both partners have not practiced unconditional, selfless love in our marriage relationships or in other relationships we find ourselves involved in. This *Agape* love is the unconditional love God demonstrated to us and that is written about in His word. We are to model *Agape* love with our partners, children, family members, and anyone else who we interact with - yes, even our enemies.

If we intentionally practice *Agape* love in our relationships, I believe we give up the right to be right. I believe if we commit to living our lives this way, more marriages will stay together, and broken relationships would be mended. Most of us marry a person who is our exact opposite, as we marry a helpmate. A helper is someone who completes us and fills in the gaps that are missing in our own life. Most of us have not consciously married a person who is our exact opposite, who completes our half and makes us whole. In Genesis 2:24 (GNT) God states, *That is why a man leaves his father and mother and is united with his wife, and they become one.* God intended to bring two people together to make a whole. Each half is unique and separate, until they unite in marriage. However, it is these differences that often lead to strife and angst in our relationships. It is the differences that are like a dripping tap that we tend to pick on and condemn in the other person. I am suggesting instead of condemning our spouse for their differences, we need to rejoice in our differences and embrace them, as this is what attracted us to our partner in the first place. Embrace their unique qualities, nurture them, and help them to flourish and grow. Teamwork in marriage is vital. People need to enter the marriage union believing as if they are joining a team. Together, two are better than one! Do not condemn your partner for thinking and behaving in a manner that is not like you. Instead, celebrate their uniqueness. If you married someone the exact same as yourself, you would be living a very mundane existence. Rejoice in their special qualities!

> *It takes two to make a relationship work as Agape love is a choice. People in unsafe situations should not remain as they need to attend to their own well-being and that of their children.*

If your marriage is safe and it is an environment that can be fixed, nothing is too impossible for God. I encourage you today and for the next 30 days to do something extra-ordinarily selfless for your spouse and your children. If you are not married, I advocate you to do something extra-ordinarily selfless for a few people in your life for the next 30 days. I recommend you develop a habit of speaking kind and respectful words to others near you and to use a tone of voice that is full of *Agape* love, peace and joy. By doing this, I am not suggesting you become a doormat and to turn off your mind to being wise and discerning. You must continue to develop a keen mind. What I am proposing is you decide to live more of a selfless life, not a selfish life. Let God guide you in living a life full of *Agape* love. A friend of mine recently sent the following quote to me that sums up *Agape* love:

> *There will never be peace on earth until our love of power becomes the power of love.*

The remaining three forms of love as described in the ancient Greek language are *Eros, Philia* and *Storge*. These three types of love are all embedded within *Agape* love - the selfless love. *Agape* love is not separate from these other three, instead these three are under the umbrella of *Agape* love - the power of *1* the power of *3*.

Dr. Cheryl Bauman

Eros Love

Eros is a physical passionate love, with sensual desire and longing (Liddell & Scott, 1940). This type of love as described by the Ancient Greeks is a romantic form of love without the balance of logic as it is created by pure emotion, *a love at first sight*. The modern Greek word, "Erotas" means intimate love. *Eros* love does not have to be sexual in nature; however, *Eros* is interpreted as a love for a person greater than the love of a friendship. *Eros* love can be applied to dating relationships as well as marriage. For the union of the marriage bond between a husband and a wife to be fulfilled according to the scriptures, *Eros* love is essential. If you are in a marriage relationship *Eros* love must develop and grow to be healthy and flourishing. Without *Agape* love, which is the unconditional selfless love, *Eros* love will feed on sinful nature and become selfish and self-fulfilling.

There are countless movies, romance novels, magazines, websites, and billboard screens demonstrating to us how the world would want us to interpret this romantic form of *Eros* love. The world is also dictating through movies, television shows and on-line websites how *Eros* love should be "played out" between partners. It is virtually impossible to continually measure-up to this worldly standard of *Eros* love, as the romantic love often portrayed is seen without flaw, always very passionate and sensual. *Is this why many of us in our marriage relationships know we cannot compete with the false pretenses of Eros love that are being flung at us from all angles? Or worse yet, is this why people wander off into adulterous affairs because he or she is looking for the movie set love, that is so fake it does not exist in reality?* We are being raised by media that is suggestively providing fantasizing false images of what *Eros* love is and how to get it. Pornography is so readily available in today's world. Many people, both young and old, own a mobile phone where they can quickly and easily access lewd internet sites that are a false form of intimacy. Statistics are revealing young children are now logging onto pornographic websites at alarming rates!

Do you often feel inadequate due to the pressure from media sources telling you what and how to display Eros love? Do you only enact Eros love within the confines of your bedroom walls, or have you moved the expression of romantic love beyond the bedroom to enhance your life? You do this with little thoughtful gestures that are so important to keep the spark going? Fanning the flame outside of the bedroom helps to ensure when you are in the bedroom *Eros* love is much more passionate and romantic. Because you are livening up your romantic love relationship with kindness, fun, and playfulness. Continually doing little acts of kindness for your partner and speaking loving words demonstrates to them

Agape love combined with *Eros* love. Therefore, when you do become physically intimate with each other the barriers of cruelty, distrust, and unkindness are broken, and you can envelope each other with the unconditional love that originates from God. This is the true God-given design of intimacy where no inhibitions are between a husband and wife, only trust and total surrender. For *Eros* love in all its splendor to be possible in the way God designed it between a husband and wife, the selfless *Agape* love must come first in your marriage relationship. If you are having problems with the romantic Eros love, try practicing *Agape* love with your spouse and wait for the positive results to occur.

> *For this reason, a man will leave his father and mother and be united to his wife, and the two will become one flesh. So, they are no longer two, but one flesh. Therefore, what God has joined together, let no one separate (Mark 10:7-9 NIV).*

The Tricks of the Devil to Sideline Your Relationships

If *Agape* love is not the central form of love in your marriage relationship, then *Eros* love will not have honesty, trust, and fidelity at its core root. If you and your partner do not have a transparent, honest and trustworthy relationship, then you opened the door for Satan to work his masterful tricks. The devil is the father of lies. He whispers lies to you and your spouse all the time. His main job is to be the accuser of brethren as found in Revelation 12:10b (NIV), *For the accuser of our brothers and sisters, who accuses them before our God, day and night.* Why is he the accuser, because he knows his time is short. The remaining portion of verse 10 goes on to say, *"has been hurled down"*. Satan knows in the Bible, which is the true living word of God, it states he will be hurled into the lake of fire at the time of Christ's return to earth. This is why the devil is working overtime to destroy relationships and to take as many people to hell with him as possible. This truth is found in the end part of verse 12 in Revelation 12:12b, *He is filled with fury, because he knows his time is short.*

Satan who is the greatest deceiver to ever roam this earth, deceived himself into thinking he could overthrow God. We are so fortunate God is the ultimate Almighty Powerful force of the Universe because God is love. However, many reject God's *Agape* love because they are deceived by Satan into believing they do not need God. They are deceived to think they can go it alone, do it on their own. This is a lie straight from the pits of hell. Through *Agape* love, God sent His son Jesus to live on this earth and to die on the cross. Jesus' selfless act took on all the sins of the world, so every single person who believes on His name will be saved from the eternal damnation Satan wants you to be part of. Satan knew pride blinded him to the truth with regards to the power found in God and in His Son Jesus Christ.

Due to the blinding pride that has overtaken Satan it is too great for him to admit he is wrong in what he is doing. Pride and deceit condemned Satan to be thrown into a lake of fire for all eternity. Thus, Satan wants as many people as he can convince to be condemned with him so they will also live in an eternal abyss of fear, loneliness, pain and suffering. The sad truth is many people on this earth are so blinded by selfishness and pride they do not even realize they are being deceived. One day if these confused people do not wake up to the reality God is in control, they will end up in hell. The spirit of pride is deceiving many into thinking there is not an ultimate Mighty God who rules over the earth. These people will be deceived all the way to the grave and then be sadly condemned to an eternal life of despair.

The major problem on earth is the battle between good and evil. Just look around and evil is encircling the world. People have been so deceived by the tricks of the devil they believe selfishness, pride and deception are good things. Many people believe these ways of acting are a natural way of being. Satan has fooled people into believing evil is good and good is evil. Many people think these negative thoughts that 'pop' into their heads regarding their spouse are normal, and they begin to believe these lies. Many believe these untruths to the point they begin to believe their marriage is not a good marriage, and they need to look elsewhere for *Eros* love, because they have lost that *lovin' feeling*. What a lie from the pits of hell! Every person that has fallen into this trap, and there are many people in this category, need to know Satan is laughing at you. In Satan's job description here on this earth is found a long list of things he is determined to accomplish. One major role Satan plays is to cause strife and dissension between husband and wife. Satan knows the truth that is written in the word of God concerning husbands and wives:

> *Two are better than one, because they have a good return for their labor: If either of them falls down, one can help the other up. But pity anyone who falls and has no one to help them up. Also, if two lie down together, they will keep warm. But how can one keep warm alone? Though one may be overpowered, two can defend themselves. A cord of three strands is not quickly broken (Ecclesiastes 4:9-12 NIV).*

Another scripture supporting the power of unity - *the power of 1 and the power of 3*, meaning God is always with us. He is in our relationship with our partner making the number *3*, not *2*. This is the *power of 1, 2 and 3*! In the following scripture, Jesus confirms the importance of being in unity with God:

> *Again, truly I tell you that if two of you on earth agree about anything they ask for, it will be done for them by my Father in heaven. For where two or three gather in my name, there am I with them (Matthew 18:19-20 NIV).*

Satan's main objective is to isolate people; to make them suspicious and to cause strife in every relationship so they do not gather in unity to declare the promises and goodness of God. If Satan can divide families, he won at separating people from living a life that could be glorifying to God instead of a life filled with strife. These schemes are designed to win people over to the dark side and to have people live in fear and hatred within their relationships instead of living free in joy, peace and love. If Satan is trying to win the battle in your mind. He does this so you begin to act and say the awful lies he feeds you thought life. If he does this then he has been successful at fulfilling roles found in his job description, as you have fallen into his deceptive snare. Located on Satan's extensive job description is some of the following tasks (there are too many tasks to list all of them), as he constantly lies and accuses people, which results in:

- Continuously sidelining humans so they do not fulfill their ultimate purpose on this earth
- Continuously spreading deception and lies about self in one's mind
- Continuously spreading deception and lies about others
- Continuously spreading hatred throughout the whole earth
- Continuously destroying people's trust in others so there are no strong and connected bonds of love between them and their family members and loved ones
- Continuously isolating people
- Continuously causing strife
- Continuously causing confusion
- Continuously causing fear
- Continuously causing paranoia

*Note every single job description listed above begins with the word "continuously". This is an indication Satan never stops, his role in your life with continue until you leave this earth.

> *Be alert and of sober mind. Your enemy the devil prowls around like a roaring lion looking for someone to devour (1 Peter 5:8 NIV).*

Pay close attention to the words in the above scripture that labels the devil as your enemy, the devil is not your friend. Do not be deceived. The good news is if you do not listen to the lies of the enemy and resist his schemes, this next portion of Revelation 12, verse 11 (NIV) is for you:

> *They triumphed over him by the blood of the Lamb and the word of their testimony; they did not love their lives so much as to shrink from death.*

The above scripture is a promise we will win over Satan. We win if we are people of God who love God more than we love the selfish ways of human nature the enemy continually tries to tempt us with by lying to us. The enemy tries to trick all of us into believing adultery and pornography and other addictive behaviors such as excessive drinking and gambling are better than God's ways. Satan tricks people into believing affairs are a way to increase Eros love. This is a deceptive trap I pray none of you fall into. If you find yourself caught run as fast as you can away from its snare. I do want to qualify the above is written for people who are in relationships that are not bound with physical, extremely emotional and sexual abuse. If you find yourself in this form of a relationship, run to find help at a Bible based church as quickly as possible.

How can you demonstrate through thoughts, words and actions love towards your partner?

Husbands and wives can demonstrate and say to each other love in simple ways every day that continually reinforces the romantic *Eros* love they have towards each other. I am writing this from a female perspective as we view the simple lovely gestures demonstrated and spoken to us from our spouse as a form of *Eros* love towards us. Kind gestures of love and affection are extremely important to us as females. Each couple has their own love language, their own way to *Just Say It!* "I love you". These connections need to be built on unconditional *Agape* love that only comes from God through us. For we are not capable of *Agape* love without the presence of God in our lives and in our marriage. Connected with *Agape* love is *Eros* love that must be demonstrated together with our partner to build bonds of trust, safety and comfort. My suggestion is if this is not currently happening in your home that it can. However, it cannot occur if you begin to whine and complain it is not happening. Instead, it needs to begin with you. You need to begin to develop *Agape* and *Eros* love in your home and with your partner, by praying to God and seeking His wisdom in this area. Ask and seek God's guidance as to how to develop an unconditional love towards your partner. This unconditional love results from an intentional commitment to being patient, kind and loving, not to being haughty, selfish and rude.

The enemy is tearing apart families and couples at such a rapid rate. His scheme is to trick you into believing tension and strife are necessary and normal in a marriage relationship. The enemy tricked many into being selfish with their time and with their affections. Out of this unconditional love that is birthed from the *Agape* love our Heavenly Father has for us, is the only 'road map' that will ensure your destination to true *Eros* love for your spouse. It is only through the realization *Agape* love embraces *Eros* love; you will want to selflessly demonstrate your romantic love in little gestures outside of the bedroom. Doing this so when you are in the bedroom the intimate love relationship will be phenomenal – beyond human descriptive language. It is a love language that is beyond words, a love language that is so intimate it is only spoken and understood between two people. Every couple's love language is unique and intimate to them and only them.

Ask yourself, do you and your partner have your own unique and intimate love language? If not, what are the barriers that are holding you back? Do not condemn, instead transcend. Transcend to a place where you want to seek and to find love with your partner like you have never experienced before. Love we long for. The love relationship God designed for you. This is the ultimate love QUEST between God, you and your spouse. *How do you find it?* I would suggest getting out your Bible and beginning with 1 Corinthians 13. As you go through the chapter bit by bit, ask God to reveal to you His message for you, and *how you can enact this love with your spouse? Ask God what you are doing right, according to His word?* Ask God what you are doing wrong and how you can correct the behavioural patterns that have probably become so engrained you might not even realize the damage you created. I encourage you and your spouse to read together 1 Corinthians 13 and to ask God to guide and show you where you are going wrong, and what you are doing right as a couple. Be open to the still small voice of God.

The next form of love, *Philia* love is also under the covering of *Agape* love. Without selfless love, it is impossible to enact *Philia* love.

Dr. Cheryl Bauman

Philia Love

Philia is *mental* love. The definition of *Philia* is the same in both Ancient and Modern Greek. It means the love of friendship; this type of love has give-and-take. It is a dispassionate virtuous love and is a concept that was developed by Aristotle. *Philia* includes loyalty to friends, family and community, and requires virtue, equality and familiarity (Liddell & Scott, 1940). I am blessed to have the love and friendship of so many wonderful people. I feel honored to call people of all ages my friend. I have people in my life younger than 10 years old and older than 90 with whom I value their love and friendship. For years, a group of eight of us women would meet every month in one of our homes to share a delicious meal cooked by the hostess. Together we would share in the delightful cuisine as well as in tons of laughter. Over the years, this number has dwindled to five of us. I am blessed to call these four female teachers my friends and loyal companions. The five of us span three generations, some of us are in our 40s, others are in our 50s and a few are now in their 60s. It is marvelous! We have been through a lot together in the 20+ years since we have been gathering. What a wonderful affirmation of friendship that stood the test of time.

My friend Georgia, who I have mentioned several times in this book needs no introduction. Georgia lights up a room when she enters, and makes everyone feel special. She is forever telling me wise words of wisdom and demonstrating exercises to keep me agile and quick on my feet. Georgia is always putting others before herself. Wherever Georgia goes she is always spreading the good news by giving people compliments or passing out little pieces of paper with positive sayings or prayers on them. I am overflowing with gratitude for this unique and special friendship! Another friend of mine, who is also a teacher, is Christina. Before we had our children, we would spend much more time together. Many of our get-togethers would center around some sort of exercise, sport, or activity. Even though lately we do not have the opportunity to see each other often, I know if I ever need her, or if she ever needs me, we are there for each other. My friend Mariola is very dear to me. We met in 1999, as we taught at the same school in Toronto, Ontario, Canada. Mariola still lives in Toronto, which is about a four-hour drive from Ottawa, where I now live. Even though distance separates us, every time we get together, it is as if no time passed. Everyone needs a "Mariola" in their life. Mariola is the friend who is very frank and honest, yet quite witty. The black and white nature of her character is what brings to light her forthright ways. She is an extremely loyal and steadfast friend. I consider her like a sister, and I feel so blessed that she is a part of my life. My friend Jill and I have a unique connection that dates to when I was a teenager. I value her friendship and most of all her love and devotion to God. We honor each other and continually pray for each other. God has us connected, and the discernment and "just knowing" is precious between Jill and me. I cannot put into words the belongingness I have with her. I sometimes travel for work, so we can be thousands of miles apart, yet we discern and communicate what the other needs to hear by sending one another a quick text message or an email.

I also have another dear friend Christine. Christine has come into my life within the past 10 years. She is such a woman of faith, courage, and strength. She is continually filling up my cup, and she testifies I reciprocate and fill up her cup. Christine always has a word of encouragement for me, a scripture verse, a unique story to tell that is so relatable to what is happening in my "world". Christine is a teacher, although now she is a stay-at-home mom, enjoying her devotion to her children and to helping her mother with her day-to-day life. Christine is a testimony as to a friend who always loves!

Laura Lynn, is a true sister in Christ. She lives on the West Coast, and I live in the Eastern part of Canada. Despite the distance between us, I always know that she is praying for me. Even though she has an extremely busy schedule, she always makes herself available to talk with me, counsel me, and offer up words of discernment as I navigate through the waters of an otherwise chaotic world. Our relationship is reciprocal, as Laura Lynn also calls upon me for support either through a quick text, an email or phone call. She knows she can do so any time of day or night. Carey-Lee, who has recently moved to Florida, has a laugh that is incredibly contagious. One of the most endearing aspects about her is her knowledge of truth found in the scriptures. This knowledge and wisdom have been a source of blessing. Carey-Lee's steadfast faith in the goodness of God is a real testimony to me and others. She is an inspiration to all who know her! Brenda has entered back into my life, after a long pause. It is incredible, as I have known Brenda my entire life! Even though we just recently reconnected, I believe we were always connected in spirit and truth. Time has passed, yet it is as if no time has passed at all. We picked up right where we left off, not missing a beat. It is exciting to witness how both of us have grown in our relationship with the Lord, and it is a real testimony that our steadfast faith has not wavered. Laura Lynn, Carey-Lee and Brenda are all gorgeous on the inside and outside. I count my blessings, knowing the three of them. We are kindred spirits.

Then there is a new group of friends with whom I have met since my daughter, Sara, attended university at Oral Roberts University in Tulsa, Oklahoma. This group of friends is like a "sisterhood" of beautiful women with whom God has given to me for "such a time as this". We had many discussions together in relation to what God is doing in our lives both in the present and praying with one another for the future God-given visions to come to fruition. Victoria has graciously allowed me to stay in her Oklahoma home. She is a retired principal, who decided to go back into the classroom for her remaining years of service. I believe we have so much in common, and yet we are also uniquely different. I enjoy our deep discussions in relation to the Holy Spirit. Victoria is a sister in Christ, and I feel so blessed to call her a friend. I was introduced to Victoria through Kristi. I could write an entire book on Kristi and the impact she has had on my life. Her peaceful ways, her constant steadfast faith and her never wavering friendship have been a testimony as how to live out the fruits of the spirit here on earth. As I am writing this, I can "see" Kristi's face beaming, and "hear" her laughter!

I also have friendships that span expansive distances to Australia and Italy. My two close friends and colleagues in Australia, Dorothy and Joan were at one time my supervisors for my doctoral thesis at the University of Southern Queensland. The countless hours that both Dorothy and Joan poured into me during my doctoral studies was one of sacrifice and dedication. I can never re-pay either of them for all that they have taught me, and the compassion and kindness that they willingly demonstrated towards me. I have known them since 2004. Over the years we have grown closer. First I studied with them and then we worked together for a time that has spanned over 20 years. Through our work life we then bonded as loyal and devoted friends. We have shared in one another's joys and sorrows. Grazia is my dear loyal friend from Italy. Grazia was a professor at university and is now a principal of a school in Italy. Even through we do not communicate as often as I would like, when we do, it is so easy to jump right back into life with Grazia. We never miss a beat! Despite the many kilometres (miles) separating me from my friends in Australia and Italy, it is comforting to know that we are just a text, an email or a Zoom call away!

There are so many friendships I could share with you. However, there are not enough pages in this book to write down every detail and to tell all the stories that are brimming with celebration, sadness, grief, kindness and love. The short narratives and the people highlighted are only a few examples. My intent was to not leave anyone out, but to instead share little snippets of *Philia* love combined with *Agape* love. I am now considered "mid-life", as I am in my 50s. I truly believe age is a mind-set! Although I still do not think of myself as becoming older, I do consider I am wiser because of my daily interactive relationship with God. God is my best friend, He is my Father, and He is the Alpha and the Omega - the beginning and the End. As a result, I have nothing to fear. One thing the years have taught me is to value my friends, as they are my sisters and my brothers in Christ.

A friend loves at all times (Proverbs 17:17 NIV).

This section on the four Greek words to describe love, even though it is a third of the way into the book, it was the last section to be written. I was giving additional thought and prayer as to what God wanted me to write with regards to the four types of love from the Ancient Greek language. I wanted this book to be completed two years ago; however, time and circumstances just did not allow. Now I know why. This is God's time. I am finishing this portion of the book after the COVID-19 pandemic that swept across the entire world.

During this unprecedented time of social and physical distancing, one that my generation and the younger have never before experienced, it was uplifting watching acts of kindness occurring throughout the world in the name of love and friendship. Even when we were instructed to distance ourselves, our human desire is still for connection and belonging. It is still wanting to look out for the welfare of others above our own. This is what true unconditional love is. It is this heartwarming demonstration of combining *Philia* love and *Agape* love as medical staff placed their own lives at-risk to save the lives of the sick. Also, as a neighbor kindly delivered groceries to an elder's doorstep, or as Chris Tomlin's song, *How Great is Our God*, was sung by an Italian community on their balconies as they continued to connect. The need to belong and the need for friendship is innate regardless of the culture or regardless of the circumstances. Good friends and family members make great times better and hard times easier.

Storge Love

Storge means *affection* in Ancient and Modern Greek. It is a natural affection, such as love shown by parents for their children. *Storge* was rarely used in Ancient Greek writings, and when it was it was used almost exclusively as a descriptor of relationships within the family. The way it was used in ancient writings was to express acceptance of family by putting up with situations, as in loving the difficult family member (Liddell & Scott, 1940). If you can visualize pulling an elastic band with both hands. When you stretch it out, and you keep stretching it, but it does not break, this is often the type of acceptance family members have for one another. Unless there is abuse, the elastic band has a lot of "stretch" to it. This *Storge* love is something I would contest we need to have more of. As we love unconditionally with God's *Agape* love. God provides for us His eyes to view family through so we develop more of an acceptance of their quirks and behaviors that may otherwise be offensive to us. Canadian singer and songwriter Tara Shannon has cleverly portrayed the acceptance a mother has of her children's demanding ways for attention in her song, Bein' a mommy is a Mutha'. I encourage you to listen to the words and watch the video. It will make you laugh, as it is highly relatable, especially if you are a mom!

My ancestors are from Switzerland. In terms of our cultural heritages, there are many discrepancies in the ways our families think, process information, see the world and thus make decisions. It is just simply a fact of life. The methods by which we are raised are impacted by the cultures that surround us. There is no denying this truth. I was raised by my parents to be logical and methodical in my decision making, yet to also be full of mercy and compassion. I do however realize that I must embrace differences, no matter the cultural heritages we are from as they have shaped our lives into who we are today.

My dear Zia Olga, who since passed, helped me to understand, through humor, just how to understand a culture that was foreign to me. Zia means Aunt in Italian. She was one of the only English-speaking people in the small village nestled in the Gran Sasso d'Italia. The Gran Sasso d'Italia is the highest mountain in the Italian Apennines, and the second-highest mountain in Italy outside the Alps. Up until her health would not allow her to, Zia Olga spent the summers in Italy and the winters in Florida and New Jersey, USA. Zia Olga was always a bright spot in my Italian vacations, as she made me feel loved and cared for. Zia Olga had so much energy and so much life, I would often forget she was well into her senior years. Her attitude towards life determined her altitude. Zia Olga would turn a normal everyday event into an adventure. She impacted me greatly as her zeal and zest for life are forever etched in my mind. Zia Olga taught me to always find the good in a situation, no matter what. I look forward to reuniting with Zia Olga in Heaven!

I have so many loving family stories involving my daughter Sara. I think some of our best times are when we are just hanging out playing board games, going to movies, boating at the lake, roasting marshmallows, skiing, cooking our favorite dishes, shopping, or working out together. We find ourselves laughing over the silliest things. Sara and I genuinely enjoy each other's company. We will often just pick up and go on the spur of the moment to enjoy an adventure - big or small! I am so grateful for this. Even though my parents are getting older, we continue to enjoy visiting them at the lake and spending precious time with them. My dad still has his sense of humor and remains a great storyteller. My mom is an amazing cook who always provides tasty meals and morsels of wisdom, especially when it comes to medical and health advice. The greatest gift my parents gave to me is the gift of knowing Jesus as my personal Lord and Savior. They instilled within me and their granddaughter, Sara, a love for reading the Bible and for seeking the wisdom of God. This is a generational legacy I am blessed to have.

As I was writing this portion of the chapter, I continually made the mistake of typing the word storage, instead of *storge*. I then began to think, *is this really a mistake?* As the relationships in our lives that involve family members can be so wonderful, yet some can be so strained. Difficulties experienced within family relationships can evolve into us carrying around all sorts of excess baggage we stashed away in the storage areas of our minds, such as bitterness, anger and resentment. Our storage containers or rooms in our homes can become overwhelmingly packed with unforgiveness. These items weigh a lot and are often not necessary. Take an inventory of all the stuff in your home or apartment you store up you really do not need or ever use. Think about how much these additional items in your storage space weigh. *Do you ever just want to rid yourself of the excess junk that is lying around your house, collecting dust?* The same is true with regards to the storing up of anger, bitterness, jealousy, resentment, and distrust we crammed into the empty spaces of our minds that continuously haunt us and weigh us down. This excess junk in our minds is taking up space, disabling some of us to not think and act clearly with regards to some of our family members. I encourage you to clear out the storage space in your mind and to rid yourself of unforgiveness towards family members. You will be so free and so light in spirit, mind and body. I guarantee you will be an entirely new person. Forgiving others is being obedient to God. It is also a gift for you, as you no longer must carry the excess storage around daily. It is possible to be set free from unforgiveness. Several upcoming keys discuss this topic in more depth.

I think I would be hard-pressed to find anyone on this earth that does not have a difficult member within their family. Or maybe the word member should be plural and changed to members. Even some of Jesus' family members rejected him. We find this in the scriptures where his sisters and brothers were concerned about his teaching and preaching. They thought Jesus had gone mad:

> *While Jesus was still talking to the crowd, his mother and brothers stood outside, wanting to speak to him. Someone told him, "Your mother and brothers are standing outside, wanting to speak to you." He replied to them, "Who is my mother, and who are my brothers?" Pointing to his disciples, he said, "Here are my mother and my brothers. For whoever does the will of my Father in heaven is my brother and sister and mother." (Matthew 12:46-50 NIV).*

Knowing Jesus also experienced rejection by difficult family members helps us to more fully accept not everyone is going to love us, even if we try hard. Unfortunately, some family members in my life I have strained relations with. For the longest time I was very distraught about this. However, God directed me to the scriptures in the gospel of Matthew about Jesus' life. God also gently reminded me about the lives of Joseph and King David. Some of their family members did not like them either. In fact, Joseph's brothers were going to kill him until they sold him into slavery. Due to uncontrolled jealousy, Cain killed his brother Abel. Sometimes the saying, *let go and let God*, can help all of us who face the challenge of difficult family members. Research suggests 10% of people are not going to like you no matter what you do. Some of this 10% can include family members. We just have to accept this and move on to do the will of God. I know in my life God has brought about people who replaced the difficult family members. I am so grateful to God for this. I feel very blessed. God is a God full of grace, love, and mercy. God wants us in right relationship with Him and with others so we can say, "I Belong".

Relationships are tough, especially when people do not practice and believe in the unconditional love of God and therefore, they do not seek wise counsel and a relationship with God. Some of our family members may be seeking the counsel found on television or the internet or are trapped in addictive behaviors. Or worse still, they are calling up other family members and gossiping and slandering you. Instead of trying to make amends, they are making a mess. Loving family does not necessarily translate into agreeing with everything a family member does or says. Family members can be hurtful towards other family members. Love towards family can also be the type of love that needs to distance ourselves from certain people in our families. Yet because of God's forgiveness we are called to demonstrate, we can still love them, however, we may not be able to be near them. Love and acceptance of behavior do not equate. *Agape* love and *forgiveness* do equate.

There is only one true way to find peace and love in your relationships with difficult family members, as described by the Greek word *Storge*. It is to take them to the foot of the cross, repent of what you have done wrong and then leave the *storage of burden* with Christ. I encourage you to daily read the word of God for direction and wisdom in all your relationships. Make God the foundational cornerstone in your family relationships – both the good and the not so good. If you do this, you will not stray, you will be in the will of God for your life. Others around you might stray and get off course. However, you need to remember you are not responsible for the actions and words of others in your family, only your own thoughts, words, and actions. A good way to visualize God's *Agape* love in relation to *Storge* love for your family members is there is not a "storage" container big enough to hold God's love. God's love cannot be kept in a storage container. If we allow it, God's *Agape* love overflows, by flooding our lives with love for family members who are either lovable or unlovable.

Key 15

What Does The Bible Say About Belonging To the Family of God?

Nearing the end of writing this chapter, the awareness and realization God is calling all of us into a relationship of *Agape* love with Him and *Agape* love with ourselves and others became stronger. I am not trying to continually rewrite the same concept, instead, I am rewriting this message as an emphasis that continually gathers momentum. Our love relationship through the cross of Jesus Christ and through God creating us in His own image is the true testimony of *Agape* love.

> For God so loved the world that he gave his only begotten son, that whosoever believeth in him should not perish, but have everlasting life (John 3:16 KJV).

If we believe in God and accept His Son, Jesus Christ, then this love relationship is eternal. We belong to God's family regardless of our earthly family relationships. We will always have a place to belong if we are a Child of the Most-High God. Our eternal home is in Heaven. We belong to the family of God. However, God also calls us into an unconditional loving relationship with others. It is the definition of the boundaries of these relationships that shape how we express this unconditional love. We express it to a husband, a child, a family member, a friend, a neighbor, a co-worker, a member of our church or a member of a local community organization. This is why it was so vital to have outlined the four Ancient Greek words and their definitions of love - *Agape, Eros, Philia,* and *Storge*. When boundary lines become blurred, confusion over love and confusion over how to express this love towards others can quickly set in.

Agape love is the love as Christians we are required to live out continuously as we interact with all the people we meet, not just some of the people. God is love, God loves us with *Agape* love, so we can love Him, and then in turn we can love ourselves and others.

Manifesting it is under the protective covering of *Agape* love. The keys according to *Agape* love are unlocked in the following:

- **God is Love:**
  ✓ *Whoever does not love does not know God, because God is love* (1 John 4:8 NIV).
  ✓ *Give thanks to the God of heaven. His love endures forever* (Psalm 136:26 NIV).
  ✓ *How precious is your steadfast love, O God! The children of mankind take refuge in the shadow of your wings* (Psalm 36:7 NIV).
  ✓ *And now these three remain: faith, hope and love. But the greatest of these is love* (1 Corinthians 13:13 NIV).

- **God Loves Us:**
  ✓ *The Lord appeared to us in the past saying: "I have loved you with an everlasting love; I have drawn you with unfailing kindness* (Jeremiah 31:3 NIV).
  ✓ *For God so loved the world he gave his one and only Son, that whoever believes in him shall not perish but have eternal life* (John 3:16 NIV).
  ✓ *See what great love the Father has lavished on us, that we should be called the children of God! And that is what we are! The reason the world does not know us is that it did not know him* (1 John 3:1 NIV).
  ✓ *And so, we know and rely on the love God has for us. God is love. Whoever lives in love lives in God, and God in them* (1 John 4:16 NIV).

- **We Love God:**
  ✓ *Jesus replied: 'Love the Lord your God with all your heart and with all your soul and with all your mind.' This is the first and greatest commandment* (Matthew 22:37-38 NIV).
  ✓ *Know therefore that the Lord your God is God; he is the faithful God, keeping his covenant of love to a thousand generations of those who love him and keep his commandments* (Deuteronomy 7:9 NIV).
  ✓ *And we know that in all things God works for the good of those who love him, who have been called according to his purpose* (Romans 8:28 NIV).
  ✓ *Whoever has my commands and keeps them is the one who loves me. The one who loves me will be loved by my Father, and I too will love them and show myself to them* (John 14:21 NIV).

- **We Love Ourselves:**
✓ *We love because he first loved us* (1 John 4:19 NIV).
✓ *The one who gets wisdom loves life; the one who cherishes understanding will soon prosper* (Proverbs 19:8 NIV).
✓ *You are altogether beautiful, my love; there is no flaw in you* (Song of Solomon 4:7 ESV).
✓ *And over all these virtues put on love, which binds them together in perfect unity* (Colossians 3:14 NIV).
✓ *There is no fear in love. But perfect love drives out fear, because fear has to do with punishment. The one who fears is not made perfect in love* (1 John 4:18 NIV).

- **We Love Others:**
✓ *A new command I give you: Love one another. As I have loved you, so you must love one another. By this everyone will know that you are my disciples, if you love one another'* (John 13:34-35 NIV).
✓ *Greater love has no one than this: to lay down one's life for one's friends* (John 5:13 NIV).
✓ *A friend loves at all times, and a brother is born for a time of adversity* (Proverbs 17:17 NIV).
✓ *But love your enemies, do good to them, and lend to them without expecting to get anything back. Then your reward will be great, and you will be children of the Most High...* (Luke 6:35 NIV).

In the next few chapters, we will explore what I believe is truly seeping into all areas of our world today. That which is confusion over love and how to express love depending on the type of relationships we have with people. If we do not have a daily love relationship with God through reading the Bible, listening and talking with Him, we can fall into temptation's trap. We may be *looking for love in all the wrong places.*

You are a chosen people, a royal priesthood, a holy nation, God's special possession, that you may declare the praises of him who called you out of darkness into his wonderful light (1 Peter 2: 9 NIV).

Unlocking Mystery #3

I Belong

> **Reflect:** What advice would you give to your younger self in terms of love and how to belong? I encourage you to write these recommendations down. Reflect on them and choose four people to share this wise counsel with. How has sharing this advice impacted your life? How has sharing this advice affected their lives?
>
> *Note: Depending on your age, you might not be able to fully complete this first section. However, try your best!*
>
> What advice would you like to be given in terms of love and how to belong? Where can you seek this guidance from? I would recommend you begin to surround yourself with people and resources that will provide you with wisdom in the area of love and how to belong.
>
> **Relate:** How can you continue to develop *Agape* love for God, yourself and others? What areas are you doing well at demonstrating and having *Agape* love? What areas are you not doing so well in terms of demonstrating and having *Agape* love? What can you do about this? Who can help you on your journey to unlock the mysteries of finding true unconditional love?
>
> **Respond:** As you continue the QUEST to find true unconditional love, I encourage you to make the following declarations to yourself every day:
>
> - I Belong!
> - I am Lovely!
> - I am Loved!
> - I Love Others!
> - Others Love Me!
>
> *Speak the Truth*
>
> *Just Say It! I Belong!*

Dr. Cheryl Bauman

#4
True Love Does Not Depend on Feelings

True love has its source in God since God is love. When we decide to invite God into our hearts then we can say, "I am loved, I am lovable, and I am loving." We must make a conscious choice to be loving in our day-to-day encounters with others - Christine Lockie.

Key 16

He Loves Me, He Loves Me Not;
She Loves Me, She Loves Me Not

Sally was sitting in the middle of the schoolyard, picking the petals one-by-one from a daisy, reciting, "He loves me, he loves me not". My classmate, eight-year-old Sally tried desperately to figure whether the new boy at our school loved her. As I came closer to her, I could see the tears rolling down her lily-white cheeks and hear the loud sniffles. Sally was so distraught with the feelings of what we might call "puppy love" she did not even notice me approaching. She barely even knew this young boy, yet here she was all alone, infatuated with the idea of "what if". This emotional entanglement had Sally wallowing in self-grief. All the while she was simultaneously giving up playing with classmates that enjoyed her company and loved her for who she was.

I tried to console her, by cajoling her into playing a game of skipping. The more I tried to help Sally, the louder her cries became. I remember as a child not being able to understand why Sally would leave her friends on this beautiful sunny day and instead allow herself to be deeply overrun with emotions that served no purpose. As it turns out, the new boy was not at all interested in Sally. She admitted to sending him a note to determine if he liked her. He swiftly replied, rejecting her QUEST for young love. Several weeks went by and Sally became more secluded and more sorrowful. At eight-years of age she chose to give up a period of time, on living her life to its fullest, in exchange for being stuck in emotions that had no realistic foundational truths. Sally was living in a fantasy world, hoping it became reality. At such a young age, I remember feeling sorry for her, as she made the choice to allow her untamed emotions to run loose. Sally's feelings were leading her life in the wrong direction. You might chuckle at this story and possibly remember yourself in a similar web of confusion over "puppy love". *Yet, how many of you reading this story continued to allow your feelings to steer your life into choppy waters on into teenage life and adulthood?*

As you trek forward hoping to unlock the mysteries of finding true unconditional love, believing you can genuinely love yourself, knowing you are lovable, some need to admit you are defining what love is. You do this based on false assumptions, false teachings, and false beliefs - but most of all on feelings. You may even be of the belief love is a feeling, nothing more, nothing less. If this is you, you are operating with an unstable belief system. You might be defining what love is through popular media, novels, television shows and internet articles. Many of these societal outlets interpret love as always changing, something that is fickle. *Ask yourself, is this the truth about love? Is love always shifting, like sinking sand?* Many conceptions of what love is are simply composed distortions, not embedded in truth. Certain explanations as to what love is are often based on "feeling good", or "feeling in love". *You need to wonder then if love is a feeling, what are the foundational truths "they" are using to define and describe love? Do these popular notions and beliefs change from time to time, based on what is current, what is trendy, what is hip and cool? Or do they remain steadfast and true? Is "feeling" in love a reliable assumption as to what to base love on?*

Some of you reading this book might believe that loving yourself and others relies strictly on feelings. You may believe love is just a chemical reaction, a feel-good feeling, that comes and goes. You may believe love will always take you on a roller coaster ride, and this ride is normal. You also may believe you always need to feel sick and dizzy from this roller coaster love-ride, and to be in love is to be continually tossed up and down. *Should you be hinging your QUEST for true unconditional love on feelings that are always up and down? Like eight-year-old Sally, is this really the responsible thing to do, place value in establishing a love relationship that is rooted in feelings?*

Key 17

Is Love a Feel-Good Potion?

When two people *fall in love* it is scientifically proven a chemical reaction occurs in their bodies. Falling in love causes your body to release a flood of feel-good chemicals that trigger specific physical reactions. This internal elixir of love is responsible for making your cheeks flush, your palms sweat and your heart race. *Does this reaction sound familiar to you? Are these "loving feelings" the yard stick you have been using to measure if you are in love with a person or not?* Science has proven levels of these feel-good substances, which include dopamine, adrenaline, and norepinephrine, increase when two people fall in love. Dopamine creates feelings of euphoria while adrenaline and norepinephrine are responsible for the pitter-patter of the heart, restlessness and overall preoccupation that go along with experiencing new love. *Sound familiar to any of you?*

MRI scans indicate love lights up the pleasure center of the brain. When we fall in love, blood flow increases in this area, which is the same part of the brain implicated in obsessive-compulsive behaviors. It is proven that falling in love (the chemical reaction) lowers serotonin levels. Lower levels of serotonin are common in people with obsessive-compulsive disorders. This may explain why some people concentrate on little other than their partner during the early stages of a relationship, when they are "falling in love". This is the stage when a "love addiction" occurs in people who need to constantly have their serotonin levels lowered and are prone to obsessive-compulsive behaviors. These people may not recognize the addictiveness of their obsessive-compulsiveness and may "jump in" and "out" of relationships on a continual basis, as they need the "high" the "new love" is providing them. Stability and a sense of right and wrong are tossed aside and replaced with an unquenchable QUEST for addictive pleasure, at any expense. This is typical behavior found in people who are unable to "settle down" or who have continuous adulterous affairs while married. Their bodies crave the "high" new love offers them, with lowering serotonin, and as a result they leave a wake of destruction in their selfish unquenched path.

Doctors caution these physical responses to love may work to our disadvantage. The phrase *love is blind* is a valid notion. When people are in the early stages of a relationship, they tend to idealize their partner and see only things they want to see. This is like eight-year-old Sally who did not even know the new boy at school. Quite simply put, negative behaviors or warning signs a person is not the right fit for you, may be overlooked due to that *lovin' feeling*. Outsiders may have a much more objective and rational perspective on the partnership than the two people involved do. If you are just recently in a new relationship, I would affirm you need to seek out a wise perspective on the partnership you are involved in. Good sound advice is especially needed if you have a history of finding yourself in relationships that end early or have no hopeful future. Especially if you have been mistreated in the past by a parent, spouse or a significant other in your life.

Seek wise guidance regarding your love relationships. I would testify God has the most rational and wise perspective on the partnership you are currently involved in. Seek Him for His guidance on this relationship. Be willing and open to listening to His voice and His direction. Be obedient to what God is telling you, above what your body is telling you, as we have just learned, we can be deceived quite quickly by "new love". As well, ask trusted friends and family who will also seek God's wisdom and discernment in helping you to know if this relationship is right for you.

Key 18

Three Phases of Love

Our human bodies are creatively and wonderfully designed by God to enjoy falling in love and remaining in love with someone. Research science resolved and concluded there are three phases to love, which include *excitement*, *attraction*, and *attachment*. *Excitement* is a hormone-driven phase, and this occurs as we experience the desire for another person. The second phase, *the attraction phase*, occurs when blood flows to the pleasure center of the brain and we feel an overwhelming fixation with our partner. The result of the behavior from phases one and two fades during the *attachment phase*, as the body develops a tolerance to the pleasure stimulants. The endorphins and hormones, vasopressin and oxytocin also flood the body at this point creating an overall sense of well-being and security that is conducive to a lasting relationship. The attachment phase relates to *intentional* behaviors and choices.

I think all of you reading this book know of some couples who lasted throughout the years, overcoming many trials and tribulations that being married and staying committed to a long-standing relationship involves. *What makes these couples stand apart from others?* It is the *intentionality* of their love and commitment to each other. I know an elderly couple, Mary and John, who have been married for over 60 years and are still going strong. They do not have a perfect relationship; however, they decided no struggle is too difficult for them to overcome with the help of the Lord. Mary recently said to me she always tried to see John through the eyes of the Lord when they experienced trials in their marriage. She said this perspective helped her to overcome any situation or behavior that tried to come in between them. Mary has not allowed "feelings" or "being on a roller coaster ride" to affect her decision to remain committed and steadfast in her relationship with John.

Mary learned to *intentionally* love John, and she has chosen to go with the compatibility factor talked about earlier in this book. She has *intentionally* developed patterns of behaviours in her marriage that created the continuous compatibility factor with her husband. She has learned how to keep love alive by *intentionally* choosing to work through life's good times and bad times. Mary and John are both intentionally committed to their marriage relationship and are in it until death due them part. Mary and John both relentlessly pursue God, as God relentlessly pursues them. They seek and find strength in God to love one another when that "lovin' feeling" is nowhere to be "felt". I am grateful we have role models such as Mary and John modelling *intentionality* in their marriage, so many of us can benefit from their intentional commitment. *Do you know a couple like Mary and John?* If you do, I encourage you to sit down with them and ask them some questions as to how they made their marriage last throughout the years. In the book of Proverbs in the Bible, King Solomon states wisdom is more precious than silver or gold. You can have all the money in the world, but if you do not have wisdom as to how to guide your relationships, you will be tossed to-and-fro by your emotions. Intentionally choose to rely on God through the Holy Spirit for wisdom to guide your decisions as a married person. If both people choose to rely on God for wisdom to guide their decisions in their marriage, then they will have someone to witness the moments of their life. Moments become memories, and memories become legacies.

Some of you reading this book may be confusing *lust* (excitement phase) with love or the *attraction* phase with love. If this is you, you may find yourself hurt as a result, as neither are true love; they are simply chemical responses your body has towards another human. Often people become fixated on the need for phase one and two – *excitement (lust)* and *attraction* – and once these two phases fizzle, they think the love between themselves and someone else has vanished. However, according to medical science it is quite the opposite, the love has moved on to a more mature phase, which is an *attachment* phase. The attachment phase is one we should all be striving to attain with a significant other. This is how we were designed by God, to leave our parents and to begin a new monogamous, lasting relationship with one other person. In the words of Jesus when tested by the Pharisees, he answered, *"Haven't you read," he replied, "at the beginning the Creator made them male and female." Then He said, "For this reason a man will leave his father and mother and be united to his wife, and the two will become one flesh? So, they are no longer two, but one flesh. Therefore, what God has joined together, let no one separate"* (Matthew 19:4-6 NIV).

Confusion can set in when a person, in a marriage relationship, is addicted to that *lovin' feeling* and thus is experiencing mixed messages. Their body is telling them they are *attaching*. Unfortunately, the person in the marriage relationship that is addicted to that *lovin' feeling* (lowering serotonin) often flees the scene thinking love is lost because *the emotional rush is gone*. If they do not leave the marriage, they may begin adulterous affairs or turn to pornography to get their "fix" of that *lovin' feeling*. People who act in this manner are confirming love on feelings (hormonal reactions) and not on true love between two people, the way it was designed by God. Some people who flee marriages are trying to find that *lovin' feeling*. They often leave their partner heartbroken and bewildered, as they are unable to fully commit to the *attachment* phase. This is due to being addicted to the need to have their serotonin levels lowered. This is a very big and a real problem in our society today. More people are lacking the ability or the intentionality to fully commit to one person in a marriage relationship as they are acting extremely selfish and lacking in self-control. They want to feel in love continuously. It is like the patterns of behavior of any other form of addiction such as alcoholism or gambling. People, who are addicted to the *excitement* phase (*lust*) and *attraction* phase need to have this addiction fed. If they do not leave the relationship, infidelity in a marriage often occurs. Infidelity can take on many forms, such as an adulterous affair, addiction to pornography, or flirting with the opposite sex.

If a partner is unfaithful and does not leave their spouse but stays in the relationship and continues the affair, they are using and abusing their spouse. The unfaithful addicted partner often wants to be married and receive the perks involved with a marriage – having a roof over their head, spending time with their children, being fed, laundry done for them etc. Yet they also want to have affairs due to their uncontrollable selfish desires to continuously loop in and out of the *excitement* phase (*lust*) and *attraction* phase. Unfortunately, these people are addicted to that *lovin' feeling*.

Does this sound like you or anyone you know? Is this you, where you experience pleasurable feelings at the beginning of a relationship, and then once these feelings die off you think love is lost? Are you a person who has difficulties attaching to others? Do you crave the roller coaster style of love, at all costs? If you are addicted to sex and are in and out of affairs with others, after a while the one affair becomes blasé, and you desire to move on to someone else. If you have problems remaining attached to one person, I recommend you give the above explanation regarding the three phases of love some serious thought and reflection. Bottom line, just as an alcoholic needs help and support to stop their addiction, so do you.

As science proves, for long-standing relationships, our bodies are not designed to remain in the *excitement* phase (*lust*) and *attraction* phase. Our bodies are designed to move on to

Dr. Cheryl Bauman

the *attachment* phase. *Are you addicted to lust and attraction, thus placing your relationship in jeopardy of not lasting long-term?* If this is you, I would recommend you seek wise counsel to move past these very addictive states, and to try to move on to the attachment phase. Give your problems in this area over to God, ask Him for His help and guidance. No problem is ever too big for God to solve and to forgive. As well, find people you can trust to help you be accountable for your behavior, so you can truly walk in freedom and engage with the prosperous life God created for you. Also find a reliable, reasonable, and understanding counsellor who will help you to maneuver through the mess created by your addiction to that *lovin' feeling*.

Key 19

Have You Lost that *Lovin'* Feeling?

I know a man named Earl. He was always in and out of relationships. The door never closed on a current relationship before a new one opened and he would walk right through it. As he would enter a new relationship, He would leave the last one in a mess. It became a way of being for Earl, a well ingrained pattern. Every time he would meet someone new, he would tell me, "This is the one, I know she is for me, I just get this great feeling." Then I met up with Earl months later and ask him how his relationship was going. He relayed to me he no longer felt anything for her and so he moved on to someone else. To this day, Earl has not been able to commit to a long-term relationship. He married several times, yet the marriages ended quite quickly in divorce, as he has repeatedly overlapped his marriages with affairs. He seems lost as he has recognized he wants comfort and wants to belong.

Earl is seeking love in all the wrong places, and he is confused by the "loving feeling" that occurs in his body and then fades after a while. He is addicted to the high he receives because of falling in love. He is on an endless, unsatisfying roller coaster being led around by his feelings. Sadly, Earl had a mother and father that never embraced him with the love parents should. He was very much rejected and mistreated by his father and mother. Unfortunately, he is reaping the long-term destructive devastation that was taught to him as a young child by his parents. Earl was rejected and made to believe he was not lovable. So, he does not know what true love is and how to love himself just as he is. On his QUEST, he is seeking love in another person, yet he has never found it. *Why was Earl able to "fall in love", yet he was unable to "remain in love"?*

The root cause of all Earl's affairs center around Earl not knowing who Jesus Christ is and by not making Jesus Savior and Lord of his life. Earl does not have a relationship with God. He needs to establish a right relationship with God and submit his WILL to

God's WILL before he can be satisfied with anyone or anything else. At the beginning of this chapter, you were introduced to Sally, who at eight-years of age had a difficult time managing her emotions around love. Earl is an adult version of Sally who is struggling with the root problems of self-identity. These two people need to view themselves as worthy of God's love, and the life He created for them. This is the most important aspect so they can then have hope of upholding a healthy relationship with a partner. Self-identity is key, coupled with identity in Christ. Both Sally and Earl are looking to others to find true love that will take away all their pain, which is too much of a responsibility to place on anyone. Instead, they need to love themselves and know they are loveable. How they view themselves is how they will project to others who they are. Comprehending their joy is found in the Lord, the Maker of Heaven and Earth, and their identity is in Christ, and not in feelings is essential for both to fulfill a healthy, purposeful life. Satisfaction needs to come from the love of God and realizing selfless, *Agape* love, is what Earl needs to envelope. But this is only made possible through surrendering to God and by Earl giving up his selfish ways.

If you are addicted to the roller coaster style of love, what happens to you after these hormonal chemical reactions in your body level out? Do the "feelings of love" for the person then vanish? Do you believe love is lost because it was based on feeling good? When you don't feel good anymore about the person you are with, do you look for another person to love, to boost up your hormonal levels to feel good again?

Ask yourself are you currently basing your earthly romantic relationships on the lyrics to the song, "you've lost that lovin' feeling?" If you are, science is suggesting the *lovin' feeling* happens in the beginning of a romantic relationship. As your relationship matures the *lovin' feeling* is overtaken by a surge in hormones designed to naturally bring about comfort and stability within your body. *Are you confusing comfort with losing that lovin' feeling? Is this you? If you are being honest, do you think the past relationships that didn't work were founded solely on the excitement phase (lust) and not on working through to intentional, committed love (attachment phase)? Have you even given lasting love with another human being on this earth a chance, or have you scampered away after the lovin' feeling disappeared? Or have you been hurt by someone who left after the excitement and attraction phase ended, leaving you reeling in pain and confusion, sceptical about entering another relationship?*

I am suggesting we all need to let go of the idea lasting, committed love is a *feeling* that comes and goes. We need to understand to love another person fully and unconditionally, we need to love by intentionally choosing to love our partner. *Have you found yourself in a marriage relationship you made a commitment to when you said your vows, "I do", "until death do us part"?* Then you owe it to yourself and to your partner to work on the commitment you made by honouring the promise of words spoken on the day of your marriage. Words hold power. Words bring blessings or curses. Words are covenant when spoke as a commitment in a marriage union. You owe it to yourself and to your partner to intentionally change your ways, regardless of the past. The good news is you have the present and the future to look towards. You cannot do it alone, and do not even believe for one second you can. Seek God and seek wise counsel. Genuinely admit your faults and work hard at reversing the curse you have brought on yourself and your spouse through the addiction to that *lovin' feeling*. We all need to learn how to keep love alive with our partner by seeing them through the eyes of God. On our QUEST for true unconditional love, we need to understand feelings fade, they come and go. Love is a choice, and this choice involves genuine commitment through good times and bad times, past the feelings. For many of us this may lead to a deeper realization love is a long-term commitment based on compatibility not based on a chemical reaction. If you want to make love last, you should focus less on chemistry and more on commitment.

Key 20

What Does the Bible Say About Basing Relationships on That "Lovin Feeling"?

Some of you reading this book may have been abused or are currently being abused by someone with whom you thought loved you. However, by reflecting on the relationship, you may now be supposing they were only relying on their feelings, and when the feelings left, so did they. Know the roller coaster ride you experienced is not love! It has been caused by a person unable to work through to the *attachment phase*, as they themselves do not know what true love is. There is a profound saying, *hurt people hurt others, healed people heal others*. This is so true in all our relationships with people in life, particularly in romantic relationships.

The abuse and mistreatment you suffered probably left you feeling confused about what true love is. It could be leaving you not really wanting a loving relationship or knowing how to love. I compare feeling the pain of someone who suffered abuse from a partner's addictive sexual behavior, to placing your hand on the burner of a stove that is turned on. Once you place your hand there you feel immediate pain, and the pain can last for some time as you have been physically burned. Depending on how hot the burner is and how long you left your hand there, may depend on whether you have a permanent scar. So, to compensate you avoid stoves, or you avoid putting your hand on a burner that has been turned on. You learned your lesson, which is a good lesson to learn, if you put your hand on a hot burner, you will feel pain.

In the same way, it is important you do not enter a dating or marriage relationship with people who have these sexual addictive behaviors. If you do find yourself in a marriage with someone who does have addictive sexual behaviors, seek help from a professional. Someone who understands sexual addictions as well as ask God for His guidance and support in sorting through your mess. Be obedient to what God is directing you to do, as it takes two to make a relationship work. Trust and obey God in this situation and seek help for it.

I encourage you to read the word of God daily and meditate on it for strength and guidance. The Apostle Paul has stern words in relation to Christians associating with sexually immoral people. Here is what Paul says in 1 Corinthians 5:9-13 (NIV):

> *I wrote to you in my letter not to associate with sexually immoral people—not at all meaning the people of this world who are immoral, or the greedy and swindlers, or idolaters. In that case you would have to leave this world. But now I am writing to you that you mustn't associate with anyone who claims to be a brother or sister but is sexually immoral or greedy, an idolater or slanderer, a drunkard or swindler. Do not even eat with such people. What business is it of mine to judge those outside the church? Are you not to judge those inside? God will judge those outside. "Expel the wicked person from among you."*

As the Apostle Paul teaches, you cannot tackle this problem alone, and do not even think you can. Isolation will continue to keep you in the cycle of addiction. Sexual addictions are straight from the pits of hell, and therefore they need to be cast back into the pits of hell for a person to be completely free from them. If your partner is willing to seek counselling with you and is willing to be accountable for their behavior, then this is a step in the right direction. However, the sexual addictive behaviors will not just need thoughtful prayer to overcome, they need intentionality to overcome them from the partner who has a sexual addiction. The partner must admit they have a problem and seek help to overcome it. The partner also needs to find people they will be accountable to so they can overcome the desires that are attached with sexual addictions – with the help of God. Without acknowledgement, accountability, repentance, and changes in behavior, it is very likely the partner will continue with their addiction.

True, unconditional love does not parallel to sticking your hand on a hot burner, yet some of you equate it exactly this way. You may be feeling so emotionally burned and scarred from what you thought was love, once you begin to experience the possibility of attaching to someone you either consciously or sub-consciously experience immediate pain. This may be due to being abused and mistreated by a partner from the past who had a sexual addiction. You might be reluctant to experience the pain again, because this pain was so deep it ripped you apart. Therefore, instead of healing your wounds, you flee, potentially wounding others and never fully experiencing love and true intimacy with a partner as was designed by God.

You are probably scared to seek out and to find love from another person, even though no human can offer you perfect love. Love and being genuinely cared for by another will meet the belongingness need and the loneliness need. If fear is gripping you due to past pain, I encourage you to seek help, to pray, and to ask God for guidance as you work through this very difficult past. Yet, I also want to encourage you your past does not predict your future. I challenge you to muster up the courage to work through these negative experiences so you can find the true love this book writes about. The true unconditional love you are seeking is only found in God and a relationship with Him. The journey to finding this true unconditional love is worth the pain you might be experiencing. God stands and stays. When it seems as if the whole world is walking away from you, God runs in your direction with wide open arms. God affirms nothing can separate you from His true unconditional love.

> *For I am convinced that neither death nor life, neither angels or demons, neither present nor the future, nor any powers, neither height nor depth, nor anything else in all creation will be able to separate us from the love of God that is in Christ Jesus our Lord (Romans 8:38-39 NIV).*

You might be asking; how can you focus on intentionally loving your partner when you are currently in a broken relationship where your partner has cheated on you and is not remorseful? Or you may have walked away from a marriage relationship because the *'lovin' feelin'* left and you tried to chase after it with someone else or something else. Being addicted to feelings, and to wanting your partner to be everything for you, is leading more married people straight to the divorce courts. Addictions in today's society are replacing the much-needed constant building and rebuilding required in marriage relationships. This can only be based on intentional choice and intentional commitment. Non-commitment and unbalanced priorities are robbing us of the time that is needed to develop strong, lasting relationships with our spouses and our families. Addictions are stealing prosperity and wholeness from our lives. You may be addicted to pornography, affairs, drugs, alcohol, the shopping channel, the internet or countless other additions that are not named here. Whatever your addiction, if you are serious about making drastic changes, say good-bye to the addiction that has been wedged in between you and your partner. And say hello to the beautiful person you made the commitment to at the marriage altar. If you are genuinely wanting to change, repent of your past and look to your future with hope.

"If my people, who are called by my name, will humble themselves and pray and seek my face and turn from their wicked ways, then I will hear from heaven. And I will forgive their sin and will heal their land" (2 Chronicles 7:14 NIV).

Life is not perfect, neither is earthly love. Yet, making the commitment to work on a relationship between yourself and another person is a choice. Some of you are not taking full responsibility for the marriage commitment you half-heartedly made to your partner. Some of you are taking your partner for granted, and if you are honest, you are not fully committed to the institution of marriage in the way you should be. Instead, you are fooling yourself and fooling the person you are with by acting irresponsible, unaccountable, and selfish. If this is you, and you sincerely want to make a change, humble yourself before God and before your partner, and commit to working it out.

But he gives us more grace. That is why the Scripture says, "God opposes the proud but shows favor to the humble" (James 4:6 NIV).

If you really want to end this lifestyle of being addicted to that *lovin' feeling*, I encourage you to admit you are powerless on your own and to surrender to God. Surrender all the pretending and pretenses. Take off the mask and expose your true self. Stop trying to cover up the pain and the sin in your life. The only way to full recovery is to first admit what you have done wrong, seek repentance, and then to ask your partner for forgiveness. God promises to redeem a heart that seeks after Him and a heart that is genuine and is not covering up lies and untruths.

"Humble yourselves before the Lord, and he will lift you up" (James 4:10 NIV).

I encourage you to seek help to gain freedom. Freedom is possible, you need to believe it is possible and to act on this belief. Seek out a professional counsellor that understands the three phases of love and understands the addictive behaviors that enslaved you. If this is you, you are currently trapped in an addictive maze trying to find your own way out. Know you need support; there is no way of escaping on your own.

You may be reading this chapter and thinking your marriage is not salvageable, it is too far gone. Or you may believe you have done too many unthinkable acts, and your life is way off base, it can never be reoriented and set back on track. These are lies and untruths.

God loves to help those who have a repentant heart and want help from Him. Draw close to God and He will draw close to you. The Lord is compassionate and gracious, slow to anger, abounding in love. He does not treat us as our sins deserve or repay us according to our iniquities. God loves us unconditionally. *As far as the east is from the west, so far has he removed our transgressions from us* (Psalm 103:12 NIV). Have you ever wondered how far the east is from the west? It is not measurable, as it goes on and on. God is a covenant God, and therefore if He states He removed your transgressions as far as the east is from the west, then what is written in the Bible is an everlasting truth. If you are seriously committed to slaying the addictive GIANT, then God is serious about helping you and removing your sins forever and forever. You can walk in freedom.

"So, if the Son sets you free, you will be free indeed" (John 8:36 NIV).

Let every heartbreak and every scar be a picture to remind you of where you have come from. Yet do not let this addiction to that lovin feeling define who you are from this day forward. Tell your heart to beat again. Close yesterday's door on the addictive behaviors. Do not be afraid to say good-bye to where you have been and tell your heart to beat again. Get back up and do not remain in addiction, bitterness, strife and pain. Decide today to change. You do not need to live in this space of uncertainty and dissatisfaction anymore. With honesty on your part and support from godly people, you can step into God's unconditional true lasting love and begin the change process.

Trust in the Lord with all your heart and lean not on your own understanding (Proverbs 3:5 NIV).

Unlocking Mystery #4

True Love Does Not Depend on Feelings

> **Reflect:** Do you want to rid yourself of being addicted to that "lovin' feeling" that has kept you chained down, as a prisoner, never being free?
>
> **Relate:** In the past, how have you tried to rid yourself of being addicted to that "lovin' feeling?" What has worked? What has not worked?
>
> **Respond:** If the answer is yes you do want to rid yourself of being addicted to that "lovin' feeling", then I challenge you to intentionally develop the following habits:
>
> - Find a quiet place, free from noise and other distractions.
> - In the stillness begin to meditate on God's goodness.
> - Start to erase and reject the messages and voices that keep playing repeatedly in your mind as to how 'bad' you have been.
> - Close your eyes and slowly breathe in and out 10 times.
> - Visualize yourself stepping into the light of God's grace and mercy.
> - Visualize yourself closing the door and throwing away the key associated with the addictive behaviors of always wanting that "lovin' feeling" (or the addiction that has you trapped and imprisoned).
> - Visualize yourself following the VOICE of TRUTH to a new door.
> - Visualize yourself unlocking this new door and stepping through it by accepting forgiveness, grace, mercy, peace, and a love that can only come from God.
> - Speak the following truths out loud: I am lovable! I am lovable just as I am! The words I say are powerful! I am intentionally committed to love myself and others without relying on feelings! God's love is perfect; and perfect love casts out all fear!
> - Humble yourself. Do not stay in shame and condemnation. Instead, seek out godly counsel. Find people you can be accountable to for your actions.
>
> *Speak the Truth.*
> *Just Say It! True Love Does Not Depend on Feelings.*

Dr. Cheryl Bauman

#5

I Can Believe in the Impossible

Love, upon hearing it so often has lost its meaning to the world, when it should really mean the world upon hearing it - Kyla Heyming.

Dr. Cheryl Bauman

Key 21

Private Pain

At a local charity event, a distinct encounter with one of the event organizers caused me to reflect on the issues surrounding private pain and its connection to the mysteries of the QUEST. During one of the intermissions, I met a very attractive, well-dressed woman who was roughly 65 years of age. She approached me and relayed she had recently read my book, *Just Say It! 4 Phrases That Will Change Your Life Forever*. I was so excited to talk with her about the book, as the true purpose of my writing is to bring people into a closer relationship with God, themselves, and others. She explained the book, *Just Say It!* changed her life, as she had become more aware of the way in which she speaks to her family members, particularly her grandchildren. I thanked God the entire time we were speaking, as I write so people's lives are transformed forever, setting them apart to live Holy and blameless lives. My prayer is the words I write are all Holy Spirit empowered so people will undergo a transformation that will be eternal.

As the heartening conversation with this woman evolved, I decided to tell her about this book I am currently writing, which explores the topic of love. Suddenly, the entire expression on her face completely changed. She said in a matter of a fact tone, "I really don't know if true love is possible." I was immediately taken back by her statement, as I was not expecting it due to the lively conversation in which we were engaged in. She must have seen the look on my face, as I was having a difficult time hiding the sadness that quickly crept over me. I was immediately moved with deep compassion for her. As she spoke, I saw beyond the beautiful outer appearance and into the darkness that was invading and preying on this woman who does not know what true love is, or how to experience it. At that moment I became grateful and honored she was willing to share her private pain with me.

She quickly gathered her thoughts, and started to stammer and mumble as she said, "well...I think love is possible between a parent and a child, or a grandparent and a grandchild, but that is it. Love is only possible under these circumstances. I have been married for over 40 years, and I have never felt loved or even know what true love is between a husband and a wife." She blushed as she was speaking and as we continued to talk, I could hear and sense the deep inner, private pain that held this beautiful woman in captivity all these years. She had an empty void within her she was longing to have filled. This woman believed having a loving relationship with her spouse as being impossible, and greater still, she believed true unconditional love between a man and a woman was not possible.

Does this story remind you of yourself or someone you know? When only three in ten couples report they are happily married, this statistic sadly represents many people living with a door slammed shut on any possibility of true unconditional love between themselves and their partner. *Why is this so?* What happened to us in this world, where things are seemingly easier for us convenience wise, yet out of our own selfish ways we are tending to make our relationships much more impossible. *What is fundamentally happening to us and our human existence?* From these disturbing statistics, we can suppose many do not find true love in relationship status. *How many of you who are married do not know what true unconditional love is between you and your partner? How many of you have a beautiful, polished outward appearance, yet have never experienced true love in a committed long-standing relationship? Do you believe you are worthy of true love? Do you believe as you seek true love from other human beings you must also seek it from an eternal source? How many of you cannot remember the last time you heard the words genuinely spoken from your spouse to you, "I Love You"?*

Key 22

Heart-to-Heart

Believing all things are possible with God is a good place to start on your QUEST. *Are you able to believe in the impossible for your life when it comes to relationships that have gone astray?* Literally believing and understanding you are worthy of true unconditional love from God, and you have the capacity to love and be loved by God and others is essential. You need to have a realization and understanding love is transferred directly from God's heart to your heart. The true unconditional love you are worthy of is not a *feeling*; it is not some chemical reaction that occurs every once and a while that is fleeting in its existence. True love lasts, true love remains, true love is eternal! True love has always existed. What seems impossible is possible through the love of God!

> *Know therefore that the Lord your God is God; he is the faithful God, keeping his covenant of love to a thousand generations of those who love him and keep his commandments (Deuteronomy 7:9 NIV).*

To truly know you are loved and believe you are loved by God requires you to know Him in all His fullness. Even though God is love and His love never changes; to experience His love, we must regularly read His words that are found in the Bible and communicate with Him. The Bible was written to demonstrate to us the power of relationships with God, with ourselves and with others. We need to align ourselves in this order before we can truly love others. We must first love God and then love ourselves before we can love others. Most people in this world are not abiding in true love, because they are not aligning themselves with the only one who is true love, and that is God. Popular culture tells us God is a thing of the past and many are falsely fooled by these secular beliefs. God's true unconditional love is the only lasting thing that can fill this empty void in all of us.

The word of God is sharper than a two-edged sword and it proclaims God as the great I AM. He was, He is, and He will always be. This is an absolute, regardless of your belief or the belief of popular culture. Our world is in a state of disaster due to these false beliefs that are not founded in any truth.

God was love and God is love and God will always be love.

Think about someone you are currently or were deeply in love with. *How did you come to love and cherish that person? Before you could even begin to love that person, did you have some form of attraction to them? What physically happened to your body when you fell in love? Is this how you gauge what true love is, a physical, chemical reaction that does not last? If so, is this why so many of you are walking around with private pain with a deep lonely void that cannot be filled up by the people in your lives?* Yet, you somehow falsely believe it can, so you keep searching and questing, yet the QUEST never ends. Your thirst is never quenched.

Let me ask you, how were you first introduced to the person you fell deeply in love with? What did the introduction look like? Was it a casual chat? An email? A friend-request? A phone call? Did you meet at work, at a social gathering, at church, on a vacation, or through mutual friends or family members? However, you met, it did not end there. *How did your love begin and how did it grow?*

I will assume if you were developing a relationship with a significant other you kept communicating with that person. You invested time and effort in them, and they in you. *How well would the relationship have gone if the calls and emails became less frequent? What is the time spent together dropped to nothing, and you each started going about your daily lives as if the other person was not important enough to contact?* These are not the best conditions for a relationship or for love to flourish. Yet, many of us in relationships are doing just that. We are busying ourselves with the worries and cares of life and not taking the time to nurture the people who are the closest to us. These are the people who have been given to us as gifts, our spouses, our children, our grandchildren, and our parents.

How well would your relationships on this earth fare if you only sought people out when you were in desperate need of help? This type of a relationship is based on a self-centered, manipulative approach, that often does not work out well in the end. Yet, many of us make choices throughout our day that push God aside and we do not choose to spend any time with Him. Many of us do not take the time to pray and to develop a relationship with Him. Some of you reading this book are probably not even inviting Him into the most intimate areas of your life, where He wants to be involved. Instead, you shut Him out. You treat Him as unimportant, or you send Him off to the sidelines only calling on Him when you absolutely need to. Or worse still when something tragic happens in your life, you blame God. Yet you do not even know Him because you rejected a personal relationship with Him by not spending time with Him. *So, how can you blame God for tragedy when you do not even know Him or acknowledge Him?* Yet many of you who reject God, suddenly when tragedy strikes, you blame God. This seems to be a flawed way of thinking. So, the good things that happen to you, you take all the credit for, yet the bad things that happen to you, you blame God. *How rational is this? How fair is this?* It sounds very self-centered and not very logical.

How can you expect a relationship to grow and flourish with God in the good times and the bad times, if you don't spend time with Him? Many people said to me they do not know how to pray. It is as if they believe there is a step-by-step method to prayer, and if they do not know the method and follow it, they are unable to pray. This is a myth. Praying to God is just like talking to a close friend. Try to talk with God throughout your day. You do not require an elaborate, long prayer. It can be a short and simple discussion with God, sharing your life, talking out loud (or in your mind) about your day, about the joys and sorrows of the day and asking for guidance. Prayer with God is not a "wish list", in fact, quite the contrary. It is an easy flowing conversation with a Higher Being that is all loving and all kind. It is thanking God for all He has given you. As well, it is presenting dilemmas to Him so that in His wisdom He can guide you into all truth. I have also heard people comment they do not have the time to pray; it takes too much time. Prayer is a continual conversation with God throughout the day, much like short little text messages sent to your loved ones. Sometimes prayer can be longer, like an email outlining greater detail. The length of your talk with God is not what is important, it is the fact you develop a habit so your communication with God is a continual part of your daily life.

Some people seem to think they must tell God their issues for Him to know everything. This may come as a shock to some of you reading this book, but God knows everything. He does not treat you like a robot by forcing a relationship on you. Instead, He wants you to develop a relationship with Him by always wanting to talk with Him, so His WILL for your life aligns with your will. Better than talking, often being quiet and still in the presence of God, listening to what He is telling you is the key to following His WILL for your life. If you talk with God and listen to God, He will make the impossible in your life become possible. Some of us tend to seek God for His guidance, but when we do not like His response, we rebel and do it our way. Then, when things go wrong, we turn around and blame God. Spending

119

time and developing a trusting relationship with God is paramount if we are going to fight the temptation of selfishly wanting things "our way". Just like your earthly relationships, if you don't spend time with the people in your life, you drift apart and never truly get to know them and trust is never developed. Now, some people in our lives we do need to drift away from. This topic is discussed in greater detail in other areas of this book. However, bottom line, we all need to grow closer to God every day.

Think about the following questions: *How can you expect your love to grow when you are not spending any time with God, by reading His love letter to you, the Bible? How can you expect your love to if you do not talk with Him and by listening to what He is saying to you? God is always available. Are you continually making the choice to treat Him unkindly, by rejecting His promptings to spend time with Him? Are you only seeking Him when you are in trouble? Or have you developed an intimate relationship with God you are continually nurturing?* It is through nurturing a relationship with God true love is transformed from His heart to your heart. It is a life altering, transformational experience that lasts a lifetime, if you allow it to.

Key 23

Peace in Times of Trouble

Do you believe peace in times of trouble is impossible? Or do you believe in the impossible by having a peace that passes all understanding no matter what? If so, I would guess you are spending time with God, developing a relationship with Him so when troubles come you are not swept away by feelings. Troubles do come in this world, as it is a flawed world. Are you currently facing difficult times? Are you shipwrecked and being tossed about by the winds and waves that continually crash down on you? Or are you able with all conviction and belief to sing the words to the song, 'It is Well with My Soul', written by hymnist Horatio Spafford. Horatio Spafford wrote this song after losing his four daughters in a shipwreck on the Atlantic Ocean. His wife survived the wreck. Spafford knew who the true captain of his ship was. That captain was and is God. Instead of allowing this tragic circumstance to control his life, Spafford put all his faith and trust in God, even when his children were taken from him, even when his world was turned upside down. Spafford knew God is true love, even in the most devastating circumstances.

In a time that seemed so impossible, Horatio Spafford decided to put pen to paper and write out his sorrow in a song. He declared to the Maker of Heaven and Earth and to the entire world he knew who was in control, he knew where his hope came from. The song, 'It is Well with My Soul' was written in 1873. The truth founded in tragedy continues to echo throughout the centuries bringing comfort to many of us today. Spafford's faith continues today! He could be listed in Hebrews 11, where the great people of faith are listed.

I encourage you to look up the lyrics of this song and to sing it out loud during the stormy times in your life. *Do you have that kind of faith and trust in our loving God, as Horatio Spafford did, a faith that can withstand the storms of life, no matter what comes your way?*

Dr. Cheryl Bauman

Or do you have a wishy-washy faith, based on feelings, based on the circumstances that will toss you back and forth if you allow them to?

Just as this book is being prepared to go to "print", on September 10, 2025, Charlie Kirk was assassinated by a gunshot while he was sharing his faith with a large gathering of students at a University in Utah, USA. The world was saddened and shocked. His memorial service was held at State Farm Stadium in Glendale, Arizona. It was attended by over 90,000 people. Apparently, some 200,000 people showed up, but many were turned away, due to the stadium being filled to capacity. Turning Point USA, which is the organization that Charlie Kirk founded, stated that worldwide livestreams of the memorial exceeded 100 million. The service ran for more than five hours. In the words of one person who spoke, Charlie was "a patriot whose heart still had so much more to give." During the memorial, Charlie's widow, Erika Kirk, stood up courageously in front of millions, and forgave her husband's assassin. *How many of us given similar circumstances could honestly say that we would have the same resolve and trust in God as Erika did to forgive a person who murdered a loved one of ours?* This brave act of faith demonstrated that Erika Kirk has a deep, unshakeable relationship with God.

How is your relationship with God? Have you been tossed about in life, by allowing circumstances to throw you back and forth? Do you want to stop being tossed and instead do you want to be firmly planted, no matter the circumstances? If the answer is "yes", then you need to develop a closer relationship with God. You may not know how to develop an intimate relationship with a Higher Being. However, God wants and desires for you to get to know Him. To know Him in all His love and in all its fullness, so you can rejoice with Him in the good times and have Him hold you in His righteous hands in the difficult times. That is what true love is. That is peace among the storms of life. It is so simple. There is not an eight-step plan. In fact, I encourage you to start today by talking to Him, by sitting still and listening to what He will say to you. Read and meditate on the Word of God found in the Bible, it will speak to you if you allow it to. Ask God to help you understand the passages you are reading in the Bible, with the help of the Holy Spirit.

The Lord wants to show up supernaturally in your life, just as he has done in mine. It takes the supernatural to walk through the storms of life. You can only survive the tempest when the Lord comes to you on the waves and calls out to you to walk on the water with Him. You may think you can, but there is no way you can pull it off in your own power. The storms of life are much larger than you!

An intimate relationship with God is required to get to know Him and so when life's storms come, you can have a supernatural steadfast faith and peace in knowing God is in control. According to the Merriam-Webster (2019) dictionary, intimate is defined as, "having a close relationship; very warm and friendly; personal or private." If we are intimate with someone, we must spend time with them, we need to get to know them personally and privately. This very close relationship must be warm and friendly. *How many of you reading this book can honestly say this defines your relationship with God? Can you honestly declare you are intimate with Him; you spend time alone with Him; your relationship with Him is warm and friendly? Do you even believe you can have a cozy intimate relationship with the Maker of Heaven and Earth? Do you believe you are lovable enough and you deserve such overwhelming love only found in God that will flood your entire being if you allow it to?*

You might be skeptical or unaware this form of a relationship with God is even possible. Many people believe God is an angry God, ready to catch them off guard and to punish them. This does not define the God you can serve. It is a false belief; one you need to erase. I challenge you to try to build intimacy with God and see what happens. You will not know until you try. But I guarantee you, if you put forth the time and energy, you will not be disappointed.

The form of intimacy God wants to develop with you is founded on His relentless pursuit of you, as He loves you so much. When you develop an intimacy with God, you will have a peace that is unexplainable. I want to challenge you to begin to develop a relationship of depth and intimacy with God. *What do you have to lose?* For to be close and warm and friendly, regular time spent together must occur – and I am not just suggesting on Sunday mornings either, I am encouraging daily time spent between you and God.

Some people do not want to know God or to take the time to know Him or even believe there is a God they need to know. However, one day, we will all know who God is and how we should have lived our lives if we do not purposefully live them according to His WILL. Even if we do not believe someday, we will all know God and be judged accordingly, our unbelief will not stop this powerful truth from occurring. You and I nor any human being holds the type of power to be able to control the universe. You may be, very powerful in your job, in your family and in your community. If this is you, then you obtained some form of earthly power. You may have financial means beyond many. With financial stability, there is a peace in life that does help you get through tough times, as you do not need to worry about finances. Yet you do not hold the keys to life-and-death. At some point, everyone must face death, regardless of your financial situation. Unfortunately for Charlie Kirk, he experienced death at the very young age of 31. Most of us would agree that it was too soon. However, all of us know that Charlie is safe in the arms of Jesus, enjoying Heaven. Charlie is looking down upon all of us with his big wide grin.

As a human you must come to an understanding there are absolutes regardless of how much power and influence you have on earth; you do not control these powerful eternal absolutes. You may be fooled into thinking you do, but you don't. You did not have the choice to be born and where to be born and you do not hold the keys that withhold death from occurring in your natural body. But you can make a choice as to where you will spend eternity after you die. Depending on the choice you make, as there are only two, it can bring about peace, or it can bring about constant worry. Your unbelief is not powerful enough to keep you out of being eternally dammed to Hell if you do not believe Jesus is the truth and the only way to God the Father. Instead, what your unbelief is powerful enough to do is to trick you into a false sense of security in yourself and in your abilities. You might be fooled into a false peace and a false hope. You may be quite accomplished, and your abilities may be numerous, but they do not hold the keys to life-and-death – you are mortal, you will perish.

I know the Almighty who holds the keys that will take away the sting of death and give you life everlasting. That person is Jesus Christ, the Son of God, and the Son of Man. Jesus can give you a peace that passes all understanding. However, if you do not live according to His WILL and ways and not accept Jesus, when you die, regardless of status, you will be separated from Jesus and from your loving Heavenly Father forever. This is an absolute truth, found in the living Word of God. You may be chuckling right now at this suggestion you are not powerful enough to control your eternal destiny. This chuckling behavior is pride hindering your eternal reality. Even if you do not believe, it does not take away the truth of the living, breathing Word of God who came down in flesh and dwelt among us. Your unbelief does not change the truth as to how to obtain everlasting life. Just because you hold unbelief, you do not hold the power to alter what God has ordained.

Part of God's will for our lives involves developing a relationship with Him where we daily walk and talk with Him. You might ask, *how do you walk and talk with God?* You walk and talk with God through reading the Bible and by praying to Him and then listening to His voice. You can hear His voice deep within you. Which is the way most people communicate with God. However, some people heard God's voice audibly, while others had visitations by angels and by Jesus. These are supernatural experiences that are becoming more frequent as our times are becoming more troublesome. People ask me how long I pray each day, and I honestly do not have an answer for them, as I do not place a timer on during my prayer time. I pray continuously throughout the day. I never cease from praying; I am always in communication with God. If we communicate and abide in God, then He abides in us, so when the storms come our way, we will not drown. Instead, we will be saved by His grace and filled with His peace; as His peace will never leave us. His peace is present if we continuously talk with God and trust in the power of the impossible. When I speak of God throughout this book, I am often referring to God as the Trinity, three in one, Father, Son and Holy Spirit.

Erika Kirk, Charlie Kirk's widow, is grieving. Yet she knows who holds the keys to life and death. Erika Kirk has the assurance as to where her husband is now. Charlie is in Heaven. She also has the guarantee that one day she will join him. Even though a huge storm has swept over her life, it is very evident that Erika knows the author of her present and future. What a testimony of true faith, as she stood in front of millions of people and forgave her husband's killer. What courage, what steadfast confidence in her testimony to the world as to her belief as to who she is in Christ, where Charlie is now, and where all of us can be someday - Heaven!

Some of Jesus' final instructions to us before he departed from this earth were:

Peace, I leave with you; my peace I give you. I do not give to you as the world gives. Do not let your hearts be troubled and do not be afraid (John 14:27 NIV).

Key 24

Don't Underestimate the Power of The Impossible

Don't underestimate the Power of The Impossible. This statement may seem so far reaching for you to even think, believe, or say. However, God is a God of the Impossible!

And my God will meet all your needs according to the riches of his glory in Christ Jesus (Philippians 4:19 NIV).

What are you believing God for? Does this dream seem impossible in the natural realm? If so, God specializes in supernaturally making dreams, that are part of His will for your life, come true. He is a supernatural God. God takes what in the "natural" seems impossible and adds the "super" to it and it becomes a "supernatural" miracle only He can take the credit for. As in the "natural" it would be impossible for us to accomplish. God also takes our "natural" abilities and talents" and connects them with his "Superpowers". If you allow God to work His will in your life, what you end up with is a "supernatural occurrence" through the power of God.

God is in the business of surprising us, as we are His children, and He loves us. As a parent, grandparent, aunt, uncle, teacher, or if in some capacity you have children involved in your life, you can relate to how you love to surprise these precious little ones. You love to make them happy by blessing them beyond what they might imagine. Well, think about our Heavenly Father and how much more He loves us. God owns everything. God is all-powerful, all knowing, all present, and all loving. Thus, God has the will to surprise us as well as the means to do so!

You might be thinking your situation is so impossible, you cannot see a way out. God performs the impossible when He rescues us from a situation that seems so overwhelmingly impossible, such as divorce, drug addiction, a child who has gone astray or the loss of a job. Remember, God delivered the children of Israel from slavery. As they were escaping, Pharaoh changed his mind and ordered the Egyptian army to chase them down and bring them back to Egypt. You can imagine the distress of the Jewish people! God supernaturally rescued them from the clutches of Pharaoh and now they were once again being hunted and haunted. Their situation seemed once again to be impossible! However, to miraculously demonstrate He is all-powerful, God "supernaturally" parted the Red Sea for His chosen ones He loved so much. The Jewish people were able to walk on dry ground and reach the other side of the Red Sea unscathed. This supernatural parting of the Red Sea allowed the Israelites to escape from their enemies. Then when their enemies tried to cross through the Red Sea, their chariot wheels became "stuck". God stopped drying up the bottom of the sea, and it was no longer dry ground. Their wheels were stuck in the mud of the Red Sea. The Egyptians were unable to advance forward. Next God withdrew the miracle of the parting of the Red Sea and the water gushed over top of the Egyptian army drowning many of them. Due to God's miraculous signs and wonders, the Egyptians were unable to recapture God's chosen people, as it was God's chosen time to save His people. The all-powerful God demonstrated His supernatural power in a situation that seemed utterly impossible.

What impossible situation in your life do you need to believe God for so you can walk on dry ground to get to the other side? Can you visualize "the other side", yet like the Jewish people, you don't know how to get there? The same God that performed these supernatural miracles all these millenniums ago is the same supernatural God of today. God never changes, He is the same yesterday, today and tomorrow. Know the Creator of Heaven and Earth desires to part many "Red Seas" in your life. God wants to "show up" and to demonstrate His miraculous powers. *But are you willing to surrender ALL to God by believing and trusting His ways are higher and better than yours?*

Whatever your need is, God loves you so much He promises in His word He will supply all your needs. He just asks you to believe by faith and to trust in the promises found in His word. These promises are also accompanied with stipulations. You must live your life according to God's word so things will go well with you and your household (Deuteronomy 12:28; Ephesians 6:3). The power of the impossible is possible through the supernatural power of God for areas of your life such as:

- That son or daughter who strayed from God.
- The void of loneliness to be filled for those of you who are widowed, divorced or single.
- A new job with better pay and benefits (an upgrade).
- A new house in a safe neighborhood.
- Debt cancellation and wealth transfers.
- Good grades at school.
- A circle of reliable Christian friends; and
- A good Bible-based church to attend and to fellowship with other believers.

The Days of Noah

As is predicted in the Bible, the last days before the return of Christ are to be like the days of Noah. I believe we are currently in these days as they parallel the days of Noah. *Remember the Bible story of Noah?* God looked down on the earth, and it was so corrupt. God only found one man who sought after His heart, who developed an intimate relationship with Him. This man was Noah. God directed Noah with very precise directions as to how to build an ark. Even in the face of adversity and mocking from everyone living for miles around, Noah continued in obedience for well over 100 years building the ark. The number of years is debated by scholars, yet one thing I know for sure, is it was a long time from the start to the finish. Noah trusted in God and was obedient to His instructions. Over 100 years, he built an ark all the while continually to hear the constant ridicule and mocking coming from people that lived in his village. This must have been horrific for Noah and his family, yet he kept steadfast for so many years, believing in the instructions that were given to him by God.

Noah Believed in the Impossible!

In today's society, we are so pampered by "stuff". Many of us cannot even endure a little bit of persecution for a short time before we begin to doubt God's word and His instructions to us. Yet Noah endured more than 100 years of trusting and believing in God's love and instruction to him, even in the face of continuous ridicule and rejection. Think about it, before the great flood it never rained before on the earth. So, for Noah to believe the ark would one day "float on water", was believing in the impossible – some phenomena he had never "seen" before. Noah's neighbors were not patting Noah on the back, making Noah feel good every day about his accomplishments and about his hard labor. In fact, they were doing just the opposite. Noah did not hear words of praise and encouragement from the people in his community. Noah wasn't experiencing or feeling neighborly love! However, instead of bending to the popular voice of that time, Noah remained unshakeable as he praised God, trusted Him, and followed the clear instructions from God. *How many of us give up in discouragement because we do not hear praises from the people around us or because we do not feel loved? How many of you have given up on the assignment from God for your life because the people around you doubted what you were doing and made fun of you? Who are you seeking praise from, and who do you praise? Who are you taking instructions from – God or people?*

I am grateful Noah persevered and believed in the impossible. As through his obedience and trust, he altered history forever. God knew with whom He could entrust this task to. He knew Noah was steadfast and of strong mind and strong character. For in the Bible God promises that "*Whoever can be trusted with little can also be trusted with much, and whoever is dishonest with little will also be dishonest with much*" (Luke 16:10 NIV). *Is this you, are you able to be trusted with little, so this little can grow and grow into more responsibility? Or are you too fickle and frail any little wind of adversity that comes along you are toppled over and trampled on? Do you want a lot, yet are you unwilling to have the faith to believe for a lot? Do you have the faith to stand in the face of adversity, trusting in God's love no matter what the circumstances around you seem to be predicting? Do you believe in the impossible? Do you believe in the voice of God who loves you unconditionally – who wants the best for you?*

Just as God promised to Noah, when the ark was complete, Noah and his family entered the ark, closed the door and the flood came. The flood destroyed every living thing on the earth except Noah, his family, and the animals on board with them. Due to Noah's obedience because of his intimate relationship with God, a relationship that was built on trust and love, God spared Noah and his family. When the rains of life pelt down on you, *do you have this type of an intimate love relationship with God, no matter what happens you trust Him?* If you cannot answer yes to these questions, I urge you to develop an intimate love relationship with God, the type that Noah had. He completely trusted God and loved Him so much he feared God and not people. It was a reciprocal relationship, as God saw Noah's obedience and trust grow and develop over time. Therefore, He entrusted Noah with more responsibility.

There is coming a day (I suggest this "day" is here) if you do not have an intimate relationship with God, listening to His instructions, as in the days of Noah, you too will be deceived. There is great deception falling on this earth like we have never witnessed before. Deception is taking on many forms in today's world. Everywhere you and I turn around, there are untruths being spoken and fake news being presented as truth. It is difficult for any of us to know what truth is. The only lasting truth is the word of God. The TV media and social media are being used by the devil to transport this deception. No longer are the reporters of the news reporting truthfully. There is a false narrative that is designed to cause confusion, as it is being spoken out by the reports on the newscasts. These false stories and inaccurate details are altering people's views of reality. This altering of reality is intentional and is dispelling a socialist and communist belief system into our Westernized democracies. In the last days Jesus said, *"Watch out no one deceives you. For many will come in my name, claiming, 'I am the Messiah,' and will deceive many"* (Matthew 24:4-5 NIV).

Are you currently being deceived? Do you want to be deceived? Do you want your children and family members to be deceived? I hearten you right now to take a few moments to reflect on this chapter. If you are not walking in an intimate relationship with God, I urge you right now to ask Him to show you how to. I encourage you to choose a life of trust in God, faith in the assignment He has given to you and obedience to the precise instructions He will give you. This is the only way you will achieve an abundant life, free from deception and an intimate love relationship with God. The other choice you have is a life that will lead to destruction. There are only two choices. You may be deceived into believing there are more avenues for you to choose to go down, but there are not. The choices are black and white, with no hint of grey. If you are tired of a life filled with untruths and deception, you will soon discover if you choose the way of God, which is life everlasting, what seemed impossible, will suddenly be possible. You will see the surprises of God unfold in front of you every day, that is if you are alert and if you are expecting them. Pay attention!

God promises in His word, *"This day I call the heavens and the earth as witnesses against you that I have set before you life-and-death, blessings and curses. Now choose life, so that you and your children may live and that you may love the Lord your God, listen to his voice, and hold fast to him. For the Lord is your life, and he will give you many years in the land he swore to give to your fathers, Abraham, Isaac and Jacob"* (Deuteronomy 30:19-20 NIV).

Without knowing God and His perfect love for you, without believing and experiencing God's perfect love, it is difficult for you to truly love yourself and others the way God designed you to love. Human love is incomplete. God's love is complete and whole, without flaw and without strings attached. God's relentless love gives us the safety, confidence and courage to believe in the impossible! Just as Noah stepped out and believed in the impossible, *are you willing to step out and believe in the impossible, so God can make all things possible? What direction will you choose to go, to live forever enveloped in the true unconditional love of God, or to die and to be forever tortured and banished from the genuine everlasting love of God?* Even if you do not believe what I have written in this book to be true, or the truth found in the Bible, your unbelief does not change the truth.

Key 25

What Does the Bible Say About How You Can Believe in the Impossible?

As I was writing this portion, God directed me to Ezekiel Chapter 4 – *The Siege of Jerusalem Symbolized*. God showed me this portion of the Bible for a specific reason. It was to demonstrate how precise God is as He talks with us, and He often uses symbolism to get His message across. If you read Chapter 4 of Ezekiel you will note how specific, right down to the measurement of food God instructs Ezekiel to portion out and eat. This is the type of communication God wants with each one of us. He wants to instruct us in a precise manner so we will fully live out His WILL for our lives. He cares so much for us, and He always takes care of us even when others around us are not taking care of us.

Note from this portion of scripture the obedience of Ezekiel in trusting God and in following His instructions. It is obvious Ezekiel had an intimate relationship with God. Ezekiel trusted God. Ezekiel loved God and God loved Ezekiel. Ezekiel also had faith in God, he trusted Him so much he believed all God was telling him to do, even when it was not an easy task. Such as laying on his left side for a period of time each day for 390 days and then laying on his right side for a period of 40 days. Laying on his left and right side symbolized northern Israel would be in captivity for 390 years, and the southern kingdom of Judah would be in captivity for 40 years. The number of days he laid down corresponded to the number of years in captivity. This was not easy news to give to Israel; however, Ezekiel was obedient in the actions and instructions that were given to him by God. God loved Israel so much he knew they needed to have a consequence for their actions of disobedience. True love corrects. True love chastises. True love cares.

As strange as these actions may have seemed, Ezekiel was obedient to his calling as he prophesied to the people the stern judgement from God that was behind the peculiar symbolic actions. His friends and neighbors must have thought Ezekiel had lost his mind, as he rationed his food, carried furniture out of his house, doing various things to represent the disaster soon to overtake them. Some of us reading about these accounts in the Bible may be glazing over the profound acts of trust and obedience Ezekiel placed in God. You might also not be fully comprehending the profound acts of love God displayed for His people, as this all took place in the Old Testament, so, *how can it be relevant to today?* It seems all so unrealistic. But remember, all these precise and unconventional symbolic acts were a prophecy to the nation of Israel that affected us in today's world. Israel was being judged by God due to their disobedience. Real love corrects. God also corrects us in today's world, as He is the same God today as He was yesterday and as He will be forever more. This story of Ezekiel is placed in the Bible for us to understand the same God of Ezekiel is seeking out willing and obedient servants on this earth. Servants to listen to God's voice and do exactly what He is asking of us. If we do not listen to God, there will be consequences for our disobedience.

This took a lot of courage and bravery on the part of Ezekiel. As well as believing in the impossible by not caring what others thought of his actions as God gave him specific instructions that accompanied his obedient actions. Ezekiel very much loved the nation of Israel, his relationship with God and his obedience to his calling. He also cared about the assignment given to him by God much more than he cared about what others thought of him. Ezekiel was not operating on feelings; he was instead intentional in his choice to obey God because he loved God. The doubters and the scoffers must have had a hay day with Ezekiel. Ezekiel had to withstand a lot of peer pressure and persecution. Yet, look what happened. Exactly what Ezekiel said would happen did come to pass. All these millenniums later, we are reading about Ezekiel's obedience and bravery, about Ezekiel's belief in what seemed to be impossible instructions he was being given by God. Ezekiel is an example as to what happens when we listen to God, trust Him, and obey His instructions. This narrative of Ezekiel's obedience and love towards God gives strength, wisdom and courage to all of us that we are not to rely on feelings but on God's loving instructions to us.

Some of you reading this book may be questing after wealth, fame, and prestige. You may want all God promised you instantaneously, and you may not be willing to make the sacrifices God requires of you so you can fulfill your ultimate calling on this earth. God often gives His children things in bite sizes, so we can learn and grow. If we "pass the test", and remain obedient to God, He then can trust us with more. He loves us so much He does not give us everything at once. He knows for most of us, giving us exactly what has been promised to us all at once could eventually destroy us, as we will become reliant on ourselves instead of God. God has given you the exact gifts and talents to fulfill your destiny on this earth. Yet you may need a season, or two or three, to gain more skills to enhance these gifts and talents. This time of "seasoning" maybe essential to further develop your character, so you become more like Christ and thereby acquire the want to serve others, not the want to be served. It is only when you developed the heart, mind and character of Christ you can confidently walk at a higher level in your calling. As well as confidently do the radical, impossible things for God such as Ezekiel did.

All things God has for you to accomplish on this earth can only be done through God's supernatural power. God will begin by trusting you with a few things, and when you can demonstrate your obedience to Him, then He trusts you with more. To believe in the impossible like Ezekiel did, you too need to place your entire trust in God. This will happen when your character is steadfast, and you are producing the fruits of the Spirit. Do not just say it, believe it, and then do it! If you do what seems impossible in the natural, it will start to be possible with the supernatural belief in the ways of God.

I will not be going into any further detail on the book of Ezekiel, because I could write an entire book analyzing its contents. It is worthy to note the book of Ezekiel is the most logically arranged of any of the prophetic books. It contains three sections, each of which addresses a different subject matter. The first section, Chapters 1–24 concern the fall of Jerusalem. The second section, Chapters 25–39 contain a series of oracles addressed to foreign nations, concluding with a portion in which the future of Israel is contrasted with that of the foreign nations. The third section, Chapters 40–48, presents a plan for rebuilding the Temple and reorganizing the restored state of Israel. Ezekiel's prophecies did much to dispel the notion God dwelled exclusively in Jerusalem. He emphasized the importance of individual responsibility, and he urged the Sabbath be kept holy by ceasing to work—for the holiness of the day was a special sign of God's relationship with His people.

Is this the type of relationship you want to have with God, like that of Ezekiel's or Noah's? A relationship so close and intimate you know every single step you take is ordained by God. You become so close with God you walk in the power of His Spirit all the time, not looking to the left or to the right. Following the straight path that leads to fulfillment of your assignment and eventually to eternal life. God trusted both godly men with increased responsibility as He spoke, and He moved precisely in their lives because both were obedient with their assignments. God used the obedience of these two men to shape and alter history. *Are you a Noah or an Ezekiel? Are you willing to surrender to God's instructions as they become so precise, and unconventional, similarly to what occurred in Ezekiel's and Noah's assignments?* If so, you developed a true sense of security, a true confidence and faith in the unwavering love of God. Faith is believing in what you do not see but trusting in God to guide you by fulfilling His WILL through your life. Faith is not seen. Instead, as you develop a closer relationship with God and learn to listen to the voice of God, faith is believing implicitly in what God says.

Many of us allow fear and discouragement to get in the way of the next level God wants to take us to in our unique earthly assignments. We allow doubt to creep in as we do not believe it is the voice of God telling us to do something that may seem so radical. However, if you have a close relationship with God it states in John 10:27-30 (NIV):

My sheep listen to my voice; I know them, and they follow me. I give them eternal life, and they shall never perish; no one will snatch them out of my hand. My Father, who has given them to me, is greater than all; no one can snatch them out of my Father's hand. I and the Father are one.

You might say, "well, I do not know how to hear the voice of God. I tried, but I don't think He hears me. *How can I be sure it is God's voice that is speaking to me?"* To hear from God, every day you need to read the Bible and to talk with Him. Then you need to wait and listen. I can guarantee you, He will respond, through His written word and through speaking directly into your very being, deep down in the part of you that was once feeling empty and lonely. The void of doubt and fear as to hearing God's voice can be replaced with the goodness and the love of God. As you begin to believe in the impossible you will begin to be transformed into the likeness of Jesus.

And we all, who with unveiled faces contemplate the Lord's glory, are being transformed into his image with ever-increasing glory, which comes from the Lord, who is the Spirit (2 Corinthians 3:18 NIV).

If you have not already begun, I urge you to give developing a relationship with God, founded on His true unconditional love, a try before it is too late.

Jesus looked at them and said, "With man this is impossible, but not with God; all things are possible with God" (Mark 10:27 NIV).

Unlocking Mystery #5

I Can Believe in the Impossible

> **Reflect:** Do you believe in the impossible? Do you have the faith to believe anything is possible with God? Is the reasoning power of intellect holding you back from surrendering to the supernatural power of God? Is fear ripping away your faith?
>
> **Relate:** What situations in your life do you need to experience a miracle, yet you cannot fathom how this will happen?
>
> **Respond:** I encourage you to intentionally establish a bold faith that believes in the unseen. Believe in it before you can "see it". You can do this by:
>
> Continuously declaring such as, "Thank you God for the bold faith and courage you have given to me. I praise you God I believe all things are possible with you!" Never stop declaring these things.
>
> Declare your bold faith in the present and future tense, not the past tense.
>
> Make a list of situations that require miraculous supernatural power from God for a resolution. Write these in the present and future tense.
>
> Take the above list and write each situation on a sticky note.
>
> Place these sticky notes in areas around your home that are visible for you to see.
>
> As you walk by the sticky notes, read them, and say, "God I thank and praise you for working through this situation for me."
>
> Just Say It! as if it were so, as if God has already performed the miracle.
>
> Watch and believe, as God is a God of surprises! God will surprise you every day!
>
> An endnote to keep in mind, the answers/solutions you are believing God for in your situations must be founded on the Biblical truth and principles found in the Bible.
>
> *Speak the Truth.*
>
> *Just Say It! I Can Believe in The Impossible!*

#6

Perfect Love Casts Out Confusion

One can only truly experience LOVE when one understands LOVE is much more an active verb than a proper noun - Alan Morissette.

Dr. Cheryl Bauman

Key 26

Do Your Words Really Mean What I Think They Do?

A few years ago, I presented at an international conference in Scotland where there were educators from over 50 countries in attendance. Among the countries represented, most people spoke or at least understood the English language. The conference was sponsored by the University of Glasgow, yet it was held at a local hotel. During break times and at the end of each day, many of the presenters and participants would meet around the elevators. One afternoon as we were waiting for the elevator to appear, a group of us, constituting about eight different countries were discussing the various terminologies we use for words such as *elevator*. In Canada and the United States, using the word *elevator* is quite a common descriptive word used. However, my colleagues from Australia and the UK use the word *lift* to describe what we North Americans call an *elevator*.

When you are travelling around the world, being able to ask where the washroom is located can be quite an essential request. Australians use the word *toilet*, not *washroom*, as do people from the UK. In the United States the word *restroom* is more common. Whereas in Canada we often use the word *bathroom* or *washroom*. In non-speaking English countries such as Italy the word is *bano* and in France it is *salle de bain*. The word for a personal handheld phone most North Americans call a *cell phone*, is a *mobile* to Australians and people from the UK. As with the example of the cell phone, even though people speak English in many countries, varying English terms label the exact same thing.

The English language has one word, love. However, there are multiple definitions to help us describe the varying forms of love that connect us in our many relationships. Thus, I would like to suggest this one word, "love" in the English language is creating confusion as to how we are currently defining our multiple earthly relationships. It is widely agreed on by scholars and theologians that most, if not all the New Testament was originally written in Greek, specifically Koine Greek. Koine means "the common dialect". The New Testament was written in the most common form of the Greek language of that time. Some authors of the New Testament often included translations from Hebrew and Aramaic texts. Jesus principally spoke a Galilean dialect of Aramaic.

Although Ancient Greek was the gold standard, a simpler version of the language, called Koine, was more accessible to diverse audiences of the time. Thus, many of the authors of the New Testament choose this version of the language so the New Testament was accessible to more people. The Koine Greek had less complexities and irregularities in the language than that of Ancient Greek. However, for the purposes of our discussion on the importance of the meaning of "love", we will focus on the Ancient Greek language. The Ancient Greek language has four words to describe types of love, and we find several of these words in original New Testament writings. If the English language had four or more words to use that described different forms of love, there would be less confusion. The Ancient Greek language helped their people, and it can help us now, to define the many relationships we have within our lives. The Greek language clearly categorizes the concept of love. It defines the love between parents with their children as *Storge* love – affectionate love. The love between friends is *Phila* love which is a dispassionate, virtuous love. Whereas the love between a husband and a wife, *Eros* – romantic love, and the love God has for us is *Agape* love – unconditional love. The four words used in the Ancient Greek language were detailed in Key #14 earlier on in the book.

A parent can also have unconditional love for their child (many do), and a husband and wife can also have unconditional love for each other, and close friends can have unconditional love towards each other. However, finally, God absolutely has pure, unconditional love for all of us. According to the Ancient Greek Language, unconditional love is a choice in every relationship we have on this earth. However, in our relationship with God it is an absolute. Whether people recognize God, or His love towards them does not factor into the equation, God has unconditional love for ALL.

The four Greek language categories as to the forms of various love relationships help to separate the confusion happening with our English language and our Western culture in relation to defining "what love is". The one word, "love", is all the English language has to offer for our often-complex earthly relationships. The Greek language supports us in our further understanding in some earthly relationships; true unconditional love will not happen. I hope this brief explanation might help some. Help them to understand and overcome hurts. Hurts that occurred in work relationships, family relationships, or friendship relationships, where you might have expected unconditional love, only to find out the other person(s) was not able to provide it. I encourage you to do more research and reading in this area, as I am just providing a brief overview.

In addition, the language Sanskrit has ninety-six words to express love in varying forms and ancient Persian has eighty words. Multiple languages have numerous words to define *love* in varying forms and contexts. When it comes to the word "love" itself, the English language does have a few words to help define what may be occurring in our varying relationships, including fondness, affection, and infatuation. Although I would argue in our Western world, we have not defined these other words as actually types of love. Yet we have a choice of English words to describe the same things and provide categorizations such as an elevator/lift or a cell/mobile.

Love can be quite complex and complicated, depending on the language we use and the relationships we find ourselves involved with. *I wonder though, are we just making love complicated simply because we really do not know what it is, or have never experienced it in its purest of forms?* Many songs and movies are written about love, and books on the topic line our shelves. The international curiosity and attention to love is endless, thus further illuminating the English language's approach to the concept of love is too simplistic. I would contest the oversimplified and under representative nature the English language has regarding the different expressions of love is causing confusion for people questing to discover love in its purest of forms.

I believe in some of our relationships, confusion runs rampant, as we only have one word in the English language to define love. Yet love is so special, unique, and beautiful in its many forms. To say, "I love this apple" is different from me saying to my daughter, "Sara, I love you". Yet we interchangeably use the only word we have in the English language, "love", all the time as we refer to varying levels of relationships with living and non-living objects. However, the meaning of "love", depending on the context and the entity, is highly variable. Saying, "Mom, I love the new coat you bought", is different from proclaiming to my mom, "Mom, I love you". In the English language, the word "love" has become diluted so much it is replacing the word "like". In certain languages, the difference is very important, and therefore other languages have provided a distinction.

The English language currently has only one word to describe something that can involve so much depth and meaning, such as a marriage relationship. However, currently in our English-speaking countries, the word love can involve something so superficial, such as the food we are eating. It is no wonder in English speaking societies the meaning of *I love you* can often be misinterpreted or overused. Part of that interpretation relies on context and the type of relationship we have with people. *How has this limitation caused confusion for you?*

Key 27

Time Spent at Home Versus Time Spent Elsewhere

As our societies become increasingly complex, moving along at such a rapid speed, we all find ourselves at varying levels of relationships with others, due to personal and professional commitments. Nowadays, many jobs have both men and women working together at facilities outside of their homes. Before the industrial revolution, many men worked from home, and women stayed at home to care for the children and tend to household needs. Prior to the industrial revolution, people were more connected to their home base through employment and household responsibilities. There was a greater need for husbands and wives to spend more time together in a compatible and collaborative relationship.

After the industrial revolution, more men were employed outside of the home, yet for the most part, women remained at home. Thus, separating work and home began. In the 1960's the number of women working outside of the home began to increase. Due to the nature of the fast-paced world we currently live in, as we rush around to meet work obligations many of us are prioritizing our work commitments ahead of our family commitments. Couples are finding less time to spend with each other at home. A survey of North American couples reported on average, partners are only spending around 15 minutes per day in meaningful communication with each other. This time does not include mindlessly sitting together in front of a TV screen. *How can couples continue to develop a relationship with the person whom they are to be the most connected with, when they are only devoting a measly 15 minutes per day to them?* Sadly, some couples reported they do not even find 15 minutes per day to spend in meaningful communication with their spouse and are reporting their relationships with their partners are virtually nonexistent.

The couples in this survey reported they believed their relationship was suffering due to the lack of "couple time". Instead, they admitted to pushing their relationships to the back burner to make time for the daily grind of work, household chores and childcare. The participants of the survey believed their relationships would improve if they had more quality and quantity time together. Given the chance, over half of those surveyed would be happy with simple things like having an uninterrupted meal together at home or cuddling up watching a movie. Of those surveyed, 16% admitted to having no quality time together with their partner at all. Almost half of the participants revealed they don't receive any romantic gestures as their other half is too busy.

This is truly a couple crisis of epic proportions!

Stop and ask yourself, where do your priorities lie? Who are the most important people in your life in terms of obligations and commitments? Who do you need to develop a deeper relationship with by spending more time with them? Are you pushing your couple relationship to the back burner to make more time for other commitments?

If you do not spend time with the people who are supposed to be the closest to you, your relationships are affected, and they become strained due to a lack of time and intimacy. This is exactly when problems begin to set in. As you are filling more time with people and things outside of the home and less time at home with the people you love and have a commitment to. If this is you, *are you valuing others above the people you should value the most? What can you do about it?* Problems and strife slowly creep in when human belonging and love needs are unattended to. This can begin a slippery slope of one or both partners acting in a selfish manner and crowding his or her time with other priorities. If left unchecked, these issues can manifest themselves in many ways. Things such as depression, addiction to social media, to alcohol, drugs, gambling, eating, pornography, or extramarital affairs. As well as addiction to trying to find love in all the wrong places. *Does this sound like a familiar setting you find yourself in at the current moment? If this is you, are you content with this current situation?*

Key 28

Can Anything Be Done About This Couple Crisis?

I am blessed with very positive and wise friends by the name of Georgia and Alan. If I wrote down all my friends' words of wisdom, I would be writing volumes and volumes. Georgia and Alan have been married for over 50 years. The more I spend time with the two of them, it is easy to know they are deeply in love with each other. They want other couples to have this same deep commitment. They are always bantering back and forth and joking with each other. Being around Georgia and Alan is fun and their love for life is contagious. Georgia and Alan share many life lessons as to how they have remained married for almost 60 years. Their love is unconditionally steadfast. Everyday the two of them dedicate special couple time together such as going pedal boating. Every night before they go to bed, they intentionally make a choice to tell each other three things they appreciate about the other. The appreciation needs to be directly related to the day. There are rules during this nighttime tradition. Both partners must not recycle past appreciations (especially recent ones) and the appreciations need to be genuine, truthful, and thoughtful. Here are examples of three appreciations. "I appreciate when you help me make supper." "I appreciate when you greet me at the door with a loving smile and a hug." "I appreciate the kind, wise, and loving way you spoke with me when I was explaining my challenging day at work".

I challenge you to use Georgia and Alan's appreciation ritual and to take the time with your partner to develop the habit of saying three things you appreciate about him or her. Do this every night before you go to bed. If you do not have a partner, find someone special such as a child, a friend or a relative you can begin this habit with.

Just as Georgia and Alan practice spending daily time together in meaningful and positive conversations, psychologist, Dr. James Dobson also agrees daily time together as a couple is essential to a lasting, healthy relationship. Dr. Dobson suggests a minimum amount of time per day couples need to spend in direct, meaningful conversations and interactions is at least 30 minutes. He also teaches to have a happy, healthy relationship, couples need to plan more extended periods of time each week in addition to the daily 30 minutes. Activities such as planning a weekly date night, taking a nightly walk together, interacting with one another through sports, or a hobby are all ways to add value to your relationships. Planning an overnight getaway about four times a year and a longer couple's vacation about once a year is also helpful to continuing to build on your relationship. If money is an issue and you have children, going away over night might be more difficult, yet not impossible. I know two couples who swap taking care of one another's kids for a weekend, while the other couple stays at home and enjoys some peace and quiet time!

If you have left your relationship unchecked, I challenge you to not let this go unattended for much longer. A slow and steady decline can suddenly shift to a fast speed derailment. Some people who admitted to having an affair relayed it did not happen all at once. They started spending less time with their partner and more time with the other person. What may have started out as a little problem, where over time, more commitments crept into a busy schedule and thus they are spending little to no time at all with their spouse. If it has been you who crowded your time with too many commitments, stop blaming the other person in the relationship for the distance. Be reflective and be honest. Look back and pinpoint where you started to spend less time with your partner. If you are wise, you will strip away the finger-pointing, and start to change your patterns of behavior, so you can rekindle the committed relationship you were once so enamoured with.

I believe some of you are chasing shiny objects around that are leading you on a wild-goose chase. You might be filling your time with too many work commitments because you are unable to say no. You might be agreeing to volunteer beyond the amount of time that is realistically possible for you and your family. You might be spending too much time in the local coffee shop gossiping with your friends or trying to catch the eye of a regular customer. Instead, you could be spending time at home communicating with your partner and trying to catch his or her eye. *What is taking away from the quality time needed to build a solid, loving relationship with your partner? What are you selfishly holding onto you need to let go, for the greater good of your committed relationship?* Whatever it is, if you want to live a life of blessings, love, and abundance, I recommend you decide to selflessly give it up.

#6: Perfect Love Casts Out Confusion

Start to develop new habits that remove these distractions and increase the interactions with you and your partner. If this is you, admit it, and start to erase patterns of behavior that need to be broken. You may ask, how can this be done? This can be carried out by making a commitment to break the old patterns and continue to set new patterns. Remember in Chapter #1 we discussed the neuroplasticity of the brain, and how it can be retrained to develop new patterns of behavior. Experts say it takes about 21 times of repetitive behaviours to develop a new habit, a new way of thinking and acting. I encourage you to begin today to set new healthy behaviours in your life and the life of your family. Here are a few examples of some inexpensive healthy habits to help you to spend more quality time with your partner:

- Play a Card or Board Game Together
- Cook Together
- Stay Fit Together
- Talk about Random, Positive Things Together
- Fly a Kite Together in an Open Field
- Play Hide-and-Seek in Your Home
- Dance Together to Your Favorite Songs
- Take Turns Giving Each Other Massages
- Go Biking Together
- Window-Shop Together
- Take a Leisurely Scenic Drive
- Take a Walk Together
- At Nighttime, Go Outside and Watch the Stars Together
- Cook Your Partner's Favorite Meal
- Write Down Your Family's Goals for the Next Five Years
- Watch the Sunset Together
- Sleep in on Weekends

Dr. Cheryl Bauman

There is no time like the present to begin developing new healthy habits, or "dust off" old positive habits that haven't been around for a while as you spend quality time with those you love. As you are developing these new habits, your attitude is vital. I encourage you to have a positive attitude and to believe in the best for you and your spouse. As was discussed in the last chapter, "Believe in the Impossible"!

Key 29

Suffering from Confusion?

There is a real tendency to misplace and confuse, *Agape, Eros* and *Philia* love (discussed in detail in Key 14). Unfortunately, current statistics are showing the workplace is the number one location where married people who engage in infidelity meet the *other person*. Regrettably, affairs in the workplace are happening all the time. Today more than ever, workplace relationships are causing a crisis of epic proportions. More men and women are breaking their marriage vows by engaging in friendships at work that slowly (or quickly) become romantic relationships. These work relationships would have been socially impossible years ago, as many women did not work outside of the home. The partitions that once separated the sexes are crumbling, as are the boundaries that once protected marriage. Pop culture, midlife crises, and spending less time with a spouse may all contribute to the decision to cheat on a partner.

Some people are addicted to that *lovin' feeling*, as we learned earlier in this book. Addiction to the chemical rush that is produced by hormones is a major problem that haunts certain people, it is just like an addiction to alcohol or drugs. If you are suffering from this form of addiction, then you are repeatedly trying to fill a void by something other than true unconditional love. You are questing for love in all the wrong places. In this portion of the chapter, I am not highlighting people who are uncontrollably going from affair to affair trying to fill an inner void. Instead, I am mainly discussing people who end up in an affair through a relationship at work that escalated out of control. However, as I state this, people who are addicted to the *relationship rush* also fit into the category of finding the people at work with whom they commit adultery with.

In Dr. Shirley Glass' book, *Not 'Just Friends'*, she says the new infidelity is between people who form deep, passionate connections before realizing they crossed the line from platonic friendship into romantic love. It is a confusion between *Eros, Philia* and *Agape* love, as we briefly learned about earlier in this book. It is a responsibility of a Christian to demonstrate *Agape* love to everyone, especially their husband or wife. *Agape* love is the selfless love that looks out for the needs of the other person above themselves. If every individual who was in a marriage union were to practice *Agape* love, infidelity would not be a part of this world. It does not mean the temptation to cheat would not be present. However, instead of acting on the temptation, the selfless love would triumph. Yet, this is not what is happening in today's world. When it comes to confusing *Eros, Philia* and *Agape* love with matters of infidelity, selfishness is currently winning.

In her years of research Dr. Glass found 82% of the unfaithful partners she treated had an affair with someone who was, at first, "just a friend" (*Philia* love). From over a decade of research Glass found 50 percent of unfaithful women and 62 percent of unfaithful men she treated were involved with someone from work. Dr. Glass is suggesting today's workplace is the new danger zone of romantic opportunity. These figures are very alarming. However, taking a closer look at today's careers, they do offer more opportunity for extramarital affairs. Group interaction with both males and females in the workplace, frequent travel and long hours create more opportunity and temptation. All these changes that ushered in the "new norm" of the work world are allowing individuals to mix freely. Years ago, these opportunities were not as prevalent, they were often segregated and restricted.

A different work environment has spawned a different kind of affair. The new infidelity happens between colleagues who at first become emotionally attached. Men and women who work closely together under stressful conditions can become attracted to each other. They often share interests and think nothing of spending time over coffee or lunch. Nevertheless, lunch between married friends or one person who is married, no matter the intentions, can have dangerous consequences. One researcher calls this new kind of affair *the cup of coffee syndrome*. Most men and women begin with safe marriages at home and friendships at work. As they regularly meet with their co-worker for coffee breaks and lunch, these relationships develop into deep friendships. Co-workers come to depend on these coffee rendezvouses, and soon they have emotional work friendships and crumbling marriages.

Glass' studies show men and women in these workplace romances believe it is wrong to have an affair. According to Glass, affair partners are usually happy in their marriages and have no plans to leave their spouses. Due to a gradual slide toward infidelity, partners often do not pay attention to their behavior until they have already damaged their marriages, and sex is often the last sign the marriage partner has been betrayed. Much confusion and distrust arise. This is how temptation, if not recognized can lead to confusion with love at very dangerous levels. If you are currently suffering from confusion, know that confusion does not come from God. God is not the author of confusion; He is the author of clarity and truth.

How to Protect Your Marriage

How do you protect your marriage when today's workplace is offering more opportunity for extramarital relationships? The simple answer is, do not even *think* about having an affair. Once you realize the temptation with a co-worker is too great, stop and step back. Healthy marriages must have proper boundaries. Once a partner begins to act on their feelings pretending, they have no other primary commitments, this is when problems arise. Good intentions are not good enough to protect a marriage from temptations at work. Attraction towards the opposite sex is a natural thing. However, when a man or woman neglects primary responsibilities and allows himself or herself to act on an instinctive attraction – even in their thoughts – they have already violated the marriage vows. Temptations happen to everyone all the time. Jesus was tempted in the wilderness by the devil; however, Jesus made the choice not to act on the temptations. Jesus combated temptation by speaking out scriptures. Acting on temptations is a choice. Many factors can play a role in causing infidelity, nonetheless, it always requires attraction, opportunity, and failure to follow precautions. Dr. Glass provides us some basic guidelines to help avoid infidelity:

- Do not allow yourself to think about being with another person, as thoughts lead to actions.

- Do not flirt, as it tells others you are available.

- Stay away from dangerous situations because everyone is sinful in nature and can be tempted.

Marriage, like a relationship with God, works best when it enters and fills every corner of life. Secrecy and infidelity are impossible when we are transparent within our marriage and with God. This transparency not only protects our marriages from harm on the outside, but it also keeps our marriages happiest on the inside. Admitting our temptations and weaknesses in this area to God and surrendering our will to His will restores our souls. However, when partners try to hide the problem and pretend God does not know, they are only deceiving themselves. Secrets of this size are unhealthy and are a sign of mental instability. Fantasy begins to overtake reality. God knows everything. He knows the end from the beginning. God is a loving God. He understands and He will guide you through these temptations. Depending on how strong the temptation is, or how often you have these temptations, you may need to seek wise godly counsel from a pastor, trusted friend, and/or a therapist. You need to make the choice to be responsible and accountable to remain living healthy and in a realistic world, not a fantasy world. Just remember, a fantasy world is not reality, it is confusion. God is perfect love, and perfect love casts out confusion.

Research suggests habitual cheaters have an addiction problem that needs to be addressed, or it could destroy him or her.

As has been previously discussed, the English language only has one word for love. The Greek language has four words to describe love. The Greek word *Philia*, which is the mental love, does have give and take. It is a virtuous love, that includes loyalty to friends, family, and community, and requires virtue, equality, and familiarity (Liddell & Scott, 1940). *Philia* love is what should be found in the workplace. Unfortunately, in our English-language, we do not have a description for the type of love found in the workplace, thus confusion often sets in when temptation begins to take over. People allow unrealistic ideals to overtake reality. This should immediately be a red flag! God establishes through His word that as Christians in the workplace we are to demonstrate *Agape* love for all, which is the unconditional love. Yet lines at work are often being blurred, and people step over these lines from *Philia* love into the *Eros* form of love, ignoring the Biblical principles of *Agape* love we are to live by.

Stopping an Affair Takes Courage and Self-Control

Stopping an affair takes courage and it takes self-control. You need to admit that becoming involved in the affair was a cowardly act of selfishness. Affairs are not founded on bravery, wellness, and self-control. Instead, you may be suffering with some mental health issues, or you may be lacking in confidence and self-identity as to who you are and who you were created to be. One, two, three or more affairs are often red flags for serious issues happening on the inside, as you are dealing with past pain brought about by rejection, abuse, anger, bitterness, grief, trauma, and despair. Having an affair is turning away from God's great plan for your life and trying to live your life your way. God has great purposes for you. Let go of the chains of adultery and let God take you places you never dreamed of! Adultery keeps you stuck in a rut! Being set free from the affair will provide you with greater clarity!

If you are involved in an affair, I highly recommend you stop right now and begin to deal with the root causes that have brought you to this point of selfishness and deception. You are lying to yourself and to others around you. You may have suffered sexual abuse. You may have been raised by a mother who suffered from mental health issues and did not love you the way you needed to be loved. You may have longed to be loved by your earthly father, but he was not a part of your life. Some of you may have been raised in a loving home, but you are simply selfish and have extremely uncontrollable desires you have been unwilling to tame. Any one or some of these unfortunate circumstances led you to a path of confusion and further turmoil, as you long to fill the empty void deep within.

If you currently are, or have committed adultery, *how satisfying was/is this affair?* The sex may be good. However, *is this person available for you 24 hours a day? Do you spend Christmas and Thanksgiving with them, or do they spend it with their family? How much time do they devote to you? Do you feel rejected by them as well, always competing for their attention, as they do not have time to spend with you because their time is spent with their own family? Does this remind you of the rejection you may have experienced from your own mother or father who might have not had the time to spend with you?* If you are involved in an affair, I am guessing you continue to feel rejected and displaced, trying to find love, trying to fill the void, grasping at any form of fake love to find happiness. *Are you happy sleeping around and lying to people in your life such as your kids or your spouse? Is living a life of secrecy making you happy?* Anything done in secret is deceptive. But sadly, you are the one who is the most deceived and you may have not figured that out yet.

> *If you must sneak around to do it, lie to hide it, or delete it so it is not seen, then you should not be doing it!*

As hard as it may be, the only solution is to stop. Having an affair is a habit of weakness you have started, and you need to stop. We all make mistakes. However, a mistake repeated is a decision. Continually being in a pattern of falling in and out of love is an addiction. If you are currently in an affair or engaged in this type of behavior in the past, you are addicted to that *lovin' feeling*. The enemy will trick you into thinking it is okay, you will never get caught, and this unhealthy affair is really a good thing, for everyone involved. *Really, is this even a logical conclusion? Have you ever spoken with people who have been betrayed by their spouse? Have you talked with a child whose father or a mother cheated on the family?* Cheating is cheating on the entire family, not just on the other partner. *If you have spoken with people such as this, were their stories filled with joy, laughter, and peace? Were their stories filled with health and happiness for all involved?* I have never heard of such a story where a partner cheats on their spouse and everyone is happy and healthy. In fact, the opposite is what happens. The enemy of your soul wants to steal, kill, and destroy everything that is good in your life and of your family's and replace it with all bad things. The devil wants you to believe the affair is surrounded with happiness, joy, and laughter. This is a lie.

If you are currently having an affair and if you are honest, I am sure you are filled with fear of being caught and engulfed in a mountain of guilt and shame. I am assuming by making these statements you are feeling guilty. If you are not feeling any shame or guilt for your adulterous actions, then I would suggest looking up the definition of a narcissist, as this is more than likely the characteristics you are manifesting. I will not be going into any further detail as to what narcissism is, as it would require quite an in-depth look into the type of person that fits this mould. Suffice to say, narcissists do not see anything wrong with their shameful behaviors, and they blame the other person in the relationship for their inappropriateness. God forgives everyone if they truly repent, demonstrate remorse and seek restoration for their sinful behavior. God is not a respecter of persons. He loves you! But you need to admit your wrongdoing, take full responsibility for your actions and never return to committing adultery. *Are you able to do this?*

If you are having an affair and you are experiencing fear, guilt, and shame then this is an indication you are aware as to whether what you are doing is wrong. If you are not experiencing remorse for your sinful adulterous actions, then I urge you to seek help immediately with your narcissistic tendencies. If you are not experiencing remorse or pain for what you are doing to your partner and family, it is next to impossible for you to recognize what you are doing is wrong. It is then virtually impossible for you to repent, to seek reconciliation of the damage done and to attempt to restore the marriage. Love, joy, peace, gentleness, kindness, patience, goodness, faithfulness and self-control are fruits of the spirit born out of God's undying love for you. Being involved in an affair does not produce good fruit, it produces rotten fruit. Good fruit is from God; rotten fruit is from Satan.

God does not want you to spend your time being tempted into an adulterous affair. This is not because He doesn't want you to have fun. No, it is exactly the opposite. He doesn't want you to give into the temptations of the flesh that will only lead to devastation and destruction. God's plan is for you to live a prosperous life, free of shame, guilt, and condemnation. There are many consequences to your sins if you continue to commit sexual immorality and try to cover them up. You only have one life to live. You can only receive life, hope and peace through the gift of love freely given by the mercy and justice of God. This is your choice; God allows you to make your own choices. Jesus chose to pay sin's penalty of death on the cross in your place. Because of Jesus, you can know what real Agape love is. You can get rid of confusion and replace it with the mercy and love of God. This is a gift you and I did not earn or deserve. However, you and I can live a life better than we could ever hope for, a life that is abundant regardless of circumstances and filled full of mercy, grace, peace, hope and love. Due to Jesus' sacrifice on the cross, we can live forever in heaven and have an eternal home.

Key 30

What Does the Bible Say About Confusing Lust with Love?

There is absolutely no place in the Bible that states or acknowledges an affair between two people is godly. In fact, just the opposite. Yet people, including Christians, attempt to justify an adulterous affair. Justifying adultery causes confusion among believers and within the body of Christ.

For God is not the author of confusion but of peace, as in all the churches of the saints (1 Corinthians 14:33 NKJV).

The author of Proverbs also contends:

He who commits adultery lacks sense; he who does it destroys himself (Proverbs 6:32 ESV).

The scriptures are filled with truth in relation to adultery. Here are a few more scriptures to support the fact adultery is sinful and ungodly.

Flee from sexual immorality. Every other sin a person commits is outside the body, but the sexually immoral person sins against his own body (1 Corinthians 6:18 NIV).

Let marriage be held in honor among all, and let the marriage bed be undefiled, for God will judge the sexually immoral and adulterous (Hebrews 13:4 NIV).

But I say to you that everyone who looks at a woman with lustful intent has already committed adultery with her in his heart (Matthew 5:28 NIV).

Yet, with all the truth found in the Bible in relation to adultery, there are currently churches and church leaders openly embracing adultery among their parishioners by not confronting these issues from the pulpit. Sadly, some church leaders are also wrapped up in adulterous affairs all the while preaching from the pulpit. As King Solomon discusses in the book of Proverbs, adultery "makes no sense". It also makes no sense that church leaders are not approaching the people involved in adultery to help them put an end to this sinful behavior by supporting them to work through these self-created messes. Instead, some church leaders are aiding in covering up these sins because they are afraid, they will lose popularity, or financial support from people. We are living in a sad day when the leaders of some churches are not tackling the very issues causing the current church to crumble. What is happening in our society today is the beliefs, values, and norms that were unacceptable a century ago in relation to infidelity and sexual immorality have suddenly become acceptable. Sadly, this acceptableness has seeped into the church body. Some parts of the church are morphing into the beliefs and norms of the world instead of standing on the beliefs and norms of the true living word of God. *What does the Bible state about adultery and sexual immorality?*

The book of Revelation in the Bible clearly outlines what God thinks about sexual immorality and adultery. That is in relation to the tolerance the churches have for it prior to the time before Christ returns to this earth to gather up his bride and prior to the great throne judgement.

The words written in Revelation are true. They will come to pass. Even if some of you reading this book are deceived and believe you can go to church on Sundays yet continue to be sexually immoral. God warned you in His word what will happen to you. Since God is all loving and compassionate, He is warning people and being merciful by giving them time to repent. It is the act of committing adultery as well as tolerating adultery God will judge. If people in the church or church leaders are not confronting adultery, and instead tolerating it, this too is sin. Note as well in the following scripture written by the Apostle Paul, as it states marriage should be honored by ALL, not just some.

> *Marriage should be honored by all, and the marriage bed kept pure, for God will judge the adulterer and all the sexually immoral (Hebrews 13:4 NIV).*

There is no confusion as to what Paul has written in the Holy Scriptures. The marriage bed is a euphemism for sexual intercourse. Paul considers the physical side of marriage as being vitally important and it must be kept pure. All forms of sexual sin come under a judging God. This is not a *novel idea* for us in the 21st century who are Christians. God literally tells us in the Bible in the end, if people who are sexually immoral do not turn from their wicked ways, they will be judged by Him.

> *Or do you not know that wrongdoers will not inherit the kingdom of God? Do not be deceived: Neither the sexually immoral nor idolaters nor adulterers (1 Corinthians 6:9 NIV).*

> *Jesus further added to the Old Testament definition of what adultery meant in Matthew 5:28 (NIV):*

> *But I tell you that anyone who looks at a woman lustfully has already committed adultery with her in his heart.*

The scriptures apply to men and women, even though some versions just use the word "men". The Old Testament law at the time of Christ merely stated, *"You shall not commit adultery"* (Exodus 20:14 NIV). Jesus further expanded on the meaning of adultery when he demanded, "You shall not *want* to commit adultery." Jesus' full warning develops the context of prohibition against adultery in the law. The seventh commandment, given by Moses, prohibited adultery, but the tenth commandment warned a man should not even covet one's neighbor's wife (Exodus 20:17; Deuteronomy 5:21). Jesus uses in the scripture the same verb as in the standard Greek translation of the tenth commandment. Jesus refers to *wanting* to have one's neighbor's wife. The principle of course extends beyond this illustration, applying to both genders and to single people. Coveting one who might be someone else's spouse someday is also implied. In Jesus' explanation of adultery, he left no room for confusion.

The Old Testament law reveals the death penalty could be imposed on those found guilty of committing adultery (Leviticus 20:10; Deuteronomy 22:22). Adultery in Old Testament law was considered an act of sexual relations between a married woman and any man not her husband. Married men could have sex with single women and either not be subject to any penalty or be subject to a penalty much less severe than those for adultery (Deuteronomy 22:28-29). However, when Jesus proclaimed he was the way, the truth and the life, the writing of the New Testament changed the definitions of adultery to include ALL – both men and women (Matthew 5:28). The Apostle Paul also further expanded on the consequences for those caught in adultery, as adultery is considered a sin.

> *For the wages of sin is death, but the gift of God is eternal life in Christ Jesus our Lord (Romans 6:23 NIV).*

#6: Perfect Love Casts Out Confusion

This verse precisely presents the Gospel truth as found in the New Testament. Our sinful nature, which includes adultery, will lead us to death. But the promise of God is eternal life in Christ if we repent and turn from our sin. Paul wrote to the church in Rome as he is contrasting between sin and mercy, death and life. Paul is defining how we find eternal life in Christ as we become dead to sin and alive to righteousness. Just as Christ died and was resurrected, we have the hope of an eternal perfect state of life. Due to God's great mercy, our sins are washed away, and we do not need to live in condemnation due to our past sin.

In Romans 6:23, The Apostle Paul uses an interesting term "wages" to describe the payment for sin. Paul is using this term metaphorically as when we work at a job for money, we hope we will get paid the wages we deserve and have earned. Due to the work of sin in all of us, we earned, and we deserve a physical and a spiritual death. At the end of the day, we are going to be paid for our sin. Paul is saying the "wages" we deserve is death. It is only by God's grace and mercy through the death and resurrection of His Son Jesus Christ we can hope for anything but death. Through Jesus Christ we are given the gift of eternal life. The only way to escape the wages of our sin, if anyone is committing adultery or involved in sexual immorality, is through Jesus. Since it is God's gift to us, it is simple to receive:

> *If you declare with your mouth, Jesus is Lord and believe in your heart that God raise him from the dead, you will be saved (Romans 10:9 NIV).*

Paul is making a stark contrast between what we deserve, which is sin and death, and what we have been given, which is the gift of eternal life. A gift is something we do not deserve or have earned. This gift of eternal life has been given to us out of God's *Agape* love and mercy. This gift is for ALL, as none of us deserve it. So, if you're currently in an adulterous relationship and not listening to God's clear direction, instead living in confusion, you can receive the gift God has given to you, which is eternal life. In His word God promises that:

> *If we confess our sins, he is faithful and just and will forgive us our sins and purify us from all unrighteousness (1 John 1:9 NIV).*

No one is actively trying to engage in as much sin as possible to be paid in death, or to see how much can be covered by mercy, right? Or wrong? Unfortunately, Jesus discussed the times that would be near his second coming to earth when he declared,

> *Just as it was in the days of Noah, so also will it be in the days of the Son of Man. People were eating, drinking, marrying and being given in marriage up to the day Noah entered the ark. Then the flood came and destroyed them all (Luke 17:26-27 NIV).*

It appears people in the days of Noah thought they were living normal lives, just before the flood took place. They were oblivious to the impending disaster, even though Noah tried to warn them. Jesus said in the last days before his coming that the society would parallel the society of Noah's day. The Apostle Peter rebukes the thinking of those alive today who imagine that the world will just keep going on as usual. He points out we are willfully forgetting the lesson of Noah's Flood. The Apostle Peter also warns us judgment is indeed coming. Peter goes on to further explain the reason for the apparent delay is God's *Agape* love for people is extending the time to trust in Him and repent. I believe we are living in a period of God's grace. I believe God is extending the days to provide as many people as possible the chance of eternal life. I encourage you to read 2 Peter 3:1-9 to fully understand Peter's words. God through His great *mercy* wants to save people. However, people need to stop living in confusion and recognize the promises that are written about in the Bible will come true.

People often complain if they believe a judge is too lenient by failing to impose the appropriate penalty for an offence that is committed. Media headlines often express outrage at judges who are "soft on crime". Back in Old Testament times a woman was stoned to death for committing adultery. Yet today adultery has become an acceptable norm in our society, and "this crime" would never appear before a judge. We expect judges to execute justice; we do not expect them simply to be merciful. On the other hand, we are fickle as we expect mercy to trump justice in our personal relationships. We expect a loving parent to be merciful with their children, and we expect friends to be merciful with one another. So, in our personal lives we equate justice and mercy as alternatives, not as equals.

Yet God is a God who *judges* with *justice,* and He is also a God of *mercy*. In the scriptures, God is beckoning ALL people, which includes the church, to turn from their corrupt immoral ways and to repent before the final judgement. God is *merciful* 100% of the time if we recognize our sin and repent of it. However, God is also a *just* God 100% of the time. God "must" be a just and a merciful God 100% of the time, not God "might" be *just* and *merciful*. Remember, the scriptures are 100% truthful 100% of the time. I am

#6: Perfect Love Casts Out Confusion

outlining a very critical verse in Revelation to emphasize what is to come if those who are involved in sexual immorality and adultery do not repent to the *just* and *merciful* God.

> *Nevertheless, I have this against you: You tolerate that woman Jezebel, who calls herself a prophet. By her teaching she misleads my servants into sexual immorality and eating food sacrificed to idols. I have given her time to repent of her immorality, but she is unwilling. So, I will cast her on a bed of suffering, and I will make those who commit adultery with her suffer intensely, unless they repent of her ways. I will strike her children dead. Then all the churches will know that I am he who searches hearts and minds, and I will repay each of you according to your deeds (Revelation 2:20-23 NIV).*

In the above scripture, God's warning with regards to sexual immorality and adulterous behavior has consequences to those who take part in lewd acts and do not choose to turn from their sinful ways. Some of these consequences, if not repented, will cost people their lives. Many people currently do not think they are really doing much wrong if they are involved in an adulterous affair or involved in sexual immorality. Nor do they believe they need to repent of their sinful ways. These people are deceived and living in confusion or denial. *Why is this so?* It is a result of the moral decay within our societies. We no longer judge adultery with the value and belief system we once did. This is the "tolerance" the above scriptures are discussing. In North America we used to believe adultery was sinful, and it was very much shunned. In Biblical times people were stoned for committing adultery. Our cultural norms have shifted so radically we are now quite tolerant to people being involved in adulterous affairs. The tolerance has tipped to justification and complacency. Adultery has slowly crept into being an acceptable societal norm. We do not have to look far to understand media played a huge part in ushering in the "normalcy of adultery".

As noted in the scriptures found in this section, God is not at all tolerant of adultery, never, ever. God is currently demonstrating mercy by stating in Revelation 2:21a, *"I have given her time to repent of her immorality, but she is unwilling".* God is merciful, yet He is also just. His justice will eventually prevail as He explains further on in Revelation 2:22, *"So I will cast her on a bed of suffering, and I will make those who commit adultery with her suffer intensely, unless they repent of her ways. I will strike her children dead."* Note the 100% mercy that is directly balanced with the 100% justice..." *unless they repent of her ways"* ...God's *mercy* still allows for repentance right up until the very end. *Yet how many* people will recognize adultery as a sin and repent of it, especially when many churches are "turning a blind eye"?

The reason God is so merciful is He is a loving God, and He does not want anyone to perish. As recorded by the Apostle John, Jesus speaks to us in the New Testament by acknowledging, *"For the law was given through Moses, but God's unfailing love and faithfulness came through Jesus Christ"* (John 1:17 NLT). The law of Moses remains, do not commit adultery. If we accept Jesus as our Savior because he paid the price for our sins, and we confess our sins to God, then we are saved and redeemed from the curse of the law. On the other hand, if we do not repent of our sins, and do not turn from our wicked ways, then we are judged according to the law, and the law for adultery is death. The eternal death sentence will be imposed by God, on all those people who do not repent of their sinful immoral ways. This is a promise of God found in Revelation 19:2 (NIV), *"for true and just are his judgments, He condemned the great prostitute who corrupted the earth by her adulteries. He avenged on her the blood of his servants"*.

Our society today is fast approaching a tipping point in human behavior from which there is no turning back. Confusion over right and wrong abounds. We are on the brink of a cultural catastrophe like that of Noah's time when it is written:

For all the people on the earth had corrupted their ways (Genesis 6:12 NIV).

The prophet Isaiah wrote:

Woe to those who call evil good and good evil, who put darkness for light, and light for darkness, who put bitter for sweet and sweet for bitter (Isaiah 5:20 NIV).

The pace of change away from what is good is dramatic. Many are in a state of confusion over what love is and what love is not in a marriage relationship as well as in other relationships. The consequences of this state of utter confusion and ignoring God's ways are frightening. Among many there seems to be little or no fear of judgment for sin. Instead, there is outright contempt for anyone who would suggest it.

The accuser of the brethren would really enjoy watching you continue destroying yourself, your family and the person's life you are having the unhealthy relationship with as well as the lives of their family members. If you are involved in an affair, it is a total deceptive lie straight from the pits of hell. It is a lie, and the enemy is trying to trick you into remaining stuck in the pit you dug for yourself. The good news is you can crawl out of that pit, and you can crawl out of it right now! One more moment in it will only plunge you deeper into desperation and deception. Why not climb out of the hole and become whole again, with the help of God!

The thief comes only to steal and kill and destroy; I have come that they may have life, and have it to the full (John 10:10 NIV).

Unlocking Mystery #6

Perfect Love Casts Out Confusion

Reflect: Do you believe you were created in the image of God? Do you believe you are a perfect mirror image of God - a perfect reflection? Do you believe you never have to be confused over true love from this moment forward?

Relate: Where do you still struggle with confusion over love?

Respond: I encourage you to step in front of a mirror every day for the next 30 days and declare:

- I am not a mistake.
- I am created in the image of God.
- I am a perfect reflection of God.
- I am a perfect masterpiece.
- I am a child of the Most-High God.
- I am holy and righteous.
- I no longer choose to sin.
- I choose to live an abundant life God perfectly designed for me.
- I believe in the true, living Word of God.
- I believe perfect love casts out all confusion.

I encourage you to give your life over to God and watch the miracles unfold right in front of you!

Speak the Truth

Just Say It! Perfect Love Casts Out All Confusion.

#7

Betrayal is a Reflection of Their Character, Not Yours

I would rather my enemy's sword pierce my heart then my friend's dagger stab me in the back - Michele Barkley.

Key 31

Just in Time

Recently, I was listening to a radio show where I heard a Christian psychologist retell a story about a woman who came to him distressed about her marriage. The woman relayed to the psychologist, during her 30+ year marriage she had grown apart from her husband. She said her husband quite often ignored her and did not spend time with her. As a result, the woman had become so bitter and angry towards her husband, she really hated him. She said she felt betrayed by her husband, as he spent most of his time working, going to the gym, watching sports on TV, or hanging out with his friends. Her husband rarely spent time with her, and hardly, if ever, suggested they do fun activities together. She found this rejection a form of betrayal, and it was becoming increasingly difficult to say or do anything nice for her husband. Now that her children were grown adults and living away from home, she wanted out of the marriage. In essence she was feeling lonely, rejected, betrayed and isolated. She believed the relationship with her husband was not worth salvaging.

After listening to her story, the psychologist decided to recommend three challenges the woman attempt over a three-month period, prior to making a final decision regarding ending her marriage. The psychologist suggested before she made a definite choice to leave the marriage, to first pray for her marriage, every single day. The psychologist instructed her to pray for her husband's love to return, as it was when they first married. The second challenge the psychologist commissioned her with was every single day for the next three months she was to tell her husband she loved him. Thirdly, the psychologist encouraged her to demonstrate random acts of kindness every day through the display of kind words and deeds.

As you can imagine, the woman was extremely reluctant to engage in this challenge. However, after some convincing, she agreed. As the woman was leaving, the psychologist said to her, "When you eventually divorce your husband, these kind words and acts will demonstrate to your husband what a wonderful person you are. And what he missed out on. It will be the perfect revenge!". The psychologist also suggested once she left her husband, he may possibly live with deep regret for the rest of his life, as he would know what a wonderful woman she is.

The woman thought this was a fantastic idea, as it would be the supreme revenge for the betrayal she felt at the hands of her husband. So, she listened to the advice of the psychologist and went home. Daily for three months she prayed for her husband, said kind words, and did kind deeds and told him she loved him. In the beginning, she reluctantly performed this challenge, as it was difficult for her, as she really did not like her husband anymore. She had a lot of anger towards him since he neglected her and rejected her. However, the thought of revenge is what motivated her to begin this three-month journey. Eventually, her husband started to notice the difference in his wife and began to respond to her kind words and deeds with his own. New habits began to form for both of them, as they were now speaking and doing kind things for each other. Both the woman and her husband were creating new neural pathways in their brains that were connecting positive words and positive actions together. This in turn created new more positive mind-sets in both of them towards each other.

After three months the woman returned to the psychologist just beaming, and exclaimed, "Wow, I do not want to leave this marriage, I want to stay, it has been an amazing three months of transformation. My husband is now responding to me in ways I never thought possible".

> *Betrayal leaves all of us at a fork in the road. We can choose to act in ways that impede or further develop our personal growth. We all decide the path we will choose on our journey.*

The above story briefly illustrates a solution to a problem that was brewing for years. The resolution is oversimplified to make a point. I realize most situations are not that quickly resolved, as betrayal, depending on the form and depth, can destroy trust forever. Many life lessons taught me I cannot control someone's loyalty. No matter how well you treat certain people, it does not always translate into them treating you with the same positive regard. Also, no matter how much you value a person it does not guarantee they value you the same. Sadly, sometimes in life the people you may love the most turn out to be the people you can trust the least. When this happens, you need to ensure you do not allow

#7: Betrayal is a Reflection of Their Character, Not Yours

betrayal at the hands of those you loved to destroy your trust in others. Don't allow them to take this from you!

It all depends on the form of betrayal you are experiencing at home. Such as a person not being present as much as they should be or not speaking kindly to you. You could change your situation around by deciding to *Just Say It*, "I Love You" on a regular basis and by demonstrating love through your actions. Now in these circumstances, I am not suggesting a situation such as infidelity, abuse or addictive behaviors will be changed with "just speaking the right words to the other person". I realize these issues are complex and require *recognition, repentance, remorse, reconciliation* and *restoration* from both parties involved. However, some situations are not as complex, and sometimes we are making "mountains out of molehills". Being humble will crush pride.

If you are having relationship problems, take an inventory as to what is really occurring. *Are the GIANTS of pride and selfishness ruling?* Pride is what leads many couples to the brink of divorce. Humility offers hope to conquer these GIANTS. You may be thinking your relationship is too far gone, there is no hope. However, humbling yourself and demonstrating love in the form of words and actions is a choice that is never too late to make. It is a choice in terms of mind-set as to how you view your life circumstances and if you believe you have the power, with the help of God, to change. Even if it is only you who changes, you will win in the end! Believing you can change by becoming less selfish and more selfless can be a huge game changer. What you believe…you will achieve. If betrayal is involved, seeking a solid Christian counselor who bases their practice on the word of God might be a much-needed intervention.

If you believe you can make a difference and change your outlook on the circumstances, if you believe you hold the power to do so, then you can with the help of God. However, if you do not believe you have any power in a relationship to being a catalyst to change the circumstances, then your situation will more than likely remain the same or become worse. I want to encourage you that you do have a choice as to how you will view your circumstances and how you view whether you have any power or control over being able to change. Your character and how you display it amid dealing with betrayal will depend on whether you give your power away, or whether you demonstrate self-control. Humility is your friend, especially under these tenuous circumstances. The language of Heaven is positive, and the language of hell is negative. Changing how you speak to or about the person who betrayed you is a big step towards the healing process within you.

Depending on the depth of betrayal this can take some time, but eventually for you to live free and whole this does need to be a goal for you to try to attain.

I recognize in any relationship there are two people involved. If the other person does not want to change, you cannot force them to. If the other person commits such horrible acts and there is little or no recognition or remorse and trust is broken forever, I suggest seeking wise godly counsel as to how to sever the relationship. In the next chapter we will discuss the importance of forgiveness, and the fact that forgiveness is necessary for your own good, even if the relationship is beyond repair. However, not all betrayals result in permanent separation, many relationships can be rescued with intervention. The act of mending a relationship from the result of a betrayal causing distrust takes two willing people who are open, honest and transparent with each other. Whether the relationship is fixable, or extremely unhealthy, you do have control over your mind-set, how you view the situation and what you will do about it. Before you decide to throw in the towel on your relationship, be it with your spouse, your child, friend or family member, I recommend you decide to align yourself with the word of God. Listen to what God is telling you, not want you "think" God is telling you. However, in the end, it does take two to genuinely work towards *reconciliation* and *resolution* for the relationship to be repaired.

Remember, Peter betrayed Jesus three times the night before Jesus was crucified. Yet Christ forgave Peter, and Peter became the "rock" on which the Christian church was founded on. No form of betrayal is too deep for God to forgive. Even if Judas repented for betraying Jesus, God would have forgiven him, and Judas' story would have ended in a completely different way. Two betrayals by two disciples occurred on the same night, one was convicted and repented seeking forgiveness while the other turned away in shame and condemnation committing suicide. Judas' story could have ended differently if he humbled himself and asked for forgiveness for his act of betrayal. God's love is too deep and wide. Nothing is impossible with God. It is our reaction that changes the outcome, not God's. God's love is consistent and steadfast, it never changes. God's love is always available to us, it surrounds us. Even if we betrayed God, we just need to reach out and take hold of His mercy, His love, and His grace. It states in the Bible, "*For I am convinced neither death nor life, neither angels nor demons, neither the present nor the future, nor any powers, neither height nor depth, nor anything else in creation, will be able to separate us from the love of God that is in Christ Jesus our Lord*" (Romans 8:38-39 NIV).

Comprehending the complete nature of God's love is a lifetime process. We need to accept there is not one human being alive on this earth that will ever be able to gain perfect love and to be in perfect unity with all the people they encounter. Betrayal will happen; it does happen. Until we leave this earth and live in Heaven forever and ever, we will face disappointment and broken relationships. God's love is perfect; our earthly love is flawed. Our lives are made whole and without blemish through the perfect love of God. Therefore, human relationships are imperfect as we all fall short of the glorious love of God. We all suffer from the human condition of sin. Our love will never be perfect, but we can continually work towards our display of love becoming more reflective of the nature of God's love. *How will we know our love is becoming more like that of God's perfect love?* It will be evident through the fruits we bear - love, joy, peace, kindness, patience, goodness, gentleness and self-control. If every human being decided to love as Christ loves the church, every person and every relationship would be transformed for the better.

Key 32

Betrayal Takes on Many Forms

Betrayal can look different depending on the people involved and the circumstances. Betrayal can be at the hands of a spouse having an affair, or a partner not supporting us in our endeavors. Or it can be a friend gossiping and slandering us, or it can be brought on by isolation and alienation of close friends or family members. Betrayal also occurs when a trusted employee steals from your company, a supervisor at work does not support us, or by church board members demonstrating hostility and aggression towards their pastor. Whoever is involved in the betrayal, it is devastating when people are betrayed by those close to them, trusted confidants.

Betrayal in today's social media world is happening at such a rapid pace as people write and speak toxic rumors and lies, across the internet. Once words are typed or spoken, they are not easily erased. Instead, the lies spread like wildfire and can result in destroying lives. Think before you type or speak, as that is a human being you are slandering. Often if it is our enemy who betrayed us, it is not as hurtful. However, betrayal at the hands of people who are our loved ones, the people in whom we have trusted, this form of betrayal is the most painful to experience and to work through. I know, as I have been betrayed by those with whom I thought I could trust. It is very painful.

> *The tongue has the power of life-and-death, and those who love it will eat its fruit (Proverbs 18:21 NIV).*

Several years ago, I tried to deal with betrayal. Unfortunately, I did not give the entire circumstance over to God, I tried to solve it. To my dismay, I only became bitter and more entrenched in my desire to see justice served. Looking back, the only person I was hurting was myself. The people who betrayed me were so obsessively narcissistic they kept on betraying me right in front of my own eyes, and they really did not care. Without going into more detail, I learned God wants us to trust Him in all our circumstances. God is our

Jehovah Jireh; He is more than enough for us in every circumstance. We are to trust God even when faced with the most unbearable situations. Trust is a big factor that hinders many of us from walking in full freedom. That was my problem. I tried to solve the betrayal on my own instead of fully trusting in God's wisdom and guidance.

Cast All Your Cares on The Lord

In past experiences where I have been betrayed at the hands of friends and foes, I tell you it is all about the choices we make and how you and I decide to live out these choices. Working through betrayal is not easy, it takes time and intentionality. However, I believe you are worth it! *Do you want your life to be built with bricks made of bitterness and strife or do you want it to be built on a foundation of love and forgiveness?* It is your choice. Knowing God's love in all its fullness by developing a close relationship with Him is key. Do not avoid placing your trust in God to help you deal with betrayal, you are already loved and already chosen by the King of Kings and Lord of Lords. You are Joint Heirs with Jesus Christ. Knowing this is enough for you to be content in any circumstance. *But are you content?* If not, I encourage you to take a step of faith and begin the healing process. I recommend, based on experience, to run straight into the arms of God, resting in His unfailing, relentless love. Humble yourself before God, do not hold onto pride and resentment, as they are the GIANTS who want to destroy you. Tell God everything. Talk to Him like He is your best friend, because He is. Pour out your heart to God; don't hold back.

For when we do not cast all our cares on the Lord and we try to solve our issues on our own, this is our pride working overtime. We begin to believe we can solve our problems, and we do not trust God to work all things out for our good. We think we have the answers, when God has all the answers. God already knew you would be betrayed. He knows the beginning, the middle, and the end. He knew it would happen before it happened. If you cast this care onto God and lean on His understanding, He will help you heal from the hurt and the bitterness that resulted from the betrayal. God will also give you a keen mind that will help you to solve the problem of betrayal. Seek God's wisdom, as it is the best answer when faced with betrayal.

> *Blessed are those who find wisdom, those who gain understanding, for she is more profitable than silver and yields better returns than gold (Proverbs 3:13-14 NIV).*

God gave Solomon, the writer of Proverbs, the opportunity to ask for anything he desired. Solomon desired wisdom above everything else. He did not desire riches or long life. Solomon did not desire to be "smarter" or more "intelligent", instead he desired and asked for supernatural wisdom. Supernatural wisdom is paramount. Desiring supernatural wisdom above everything else is what I pray for you. Having supernatural wisdom allows you to realize the only hope for you and for humanity is God. Have the wisdom to admit you can, by faith, ask God to help you sort through even the toughest of situations. Even if you have only the faith of a mere mustard seed, trust in God that He can handle all your disappointments. He will. He promises in His Word. If you have not already, I hearten you to make God your Savior and your Lord. Allow God to take over your life, so His will becomes your will. Surrender all to Him (John 3:16)!

Often when we are stuck, we are only submitting to God as our Savior and not our Lord. By making God the Lord of our life, we surrender control of our circumstances over to Him. By not making God our Lord, we keep the control, and do not submit to His supreme Lordship over our lives. I urge you to not hold on any longer, surrender all your hurt and pain over to God. His ways are higher than your ways. Worrying and trying to keep the problems to yourself is pride. Wisdom will guide you to cast all your cares onto the Lord of your Life. Make God the Lord of your life and transform your worry into faith. God has got you!

#7: Betrayal is a Reflection of Their Character, Not Yours

Key 33

Do You Believe in God's Rescue Plan?

I was almost too late in realizing I needed to totally surrender (not just a bit) to God's rescue plan from a relationship that was in deep trouble. Bitterness and strife had set in. Betrayal was looming all around. As a result of being surrounded by betrayal, I began to lose my faith in humanity. During this most horrific time of my life, the most miraculous thing was knowing God did not leave me for one second. God is so wise and so gracious. At certain low points it felt as if God had hidden His face from me. In "raw honesty", I thought He loved others more than me. I thought He had left me all alone in darkness, but He was right there, saying, "lift your eyes, I am closer than ever. Lift your voice, let me hear your cries, you are not alone. I am here with you always." God was whispering to me He was closer than I thought. He never left me. God was showing me He was closer than I imagined. He kept saying, "I am right here, by your side, walking with you step by step, and holding you up in my righteous right hand".

In the wee hours of the morning, He would whisper to me, "I love you with a relentless love. I am always pursuing you. *Are you pursuing me?*" God kept whispering to me, "trust me, trust me, trust me". He also told me because I was worrying and trying to solve the problems of betrayal on my own, I was sinning, as I was not trusting Him and fully surrendering my situation to Him.

God was always right there; it was I who had left. It was I who was not trusting and leaning on Him for support. I was not making God the Lord of my life and surrendering my circumstances to Him. I tried to keep control and to solve the situation on my own, as the GIANT of fear and worry gripped me. The betrayal had cast shadows on my own mind and fear altered my view of the situation. My mind was clouded with betrayal. I unconsciously placed the love of others and the fear of others ahead of God's love and ahead of having a reverential fear of God. I was in such despair even though I knew God is LOVE, I became embroiled in bitterness, because I was unconsciously relying on people for love instead of on God's perfect LOVE. Through much prayer and meditation, God revealed to me that wanting the love of others over God's love and being afraid of people instead of fearing God are both idols in His sight. This revelation has never left me. I now know the error of my ways; due to fear of people, I placed their happiness ahead of God and His perfect will for my life.

There is No Fear in Love. Perfect Love Drives Out Fear (1 John 4:18 NIV).

The pain, bitterness and disappointment caused by the betrayal were not healthy. I knew this amount of unhappiness was destroying the person I was created to be. I was not destined to wake up every morning unhappy, to wake up every morning with an unsettledness surrounding me. Obviously, God had not created me to be this way, or to think this way about my circumstances and the people around me. My inward being, where I was trying to hide all the private pain, was spilling over, as it was too much pain to contain. Instead, through my words and actions, my private pain I was so desperately trying to cloak, was now on display for the entire world to see. At that time, I imagined if I could view my inner self, and the sight of the contents that existed on the inside of my body, it would have been polluted with toxins. As an adult female, is made up of roughly 55% of water. So, imagine the water in my body was not clear, pure water, but instead polluted, murky water. Alarmingly this is how diseases manifest in people's bodies, as the acidic levels rise above normal levels when people try to deal with stress and unforgiveness on their own. This is why the Bible teaches us to, *"Cast all your anxiety on him because he cares for you"* (1 Peter 5:7 NIV). He does not want us bearing our pain, as God knew He did not design us to bear the pain of betrayal.

I became increasingly distressed and unhappy. I allowed fear to rule my life instead of faith in God's love and promises. God was my Savior, but I was not surrendering ALL of me to His Lordship. There is a big difference. I needed both. I wanted an easy fix, to escape the tremendous amount of pain. However, I knew deep down inside, this is not what God wanted me to do. A still small voice kept saying, "trust me I love you." I remember responding back, "God this does not feel like love, this is painful." I knew God never left me or never did forsake me, not even for one single moment. I always believed He was there, yet at times due to the darkness I was not *feeling it*. I was experiencing confusion over *feeling* God's love and *knowing* His steadfast love. Since that moment when God spoke to me, I realized that day by day, God reveals the fullness of His love to His children, if we allow Him to. God's love is not a *fuzzy feeling* kind of love. It is the real deal. God's love envelopes our entire body; inside and outside. That is why when we give our problems over to God, He purifies our bodies so there is no more pollution in our lives. The water content of our bodies can stabilize to normal levels again, and the toxicities can leave through the supernatural power of the Holy Spirit.

I intellectually knew every breath I take and every moment I am awake I needed to surrender every hurt and bitter feeling over to God. I knew the "head stuff" well. I was not as familiar with the "heart stuff" in terms of completely surrendering to His supreme rule and reign over every inch of my life. I needed to seek after God with all my heart and soul, this included getting rid of my bitterness and anger. I thought I was, but looking back I was not. I was holding on to bitterness, anger and sadness. I had not fully experienced God's true love. I was not surrendering ALL to God. I was not fully trusting Him. I had never experienced this type of deep, dark pain before. This depth of betrayal and mockery were completely new to me. I was not prepared for this battle. But God was! God tells us in His word, *"Do not be afraid or discouraged because of this vast army. For the battle is not yours, but God's"* (2 Chronicles 20:15b NIV).

Key 34

The GIANT of Pride Keeps You from God's Perfect Plan

I thought I knew what the best way was. This was the GIANT of pride convincing me. Pride and fear are convincing if we do not know how to fight the battle with God, by surrendering ALL to Him. Peter clearly instructs us in 1 Peter 5:8 (NIV), *Be alert and of sober mind. Your enemy, the devil, prowls around like a roaring lion looking for someone to devour.* Looking back, I think I was fearful of the result, as I did not hold a crystal ball in my hand. I needed to realize my choice to carry the pain was pride. I was not trusting in God's ways or relying on wisdom as my best friend. I was not believing God's plans for me were the best plans. I learned through this experience and many more since then, God knows what is best, and His love endures forever. God knows the beginning from the end, and I needed to trust Him I was going to be alright, regardless of the outcome. I needed to trust in His unfailing love and believe He sees and knows my future. God knows the paths that are best for me (and for you!). I do not know what is best, only God does. I needed to humble myself and bow to God in my brokenness. I needed to allow God to fully envelope me in His unconditional, unending love. I was stubborn and not completely humbling myself to God's WILL. Although, on an intellectual level I thought I was surrendering to God. But instead, I was trying to solve a completely unsolvable situation on my own.

Knowing in my head, not my heart, I needed to submit to God and to engage in the act of surrender, are two separate choices. One is an intellectual decision; the other is a supernatural decision. As I continued my QUEST for true unconditional love, I was not at all happy with the messages God was sending to me. In fact, being honest and transparent, at varying levels of consciousness and unconsciousness there were certain points I truly thought God wanted the worst for me. All the while the betrayal had not stopped. I was becoming extremely discouraged!

This was private pain I was carrying around, pain that resulted due to betrayal. I knew my pain was a burden too heavy for me to continue carrying. And even though God had never left my side and was willing to take the burden and the pain, I was not fully submitting to His way and to His answers. I was blinded as to the full realization the best plan was to allow God's love to completely envelope me, to fully trust Him and to listen to His voice. The devil tricked me, through rational thought, I was completely surrendering to God and He was not fully helping me. But, in all reality, I was holding on to parts of the betrayal I thought I could solve on my own. Due to being blinded by pride, as I had not fully surrendered, even though my mind "fooled me" into believing I had fully surrendered. I was "hiding" parts of the pain of betrayal, holding onto them, like a child holds onto a blanket for comfort. The betrayal and my reaction to it had become part of my identity.

As R.T. Kendall so clearly outlines in his book, *Fear: The Good, the Bad and the Ugly*, I was not fearing God, I was fearing people and what they had and could do to me. I was sinning by not demonstrating a reverential fear of God and trusting in Him for ALL things. Instead, due to my fear of people, I was giving into the GIANT of pride and not letting go that grip of fear had on me. R.T. Kendall (2022) states in the introduction of his book, "I had a head start when it comes to the fear of the Lord. Between my parental background and my church background, I was given a double dose of the sense of the fear of God" (p. 1). I too came from a background where my father was a pastor. I spent most of my childhood and teenage years helping to serve in the churches my father pastored. So, I was taught and well-aware of the fear of God. However, I allowed the worries of the world, and the fear of people to overcrowd my upbringing as well as to block out the truth found in the Holy scriptures.

My hope is for some of you reading this chapter you can connect with this story, and it helps you in your own life. *Do you find yourself in a similar circumstance and you are not even opting for God's way because it appears too distant, or too foreign? Are you stubbornly holding on, trying to work it all out on your own? Are you fearing people and not fearing God?* You might be believing God is requiring you to act in unconventional ways, ways our culture and society would frown on. Are you thinking, *'isn't it right to be right? Isn't it my right to seek proper justice when I have been wronged?' Are you so enveloped in bitterness and anger that allowing God's love to penetrate through the hardness is too overwhelming or possibly too risky?* Or like I was, maybe you are too caught up in the circumstances you do not realize you are not surrendering to God. You may be allowing pride to cloud your supernatural vision.

The heavy storm clouds of sadness and bitterness were drowning me and causing me to become spiritually deaf and blind. Sadness and bitterness became my new companions. They clung to me and were draining the life out of me. They were making me view the world in obscure ways. I had a very unhealthy codependent relationship with these new toxic friends – sadness and bitterness. Their best friend, "hurt" also frequently hung out with us. When someone is betrayed at such a deep level as I was, you can become suspicious of everyone around you. It is vital to know who to trust. It is difficult to distinguish the "wheat" from the "chaff", as there are "great pretenders" lurking in the alleyways. A coping mechanism is to believe these new toxic friends – sadness, bitterness and hurt – are good for you and are required to "get you through the betrayal".

I knew I was becoming consumed with toxicity as the "great pretenders" continued to betray me and I started not to trust anyone. It was a vicious cycle I wanted to stop. However, some of these "great pretenders" I could not just get away from so easily. I finally sought advice from a close Christian friend whom I had known for years. She is a trusted friend. I desperately wanted the pain to vanish. I was secretly hoping she would provide me with the answers I wanted to hear, knowing justice should be served. Outwardly, I was not admitting this was my motive, and I pretended in my pain my motives were pure and holy. I pretended to seek counsel, but instead I wanted to hear the advice I wanted to hear. Looking back, this pretense was at an unconscious level, as the enemy deceived me into believing what I thought I needed to hear. Through manipulation and deception, the enemy convinced me I knew what the answer was. So, I was just waiting for my friend to confirm this deception. By foolishly not listening to the wise counsel of God, I was betraying God. I was going against His voice and what He had told me. Cloaked in deception, yet willingly wearing the cloak, I was betraying God's love and care for me. I was not being obedient to His voice. I was seeking to find the answers and the support I wanted, not what God wanted. I was not willing to totally surrender to God's perfect love and wisdom that is only found in surrender and forgiveness.

> *With whom and where we seek our advice from is critical to becoming unstuck and moving forward.*

Before I continue with this story, I do want to caution all readers when we foolishly choose not to listen to the voice of the Lord, be greatly prepared for consequences. For seeking counsel outside of what God has already instructed us to do is, very dangerous. I was wrong for trying to find another answer from another person I hoped was different from God's answer. I wanted to justify my decisions, and if my friend supported me, this is all that was required for me to make my decision. I was blinded by the betrayal. Years later, I understand the great vastness of God's love, mercy, and compassion towards me, even when I was not humbling myself. Even in my own betrayal to my Heavenly Father, God cared and loved me so much. Even when I was betraying Him, He demonstrated compassion beyond any words that are suitable enough to write down on these pages. God's love is boundless; it is without borders.

I also caution you to be wary of whom you share your stories with, and in whom you place your trust. During this dark period in my life, I placed my trust in some of the wrong people, and I paid dearly for it. I encourage you to find people in your life, people you can trust, and you can share deep personal issues with. You need to find friends and family members who will not turn around and tell others or use the information to try to further destroy you. Proceed with discernment, be aware. Wisdom needs to be your best friend. In the Bible it states the Holy Spirit is the Spirit of truth, and this Spirit of truth will lead you into all truth (John 16:13). Seek and listen to the nudges of the Holy Spirit. Ask God to help you take every thought captive unto obeying Jesus Christ. And casting down every imagine, and every high and lofty thing that exalts itself against the knowledge of God (2 Corinthians 10:5).

By the time I asked the advice of my longtime Christian friend, I was really hurting, entrenched in bitterness, and experiencing deep pain. I was ashamed to tell my story, as I was consumed with shame and guilt. Fortunately for me, this friend has wisdom and discernment from the Lord. As I relayed my very long story, she listened and was extremely empathetic. She hugged me, cried with me, and laughed with me. However, in the end, my friend's advice was to love and forgive those who betrayed me. Her advice was to treat them better than I ever had in the past. She did tell me to separate myself from the toxic people, yet to forgive them.

Later, I would learn forgiveness is not the same as *trust, reconciliation* or *restoration*. *Trust* and *forgiveness* do not necessarily go hand in hand. *Trust, reconciliation*, and *restoration* are based on the genuine motivation and willingness of all the people involved in the betrayal. I was holding on and not letting God work in my life because I thought if I listened to God, I would need to trust these people to reconcile and restore my relationship with them. This false belief is what was holding me captive. You know the saying, "the vultures are circling". Well, the "ugliness of their sin" caused them to act, look and behave like turkey vultures. I do not know if you have ever come across a turkey vulture, but they are one of the ugliest birds I have ever encountered. I was concerned I would need to remain hanging out with these turkey vultures, as they were within my inner circles. I knew this was not at all healthy for me, as the vultures did not want to change.

I remember being so shocked and speechless with the advice my trusted longtime friend gave to me. Inwardly I was so disappointed and frustrated with her, however, I did not want to outwardly express my complete discouragement. In fact, I was thinking to myself (not out loud), *whose friend, is she?' 'Mine or theirs?' 'Whose side is she on?' 'Wow, how can I ever do what she is instructing me to do?' 'Has my friend lost her mind?' 'This is the most ridiculous advice ever, after all they have done to me.'* I even wondered if she had been listening to me as I recounted my very long story. I was convinced at a certain superficial level my friend must have drifted off during the most horrific details.

Yet deep down I knew she was right. I knew what I needed to do was exactly what she was suggesting, as this is also what God was instructing me to do. God was speaking through my wise friend. In the Bible, it tells us to bless those who curse us, and we are to do good to people who hate us, and to pray for the people who use us (Matthew 5:44). *Yet, how could I do this?* I knew this plan would make me eat humble pie, and I was reluctant to do so. I thought the humble pie would be bitter and dreadful to swallow. The story at the beginning of this chapter and my story are fine for us to read or hear as examples on the radio or television as to how-to walk-through betrayal and to forgive. Yet, when we are living out these scenarios, choosing to do what God wants us to do, is often the opposite as to what we are doing and what we are wanting to do. The Apostle Paul recognizes this when he wrote, *"For I have the desire to do what is good, but I cannot carry it out. For I do not do the good I want to do, but the evil I do not want to do – this I keep on doing"* (Romans 7:18-19 NIV).

Nodding our heads on Sunday morning as we listen to the preacher's sermon and enacting what is being said are two completely different behaviors with choice, motivation, and intention attached to them. Loving others like Christ loved us and forgiving those who have deeply betrayed us are difficult to do. Nodding my head to my pastor is a passive act, yet forgiving others who have intentionally betrayed me is an active act. God wants us to be active Christians, living out our lives as living sacrifices for His glory and His purpose. We can only forgive and love others as God wants us to love with

His help. We are unable to do this on our own, but we can do it with the help of God, through the Holy Spirit (Romans 7:15-24).

We all have the choice to be stuck in bad situations forever, or we can put them behind us for good. Life is full of choices!

I must admit that hearing from my friend and imagining acting out what I knew I needed to do was difficult to digest. I knew I would need to swallow my pride. I was stuck. Stuck knowing what my friend was saying was right, and it was based on Biblical principles. Yet I was entrenched in selfishness and pride. Selfishness and pride were like quicksand surrounding me. My feet were not on solid ground; in fact, I was sinking quickly. The more I tried to escape, the more pride and selfishness tried to swallow me whole. I knew if I did not do what I needed to do, I would be feasting on a huge buffet supper of pride topped with a side order of selfishness. As King Solomon in the Bible so wisely states, *Pride goes before destruction* (Proverbs 16:18 NIV).

If I continued living and acting with pride, I discerned I would surely fall, as I was already on unsteady ground. I was already tripping up, but if I continued not listening to God, I knew my fall would be long and hard. I understood I was right in these circumstances. God knows I was *right*. Yet being *right* is not always what is required to solve matters. The "Power of Rightness" takes all of us down the wrong path that leads to destruction. Being humble and submitting ourselves to the WILL of God for our health and wholeness is what is required. God sees both now and He sees the future. At a deep spiritual level, I knew my dear, beautiful, lovely friend was right. I knew she was using the discernment and wisdom of God. I knew I needed to love my enemies unconditionally, even when faced with betrayal. Even if I did not feel like it, even if I did not want to, I needed to make myself do it. But this could only be carried out supernaturally with the help of God. Even when I did not *feel* like doing it, I needed to just say out loud, "I love you" and "I forgive you".

Forgiveness as with love is not decided on by feelings, it is a choice and a commitment. Forgiveness is an intentional action. I decided to tuck this advice away. I knew the advice was godly and based on Biblical principles, but I wasn't ready to act on it. I was allowing the solid advice to simmer in my spirit being. My heart was transforming on the inside, even if my outward behaviors were not displaying the evidence. I was on an inward QUEST to find true unconditional love, as I was being transformed from the inside to the outside. I have undisputedly learned from this QUEST true unconditional love is not based on feelings.

Key 35

What Does the Bible Say About Betrayal and Loving Those Who Betray You?

It wasn't long after the conversation with my friend I started to hear God telling me to listen to my friend. He wanted me to listen to her advice, to start to step out and to just say multiple times per day, "I love you", and "I forgive you" to my enemies. I would insert their name into the phrase, "I forgive you XXXX". I did not *feel* like doing this at all. It was a real struggle of my WILL. However, I knew I had to intentionally change my mindset and the only way I could do this was by framing new patterns of behavior. As we learned earlier on in this book, I needed to create new neural pathways in my brain.

When God speaks to me, it is not an audible voice. Instead, it is a deep knowing in my very inner being, like a still small voice whispering to my heart and registering in my mind. Please note I did not even remotely *feel like* it. I didn't have that *lovin feeling*. This journey back from betrayal solidified for me love and forgiveness are an intentional *choice*; they are not based on a *feeling*. This is where many of us become confused. We think if we *feel* like forgiving someone who betrayed us, or when we are around the betrayer and we *feel* peace, then we should seek forgiveness. This is false thinking. The topic of forgiveness is covered in greater detail in the next chapter. Intellectually as well I knew love and forgiveness are not based on *feelings*. If it *feels* good, do it is a false mantra touted in our society today. Yet this belief is widely accepted in all areas of our churches today.

To walk *out* love and to *talk out* love were completely different places and spaces I needed to embrace. I needed to walk in the Spirit of God all the time, and to walk in the love of God all the time and, not to walk in pride, anger and resentment. Yet, my selfish human desires wanted to continue to hang out with the companionship of anger, bitterness, and resentment. My new friends and I had become close throughout these years of pain and suffering. *But were these good companions of mine – anger, bitterness, and resentment? Did they want the best for me?* If I was honest, I knew the answer was no.

Who Are You Hanging Out With, Anger or Love?

Due to betrayal in your life, have you found companionship with anger, bitterness, and resentment? Have they been hanging out with you for so long they are hard to break free from? So much so the relationships you are embroiled in are being torn apart because you will not humble yourself, forgive and work through things. Remember it takes two people in a relationship to be genuinely committed and motivated to work things out. I believe pride, addictions and selfishness are at the root of many dysfunctional relationships, holding back one or both parties from seeking true forgiveness, recognition, repentance, reconciliation, and restoration. As the old cliche goes, it takes two. It certainly does. For your own good you need to be honest and seek God's transforming power and seek His wisdom and counsel as to what you are to do with the brokenness brought about by betrayal. No two circumstances are the same.

What do you have to rid your life of to become free of bitterness, anger and resentment? These negative companions will try to linger as long as they can. *Are there strongholds in your life, holding you prisoner in a damp jail cell piled high with unforgiveness?* Through the redeeming power of God's love, you can be set free from these unhealthy codependent strongholds, as you do not need to be chained up anymore. Being chained in pride, unforgiveness, bitterness and selfishness are not the WILL of God for your life. Instead, on your QUEST to unlock the mysteries of humanity, you can begin to hang out with new companions such as forgiveness, selflessness, hope, joy, mercy, peace, and love.

I wish I could say my story was happily wrapped up in three short months, like the story at the beginning of this chapter. Unfortunately, it was not. This story took some long hard years of going two steps forward and sometimes three steps backward. I relied heavily on God's wisdom, mercy, love and grace to see myself and others through undoing negative patterns and embrace myself and others in a love that only comes from God. Working through betrayal and all the steps involved is a process. Layer by layer God peeled away all that was not bearing fruit in my life and transformed me from the inside out. It was like peeling back the thin layers of an onion, in the process it stings, just like pride stings, hurt stings, and pain stings. Giving up my will and letting God's will take root was painful at first. I had to eat and drink from the goblet of humility many times on my QUEST for true unconditional love. It was a step-by-step intentional surrender of allowing God to work in and through me.

Looking back now I can honestly say it was worth it. I made a committed choice to allow God to transform my mind, my heart and my spirit. I am still on the journey; it is a lifetime process, and it is hard work. The QUEST to unlock the mysteries of humanity is not for the faint of heart! To work through betrayal and to come out on the other side loving others and wanting the best for them takes strength, courage, and wisdom that only comes from the Lord.

Not Every Story Has a Happy Ending

On the journey from betrayal back to wholeness, I would often rehearse what I would say to those who betrayed me. Some conversations I was able to have, some I may never have. One conversation I had with a person who had deeply betrayed me did not end at all the way I envisioned it would. I believed God was prompting me to confront this person and to seek forgiveness, even though I had been betrayed by them. Meeting up with this person one day, I was all prepared to ask for forgiveness and tell this person I forgave them. One thing I learned on this journey is not to act unless the Holy Spirit prompts me to. I believed the Holy Spirit led me to walk up to this person in the confidence and courage of the Lord. I talked through some of the issues that led to this state of unforgiveness between us and I eventually said, "I forgive you for what you have done to me. I want to give you the gift of forgiveness." I was poised, and expectant to hear back a heartfelt, genuine apology. I even imagined us crying and embracing as we transparently apologized to one another. Instead, I heard a loud laugh as the person mockingly said to me, "forgiveness, that is not what I need, I do not need or want that from you. *What kind of a gift is forgiveness?*"

The person proceeded to ramble off a ridiculous, unrealistic list of what they thought they needed from me and what I had done to them. They were "gaslighting me". Which is a term I learned through seeking wise godly counsel. I was stunned. I was shocked. I was saddened. Their lack of remorse and genuine unwillingness to seek forgiveness, repentance, reconciliation, and restoration was deafening. I was also taken back by their dishonesty and untruthful accounts. This person was unwilling to confront their blatant betrayal and instead started to point the finger and to blame me for their sinful behavior. I knew at that moment in time our relationship was not valuable to this person. I was deeply grieved. So was God. However, in God's loving-kindness I felt a peace sweep over me as the person continued to mock and ridicule me. I knew I had been healed from the deep wounds of betrayal this person inflicted on me. In that moment I realized I was free to love, to worship and to trust God with no fear of rejection or of being hurt (John 8:36; Romans 8:1)!

I mention this narrative from my life so you are prepared not every story has the happy ending you might believe will occur. When you seek forgiveness and reconciliation with a person who betrayed you, you must be led by the Holy Spirit when you do so. You cannot predict or control how the other person will respond. As this perpetual dishonoring of me occurred by the individual I attempted to reconcile with, God in His true unconditional love for me, wrapped His strong arms around me giving me peace and assurance. During this encounter, I had a deep understanding of the vast love and mercy of God, and I know He believes in me because He created me. This peace that passes all understanding overrode any feelings of shame or of unworthiness that could have overtaken me and clouded this spiritual gift from God. I learned from this experience and others like it, forgiveness is not dependent on the reaction of the person with whom I seek to forgive. The gift of forgiveness is for me from God.

Immediately, I saw this person through the eyes of God. God allowed me to see a very hurt, bitter, and rejected person who needed to bully and to put others down to feel good about themselves. This person gained strength from abusing and betraying people close to them. For the first time I saw this person, who appears very accomplished in the world's eyes, through God's spiritual eyes. This seemingly competent person appeared secure to those around them. However, they are a "great pretender" who is covering up years of wounds and scars. God showed me through the eyes of love they were scared and insecure due to years of instability growing up as a child in a dysfunctional home. God allowed me to have an impartation at a spiritual level as a gift to understand my hurting betrayer. I finally saw the situation for what it was, not for what I had thought it to be. For years I lived with shame and condemnation brought on by the betrayer, who abused me with false words, unkind deeds and sinful acts. My obedient act of seeking genuine forgiveness from a betrayer broke me free. The scales lifted off my eyes, and I could see this person through my Heavenly Father's loving eyes.

Looking now from the other side of the fence, I can honestly say I am set free, with no fear of rejection or of being hurt. I am free to love, to worship, to trust God. I know this, because if I were faced with the same situations again today, I have a peace, a strength, and a confidence in knowing God is my true love. Only true undying, unfailing, steadfast love is found in God. I needed to tighten up my inner circle. I have forgiven them, and I know what they did to me is being dealt with by my Almighty Father. God taught me through these experiences to rely on His justice, that balancing the scales is up to Him, not up to me. I now know the QUEST for true unconditional love is not found in a human being, it is only found in our Heavenly Father. I can assure you, it is worth the process, and it is worth the pain. Trust God. God knows what is best!

God Does Not Use Our Past to Determine Our Future

If you have been wronged in the past and betrayed by those you loved, know there is hope for you now and hope for you in the future. I encourage you to step out of your past and into your future with the steadfast belief God will take care of you. God promises in the Bible, He will make you the head and not the tail, you will be above and not below. He promises in His word your enemies will be under your feet (Deuteronomy 28). You may feel inadequate and full of shame due to the terrible things that have been done to you. However, when God calls you, He is not looking for your ability, He is looking for your availability. *Are you available to serve God?* If you choose an attitude nothing is impossible with God, if you believe and accept in your heart you are a child of God's, then watch what God will do in your life. He promises to transform you from glory to glory.

The story of Joseph is an excellent example of the limitless power of God in a life that looked as if it was washed up not just once, but a few times! Joseph was betrayed by many, starting out with the devastating betrayal by his brothers, as they were envious of him. Joseph was created in the image of God, just like you and me. Just like you and I, Joseph was called by God. Despite all that happened to Joseph he made the intentional choice to be a difference maker in the world. He did not give up on his dream even though he was continuously betrayed by others. Instead of curling up in a corner and blaming God, Joseph kept believing in the promises of God. Joseph did not doubt. He kept on believing even when the circumstances around him were desperate. Some are familiar with the story of how Joseph went from the Pit to Potiphar's house, from Potiphar's house to Prison, from Prison to the Palace and from the Palace to the position of Prime Minister! It looked as if Joseph was disqualified, but God had another plan for him. If you are not familiar with Joseph's story, or if you want to refresh your memory, I invite you to read about it in Genesis chapters 37 to 50.

God demonstrates through the story of Joseph He qualifies the unqualified, and God qualifies the disqualified. God can do the same for you! My challenge for you is to let go and to let God work in your life through His redemptive power. Life isn't always easy; bumps and bruises happen along the way. But if you choose a life directed by God as He cradles you in His arms, even though storms come, God promises to give you peace. Do not give up on your dreams, do not allow your betrayers to snuff out the light of God in you. God will fight your battles. Walk with God and fight through life with Him to accomplish your dreams. Just like Joseph, your attitude will determine your altitude!

In order that Satan might not outwit us. For we are not unaware of his schemes (2 Corinthians 2:11 NIV).

Unlocking Mystery #7

Betrayal is a Reflection of Their Character, Not Yours

Reflect: Being honest, betrayal is painstaking. It is felt all in time. Whether you remain trapped in betrayal or choose to break free, depends on the intentional decisions you make. Are you ready to break free from the chains that are holding you back due to being betrayed? Do you need a new inner circle of people to associate with?

Relate: In the past, how did you try to rid yourself of betrayal and the toxic people in your life who have betrayed you? What has worked? What has not worked? What shame and guilt have you accepted due to betrayal?

Respond: I would encourage you to work through the following steps to break through the barriers of betrayal and to begin to trust again:

Throw betrayal away. Literally toss it away. Write down on a piece of paper the worst case of betrayal by the person. Ensure you detail the incident by capturing the emotions and highlighting the importance of the event. After you are satisfied that you have described the situation in graphic detail, fold the paper and get rid of it in a dramatic way. You may even want to crumble the paper up and stamp on it first. You can toss it into a garbage can, burn it or throw it into the sea. Whichever method you choose to discard the letter of betrayal, ensure you physically get rid of any traumatic traces of it. You may want to repeat this method as many times as is required if you have several betrayals to throw away. (1 Peter 5:7).

Erase the memories of betrayal. These wounds can be so deeply engrained in your subconscious mind you might not even realize some of them even exist. It is key to place your trust in God, praying to Him daily and asking Him to take away the memories or patterns of thoughts. Ask God to replace them with loving thoughts of Him and others in your life you trust. Trust in God, He loves you so much He will help you through this. Repeat this phrase as many times as you need to, "I trust you

God". I trust you to erase these memories from my mind and to give me a new mind in Christ" (Romans 12:2; 2 Cor. 5:17).

Forgive the person. Forgiving the person who betrayed you does not mean you accept the wrong behavior they did to you, or they do not have to face consequences for their behavior. Instead, forgiveness is a gift from God. It takes you off the hook of trying to seek justice and revenge and it puts them onto "God's hook". God will vindicate for you. He is your ever-present help in times of trouble. Meditate on forgiving the person every day until you are free. Visualize releasing them over into God's hands and ask God to release you from the pain and bitterness they caused you. By forgiving you are free to become all you were created to be. God will take care of them. Have faith and trust He will! (Psalm 91; Proverbs 17:9; Matthew 6:14). *Forgiveness will be discussed in greater detail in Chapter #8.

I encourage you to also say out loud you forgive this person, that you love them, and you want God to bless them. This might take some time to repeat it out loud. First, if you are just going through the motions, do it anyway. You cannot wait until you feel like it, or you may never do it. Feelings cannot be associated with forgiveness. Instead, intentionally choose to forgive, because Christ died on the cross to forgive all of us of all our sins. You can forgive because you have been forgiven. Create a pattern of behavior of just saying it. Soon this pattern will become a habit.

Start and regain faith in yourself and others. You can start slowing as your faith is not damaged in one day. Start to piece your faith back together with the help of God. You might find it difficult to trust anyone in the beginning. By faith, be willing to take each day at a time and rebuild your trust in yourself and in others. Develop a deep unshakeable faith with God and ask Him to help you trust yourself again and to believe in yourself (as you may be blaming yourself for the betrayal, which is an untruth). Surround yourself with a positive, trusting group of people. Believe there are honest people who do want to be loyal friends with you. Take daily steps with trust so it becomes a habit. Also, you may need to seek the guidance of a pastor, counselor or a true friend.

Don't seek revenge. The Golden Rule, do unto others as you would have them do unto you, was taught to us by Jesus (Matthew 7:12). It is an excellent principle to live a healthy and prosperous life. Do not seek revenge with the person who betrayed you, or do not betray someone else. Always remember what betrayal felt like and the damage it did. This will help with your recovery process, as well as it will eventually help you to help others in the same situation. Do not choose to be trapped in a cycle of recurring actions. Instead choose to give back to others in the form of wisdom you will gain.

Visualize a future that is free of betrayal. Envision yourself in a future state where no one can hurt you ever again. This does not mean others will not come into your life and betray you, instead it means you will not give your power away by allowing others to hurt you. Believe in yourself next time you will be more aware. Create images in your mind that become projections of reality in the future. What you fear the most you attract. If you can quiet your fears by being confident God is always by your side and His perfect love casts out fear, then you can control what you attract. The peaceful and loving thoughts you choose to conjure up in your mind will manifest into your reality.

Reaffirm your faith daily. Every morning as you are waking up, declare out loud, or to yourself, positive affirmations based on scriptures found in the Bible. Affirm your strong faith in God, in others, in yourself and in your future. Waking up giving thanks with faith-filled phrases each day will help to wipe away those lingering doubts. You may have to repeat these affirmations over several times during the day. Here are some faith-filled affirmations for you to use:

- I am a new creature in Christ; old things have passed away; behold all things become new (2 Corinthians 5:17).
- I have been set free. I am free to love, to worship to trust with no fear of rejection or of being hurt (John 8:36; Romans 8:1).
- I am a believer not a doubter (Mark 5:36).
- I do not hate or walk in unforgiveness. (1 John 2:11; Ephesians 4:32).
- I cast all my care on the Lord, for He cares for me (1 Peter 5:7).
- I am not afraid of the faces of people. I am not afraid of the anger of people (Jeremiah 1:8).
- I do not have a spirit of fear, but of power, love and of a sound mind (2 Timothy 1:7).
- I do not fear. I do not feel guilty or condemned (1 John 4:18; Romans 8:1).

- I catch the devil in all his deceitful lies. I cast them down and choose rather to believe the Word of God (John 8:44; 2 Corinthians 2:11).
- I use my time wisely. All my prayer and study time is wisely spent (Ephesians 5:15-16).
- I am blessed when I come in and when I go out (Deuteronomy 28:6).
- I am very prosperous in everything I put my hand to. I have prosperity in all areas of my life - spiritual, financial, mental, physical, emotional and social (Genesis 39:3; Joshua 1:8; 3 John 2).

*The above affirmation list is adapted from Joyce Meyer's book, Change Your Words, Change Your Life.

Speak the Truth

Just Say It! Betrayal reflects Their Character, Not Yours.

#8

Freedom is Found in Forgiveness

When we live with unresolved anger or hurt, the result is nearly always bitterness, broken relationships, and unhealthy behaviors. Unforgiveness not only sabotages our interactions with those around us, it impedes our own spiritual growth and inner peace – Ruth Graham.

Dr. Cheryl Bauman

Key 36

Stuck in the Moment

As I was writing this book there were many days where I would find myself getting lost in the writing process. Time slipped away. Sometimes I would even forget to stop and eat lunch. I like to jot down ideas when they come to me, and I will sometimes do so on the computer, or I will grab an available piece of paper. If you were to visit me at home, you would discover in my office you will find pages and pages of typed or handwritten notes. Yet there were other times when I would sit down to write this book where I would feel a sense of being lost as to what God wanted me to fully accomplish. At times, I would feel stuck in the writing process. I knew God was calling me to write a book about love. However, procrastination would set in, and I would keep putting off opening my computer to continue to write or to edit a draft copy, as the words were just not flowing. The yearning to write about love and God's love was not leaving me. However, I felt so unqualified to write on the topic of love, as it is so vast, it is all encompassing, it is limitless.

Attempting to write, some days I would just stare off into space. Or lay down on the grass and look up at the sky. Maybe go for a run or a swim trying to muster up ideas for this book, trying to force the words to go from my head to my heart to my fingers to the computer screen. I would lay awake at night or wake up early in the morning pondering this book, knowing it needed to be written, yet not being able to pull it all together. I was good at the "head stuff", such as the research required to support the claims I wanted to make. I was even able to find tons of scripture verses about love. Yet finding scriptures about love and truly believing and knowing God's love are two different things. The hard part came when I was trying to write from the heart as I fiddled with words, phrases and paragraphs, feebly attempting to discuss what true unquestioning love is and how to find it.

Dr. Cheryl Bauman

> *Our QUEST for genuine unconditional love seems to consume most of us at some point in our lives. Isn't life about reaching that pinnacle mountaintop experience found only when we discover unrestricted love? But not just any love, the unconditional love that is unearthed only through a two-way relationship with God.*

The more I tried to put pen to paper, the more I realized I did not know the full extent as to what true unconditional love was. I did not understand why at times, over the years, the two-way relationship between myself and God was not always right. I thought I knew. I also pondered and realized I will never have full clarity and understanding on this subject until I reach Heaven. We think we know, but we only know in part on this earth. I believe God's love will be revealed in all its splendor when we reach our eternal destination. I cannot wait! Through the writing, researching and meditating process that was required for this book, I was led on a steep learning curve from the Almighty God. I was on an assignment, commissioned by the Creator of the Universe. I was taking this assignment seriously. While writing this book God took me places on my journey that were so painful to endure. Yet I am so grateful to have experienced them, as I can authentically share them with you. By surrendering my ALL to God and giving up my WILL for His WILL, I now more fully understand His true unconditional love for me and for you. You too can have this love relationship with God, but it takes full surrender daily in every part of your life. Not my WILL, but His WILL be done one earth as it is in heaven. This is a "hard pill" to swallow at times when we know what we should do, according to His will, but we often do the opposite. I also now know he wants all of us to demonstrate His unwavering love towards Him and others. Others meaning ALL. You may wonder, *how is this possible?*

The uncomfortable events I had to face brought the words of the psalmist so alive, *"Yea, though I walk through the valley of the shadow of death, I shall fear no evil, for though are with me. Thy rod and thy staff they comfort me"* (Psalm 23:4 KJV). These words were so affirming to me as God promises no matter what I face, He is always there with me. Through His word He teaches us we need not fear, for He is an all-powerful, all-present, all-knowing, all-loving God who never leaves our side. If you are walking through some dark moments now, and you believe God abandoned you, know unequivocally He has not left you. He is right by your side. His word promises He will never leave us or forsake us. The Bible does not lie, it is the true living, loving word of God.

I encourage you to read Psalm 23 in its entirety and to reflect on the spiritual meaning of all the words. Ask God to reveal His power, and His knowledge through this scripture passage. Don't rush while you are reading and meditating on it, allow God to speak to you. He is waiting to do so. *Are you willing to take the time to spend with Him?*

Feeling so unqualified to write on the subject of forgiveness, I came across Ruth Graham's book, *Forgiving My Father, Forgiving Myself.* I also reread R.T. Kendall's book, *Total Forgiveness*, from a "new lens", with my eyes-wide open to God's loving-kindness and mercy. Kendall eloquently disseminates how to completely forgive people is the second greatest challenge God has ever given to us, other than laying down our lives in total surrender to God. As I was reading R.T. and Ruth's invitation to accept the miracle of forgiveness, I knew exactly the piece of the puzzle that was missing in my life so I could freely love others. It was forgiveness. I needed to truly forgive myself and to truly forgive others, just as God through His Son Jesus has forgiven me. I highly recommend you read both R.T. Kendall's book and Ruth Graham's book. This chapter only skims the surface on the topic of forgiveness and its connection to being able to freely love others. R.T. Kendall's and Ruth Graham's books are a testimony to the power of what forgiveness can do in a person's life. They challenge all of us to surrender the right to be right and to instead live a life filled with surrendering our WILL to God's WILL.

Surrendering our WILL to God's WILL is the essential foundational piece of a two-way relationship with God. A two-way relationship between you and God is only possibly through one method. As the Bible precisely delineates, there is only one God and one mediator between us and God, and that is Jesus Christ. Jesus announces this truth to us when he proclaims, *"I am the way and the truth and the life. No one comes to the Father except through me." (John 14:6 NIV)*.

By Jesus dying on the cross for our sins, he paved the way for ALL to be forgiven by God and then our sins are washed away. If we accept Jesus into our lives, we automatically become Joint-Heirs with Jesus - sons and daughters of the Highest God! If we ask God with a genuine heart, He then immediately forgives us of our sins, and we are clothed in righteousness. The truth is we need to ask and believe in forgiveness from everything. *"You have not because you do not ask God"* (James 4:2b NIV). When God looks at us, He sees us through the righteousness of Jesus Christ. Therefore, our sins are washed clean through the blood of Jesus. But we must confess our sins daily, hourly, minute by minute to always be in right relationship with God. Confessing our sins and asking forgiveness for them is not a once-in-a-lifetime event. It is continual, daily, and with a humble heart. Once we accept Christ into our lives, we are God's children, that never changes. However, by accepting Christ into our lives, we begin this journey of being a joint heir. It is only natural to want to develop a relationship with God, as we have professed our love and faith in God. A relationship with God is something all of us have an inborn desire to want, it is that emptiness we all QUEST after. Yet this emptiness, the missing piece to the mystery of existence, is what many human beings are not aware of or are dismissive of it. If we commit to a purposeful QUEST to establish a loving relationship with God, this as well provides us with God's relational forgiveness if we confess our sins. Getting offtrack with God happens when we are not in right relationship with God by holding unforgiveness, towards ourselves or others.

Relational Forgiveness

Unforgiveness is an unconfessed sin. It messes up our relationship with God. The Good News is through accepting Jesus as our Lord and Savior, relational forgiveness with God is possible. However, it is also necessary for our continuing in a Holy relationship with Him. When we hold unforgiveness towards others, it creates barriers in our relationship with God. We need to deal with the unforgiveness to ensure our relationship with our Almighty Father is free from any obstacles that would prevent God from moving fully within our lives. We need this two-way relationship with God to live the life we were created to live. If we are holding unforgiveness towards others we are still God's children, but our relationship with Him is fractured. For further clarity, let me illustrate by using an example from my own life.

When I was four years old, I told a lie to my earthly father. It was the day after Christmas; my siblings and I were playing with the toys we were grateful to have received. Christmas was a joyful time of family celebration in our household. It was a tradition my parents gave each of us children in our Christmas stockings a box of raisins. We all loved raisins, and it was a special treat having our own individual boxes, as normally my mom bought the raisins in larger quantities, as it was more practical, and much less expensive. During our playtime, my older brother found a penny on the floor. He decided to give the penny to my sister, and he taped this penny to her raisin box. I was jealous that my brother gave my younger sister the penny and not me. So, I decided to take the penny. It was not long after my father approached me and asked me if I had taken the penny. I quickly denied taking it.

I was caught and I lied to my earthly father. I did not confess I had been the one who committed the act of stealing the penny. In this situation, I remained my earthly father's daughter, however, my relationship with him was strained. There were now obstacles preventing my dad and I from moving forward in a right relationship, due to my sin of lying and of not seeking forgiveness.

When we sin, the enemy blinds us to the truth and instead convinces us what we are doing and saying is OK. This also places strain, and barriers are built between us and our Heavenly Father. *"But I am afraid just as Eve was deceived by the serpent's craftiness, your minds may somehow be led astray from your sincere and pure devotion to Christ"* (2 Corinthians 11:3 NIV). As a young child, I knew I had lied to my dad, and I had sinned. However, I did not want to be caught in the sin of taking the penny so, the enemy convinced me the better solution was to lie to my dad. In fact, I was tricked into lying to both my earthly father and Heavenly Father. The situation intensified even more, as the enemy continued to fool me by planting a suggestion in my mind to hide the evidence and swallow the penny. Just as Satan persuaded Eve to eat the apple. Satan, in his craftiness, convinced me by eating the penny it would take care of the problem, as the evidence would no longer exist. In my fear of being caught, I was also persuaded my sister would also not have the penny. I was blinded by fear and jealousy, so I swallowed the penny. What a mistake!!! Immediately the penny got caught in my throat…my parents rushed to help me as they could hear me choking. My sin had found me out…it almost killed me!

See how crafty the enemy can be by making subtle suggestions that seem fine, such as, 'this is just a little sin, so you can cover it up'. But the little sin almost destroyed me for good. I am grateful my mom is a Registered Nurse and somehow was able to get the stuck penny to eventually slide down my throat. I could have choked on the penny and died. To ensure I was fine, my parents decided to take me to the hospital. On arrival, the doctor ordered an x-ray and was able to locate the penny in my body. He assured both myself and my parents that the penny would eventually make its way through my body.

The drive home from the hospital was long and filled with much remorse and repentance. I asked my dad for forgiveness for lying to him and I confessed I was jealous my older brother gave my sister the penny instead of giving it to me. My dad forgave me and when we got home, he gave me a big hug and kiss. My relationship with my earthly father was restored, due to my repentance and desire for reconciliation. I believe trust was also restored. However, I was still not finished with my need to restore and reconcile my relationship with my older brother and sister. With the help of my dad, I approached them, told them the story and apologized for taking the penny and asked for their forgiveness. They were quick to accept my apology and wrapped their arms around me. I think the entire incident jolted my family, as I nearly choked to death.

On that day, my relationship with my family members was restored to a whole and right relationship. I am grateful for this lesson I learned early on in my life, as it placed a holy fear within me as to the dangers of sin. To this day, I do not have a problem with jealousy. I am grateful to God for healing me at such a young age from the terrible human condition of jealousy. God takes our ashes and makes beauty out of them if we allow Him to do so. What the enemy meant for harm for me; God turned it around and used it for His glory (Genesis 50:20). Moreover, I had to be a willing participant and confess my sin and ask for forgiveness. This narrative from my life parallels how my relationship with my earthly father was fractured and had to be mended to regain trust and a right relationship with him. My earthly father always loved me, even when I was lying to him. However, I needed to seek forgiveness to restore my relationship with him. The same goes for my relationship with my Heavenly Father. If I am dealing with unforgiveness and not willing to humble myself and confess my sins to my Heavenly Father, then my relationship with Him is fractured. However, *"If we confess our sins, He is faithful and just and will forgive us our sins and purify us from all unrighteousness" (1 John 1:9 NIV)*.

I often think about how my life would have turned out if I did not willingly admit my sin and ask for forgiveness. My guess is I would have been a very bitter and jealous person. The root of jealousy would have taken hold that day and grown in my life to the point where it probably would have destroyed me spiritually, physically, mentally, socially and emotionally. I would not be as effective today for the Kingdom of God if I had jealousy and bitterness at the root of my life. We think we are only sinning a little, but a little sin can lead to destruction quickly.

> *When it comes to forgiveness it is always our turn. Go to whoever wronged you or whoever you wronged. Forgive just as you have been forgiven so your relationship with your Heavenly Father is always right.*

Key 37

Must I Love My Enemies?

"You prepare a table before me in the presence of mine enemies" (Psalm 23:5a NIV). "Enemies, do I really need to love them? Surely not, God". In the previous chapters I discussed a different time in my life where betrayal was all around me. I kept asking God, *"Can't you just strike down my enemies with lightening?"* Would you do that for me and then it would be over very fast, and I could get on with things, such as writing this book. Oh yeah...your word also states, "love your enemies and pray for those who persecute you" (Matthew 5:44 NIV). *"Oh gee, I guess I can not just skip over that scripture, can I, God? What type of love is that for my enemies? How do I truly love my enemies, the people who torment me, how can I love them? Really, how can I do this with all they have done to me?"* God whispered, "you cannot on your own, but through my grace and through my love you can". There was a pause, and then God softly spoke to my soul, "you must not only love your enemies, but you must also pray blessings over those who persecute you". Everything within my very being cried out, "OUCH"!!

It is vitally important to depend on God and His *Agape* love, to support us through loving and forgiving our enemies. There is no other possible way to do it. Some people wronged us in ways that are unimaginable and evil. Forgiving our enemies with the help of God does not take them off the hook. In fact, it places them on God's hook. God promised in His word that, *"Though you made me see troubles, many and bitter, you will restore my life again; from the depths of the earth, you will again bring me up. You will increase my honor and comfort me once more"* (Psalm 71:20-21 NIV). If you firmly trust in God to bring about justice, He will ensure your enemies are put to shame (Psalm 71:24). God will judge the evildoers and bring about consequences for their actions. *"It is God who judges: He brings one down, he exalts another. In the hand of the Lord is a cup full of foaming wine mixed with spices. He pours it out, and all the wicked of the earth drink it down to its very dregs"* (Psalm 75:7-8 NIV).

Dr. Cheryl Bauman

Depending on what harm has been done to you by your enemies, such as physical or sexual abuse, the situation might need to be brought forward to the authorities of the law. As sexual and physical abuse must meet with consequences through the support of the laws that govern us. Forgiving your enemies sets you free from torment. Remember forgiveness does not set the other person free from requiring facing consequences for what they have done. Instead, forgiveness sets YOU free! I encourage you before acting, seek Godly, wise counsel, as to your situation and the next steps.

There is a particular man, I will call him Jack, who has intentionally brought much strife and pain into my life. God was always guiding me to forgive Jack. It was difficult to even be in the same room as him, as he treated me like an object, and did not even acknowledge the pain and hurt he blatantly heaped on me. Of course, I know the scripture by heart, *"greater is he that is in you, than he that is in the world"* (1 John 4:4b KJV). Standing and believing this scripture during the times he continuously betrayed me was what I should have done. However, many times I attempted to take on the battle on my own. This was a big mistake as in the Bible, *"This is what the Lord says to you, "Do not be afraid or discouraged... for the battle is not yours, but God's""* (2 Chronicles 20:15 NIV). God also declares in His word, *"No weapon formed against you shall prosper, and every tongue which rises against you in judgment You shall condemn"* (Isaiah 54:17a NKJV).

These scriptures are the word of God, and they are truth, they do not lie. Therefore, when God says *the battle is His*, He is telling us there will be battles. When He announces to us in His word *no weapon formed against us shall prosper*, He is acknowledging weapons will be raised against us, and these are demonic, spiritual weapons that cannot be physically held. Battles and weapons are absolute as the scriptures declare them. So, when troubles come our way, which they will, know you have been forewarned. Jesus said, *"in this world you will have trouble. But take heart! I have overcome the world"* (John 16:33 NIV). Therefore, we need to prepare for battle, not on our own, but armed with the sword of the Spirit (the word of God), as the Holy Spirit leads us. This is where my shallow plans with Jack fell apart. Many times, I thought, said and did things that were not prompted by the Spirit of God, and instead were spurred on by my own WILL, not God's. I thought I could fight this battle by myself. This false thinking was a lie from Satan, and it caused me many years of heartache.

During this time in my life, I was weakened by the demonic forces fueling Jack's selfish and sinful nature. I knew and believed I was more than a conqueror. But at the times I needed it most; I was not asking God for His help when I was amid the battle. The Bible proclaims, *"For our struggle is not against flesh and blood. But it is against the rulers, against the authorities, against the powers of this dark world and against spiritual forces of evil in the heavenly realms"* (Ephesians 6:12 NIV). I needed to take authority through the power of God over the forces of darkness, yet I was being led by fear. I did not detect with spiritual eyes all the evilness going on around me and the battle was spiritual. I have learned from this experience as to how to detect, see and rely on God's spiritual realm for power. For when I did not the evil powers did try to overtake me and "weaken" me. That is why it is important to always put on the full armor of God every day, as we all need to prepare for "daily battles" (Ephesians 6:11-13).

The words of the psalmist were very much a part of my belief system, *"You anoint my head with oil; my cup overflows"* (Psalm 23:5b NIV). But in all truthfulness, I was not standing on this word from the psalmist. Instead, I was focusing and becoming more frustrated with the constant bullying, mocking and betrayal being flung at me by my enemy. *"Surely goodness, love and mercy will follow me all the days of my life, and I will dwell in the house of the Lord forever"* (Psalm 23:6 NIV). However, for a while, the more I quoted scripture, the more Jack constantly bullied, mocked and betrayed me. *Why?* Because he felt very powerful. He was not merciful, he was merciless. In fact, he was a *great pretender*. He was extremely skilled at putting on a mask and pretending he was doing nothing wrong. In public he acted and pretended to be my friend, all the while behind my back, he was doing unthinkable things to me. Jack saw me as easily disposable, as he sought after his own wants and desires.

I found myself pleading with God. *"When God? When will all this goodness and mercy follow me you promise ...all the days of my life? When did you say this will happen?* Oh yeah, when I love my enemies, not just some, all of them. Oh yeah, all of them. *How do I love them, especially Jack?* Oh yeah, your word states, *"My grace is sufficient for you, for my power is made perfect in weakness"* (2 Corinthians 12:9 NIV). Well, I sure felt weak because I was not standing on the promises and power so readily available to me as a child of the Most-High God. Instead, I was permitting this unstable, double-minded individual to prey on me. Note, the words *I was permitting*. I was giving my power away. I was not leaning on the power within me. The same power that raised Christ from the dead.

I wanted revenge, I truly disliked Jack. Dislike is too soft of a word. Yet, it was the devil within Jack I disliked. I would rehearse what I wanted to say to him. Yet, this weakened me even more and was a complete and total waste of my time. The unforgiveness I held towards him and my lack of faith in trusting God is the judge and He would fight my battles almost did me in.

It is a good thing my friend wisdom and God's unconditional love for me came to the rescue. Knowing I was not loving ALL, especially not my enemies, I asked God to show me how to love my enemies, especially the people who were intentionally harming me. God in all His infinite grace and mercy did not give up on me, and I am so appreciative of that very fact. He led me on quite a journey of bittersweet refinement. I touched on some of this journey in the previous chapter. During this time of betrayal, God began to deal with me and speak to me deep within my innermost being, "*Do you really know I am Love? Do you really believe I love you more than anything and I will fight your battles for you? Do you really know you do not have to do anything to gain my love or to gain more of a level of my help and support?* I love you unconditionally, my love never changes, my promises of protection never change." God gently spoke, "It is your love for me that changes depending on your level of trust and your level of faith. *Are you willing to trust me completely with this situation?* Do you believe me when I say, "I am LOVE, I am CRAZY in LOVE with you, I relentlessly chase after you with my unfailing, undying love." *Do you believe me?* If so, allow me to shine my light into the hidden crevices of your very inner being. This way I can carve out the many painful wounds this world heaped on you, preventing you from truly trusting me and knowing my love in all its fullness."

The wounds from betrayal and past hurts were preventing me from loving my enemies…they were preventing me from trusting in God to fight my battles…and they were preventing me from my destiny. I needed to forgive my enemies to live whole and free so God could work more miracles in my life. I needed to forgive my enemies and to trust God so I could live a more abundant and prosperous life for His Kingdom's work on this earth. My lack of faith and not yielding my cares over to God and trusting Him to be the judge of the people who so viciously betrayed me. It was holding me back from many blessings God wanted to bestow on me. God blesses His children so they can bless others. I needed to understand the depth of God's love towards me but also towards my enemies, particularly Jack. I also needed to understand that by me forgiving Jack it did not make what he did to me right. Instead, forgiveness would free me to live a life of abundance. Forgiveness allows God to be the judge and the jury, and takes this want for justice from me, and places the responsibility of justice onto Him. That in and of itself is so freeing. Carrying around hurts and wounds from betrayal is very heavy. This weight was holding me captive, disarming me from being able to fully function in the life I am created to live!

I was under a false pretense forgiveness is moderated by feelings. If I felt like forgiving, I would forgive. If I did not feel like forgiving, I would not forgive. Similar to what many of us based love on, as was discussed earlier in this book. Many of us think love is controlled by our feelings. Yet, I hope by the time you arrive at this place within this book you learn love is a choice. Love is a commitment, a responsibility commissioned by God through His written word. In the Bible verses earlier quoted in Chapter 1, Jesus was being questioned by the teachers of the law as to which commandment is the greatest. To this question Jesus answers that there are two new commandments, that we are to love God and to love our neighbor as ourselves (Mark 29:30-31).

If we choose to follow these two vital commandments given to us by Jesus, we will live a life of peace and overflowing abundance. If we choose not to follow these two commandments we will continue to be tossed around by the problems of life and accumulating heaps of bitterness and anger. There were days during this writing process I would just pour out my heart to God. I would ask Him to uphold me with His righteous right hand; to wrap His strong arms around me; to never let me go; to always be the lover of my soul. I asked Him to teach me how to love; even when I did not want to love some people; and to forgive me for not forgiving others. The soft, gentle whispers came from God, "Stop trying so hard. You cannot do this on your own. It is only through my perfect *Agape* love you can love them. Give these burdens and hurts over to me and ask to see people through my eyes, and you will be fully transformed by my love." Through my pain I was able to allow God to help me refocus and to gain *new sight* and *new insight*!

God reminded me on numerous occasions in relation to Jack and others that hurt and betrayed me He also sent His only Son to die for their sins. Also, He loves them just as much as He loves me. Wow, this was a hard pill to swallow, especially when I was steeped in unforgiveness. I would continually question God, "*How can you love them when they have so much hatred and deception in their hearts? How can you love them when they live secret lives, pretending to be one thing and living out another?*" No matter how many times I asked, His answer remained the same, "Leave their hearts and lives to me, I want to prosper you. So, in order to prosper you, you need to let go of this pain unforgiveness is causing in your life and let me be the judge."

After countless times wrestling with God, I literally had an experience of God performing reconstructive heart surgery on me. He was carving the old, hard, cold heart out of me, and replacing it with a new, softer, warmer heart. As I surrendered my WILL to His WILL, the more He carved away at my hardened heart. *"I will give you a new heart and put a new spirit in you; I will remove from you your heart of stone and give you a heart of flesh"* (Ezekiel 36:26 NIV). I knew it was the only way I could continue to live a healthy and happy, prosperous life on this earth. I needed to surrender ALL. The surrender involved forgiving ALL:

- So that my heart was made right with the Lord.
- So that the condition of my heart was purified by going through the refiner's fire; and
- So that my heart that sought after the ways of God and His will for my life.

Key 38

Final Surrender

I will never forget the day I decided to surrender it ALL over to God, to give up trying on my own to love some and to not love others. But instead to see ALL through God's eyes of love and to ask Him for guidance and courage to see others' hurts and wounds. I asked Him to use my words to bring Him glory, so I could speak life into the wounded people, so their hurt could be healed through atoning His perfect love. I prayed this atonement would flow deep into their open sores, and God's anointing love would seal up their wounds, never to be reopened again. Being able to genuinely pray for enemies and want the best for them is a huge step in the forgiveness process. This process did not happen in the blink of an eye. I wish it did.

During the healing process, God revealed forgiving and loving these people *does not equate to accepting what they have done to me, nor does it abolish their responsibility for their actions.* Forgiveness also does not require that I closely associate with them. In the past I confused forgiveness and love as needing to allow these people who had broken my trust back into my circle. Through this process I realized there is a distinguishable difference between forgiveness and trust. I was confusing *forgiveness with trust*. I was confused by thinking to forgive I needed to trust them again. Yet they had broken my trust and deeply wounded me, and they had no desire to reciprocate and change. *Forgiveness*, *trust*, and *reconciliation* are not synonymous. The people who betrayed me were not remorseful and were not seeking repentance or reconciliation. *Reconciliation* implies there are two people who are genuinely motivated to want to forgive each other and to work through the wounds caused and repair a broken relationship. It also involves the two people making a commitment not to fall back into the unhealthy cycle of betrayal, but to intentionally develop new healthy patterns of behavior. We know from chapter one, learning about the neuroplasticity of the brain that developing new patterns of behavior and new mind-sets are possible.

Dr. Cheryl Bauman

I knew my betrayers were not at all interested in *reconciliation*, and I was afraid to trust anyone again. God provided me with a Spirit of discernment, and I was discerning the people who betrayed me were "pretending" to like me in social situations. Although all the while they were "stabbing me in the back". I have to say, it was a horrible position to be in. I did not feel at all safe with some people, and I did not feel loved by them either. I think most of you reading this book know when you are with people who just do not have your best interest at heart. It is an unnerving feeling, especially for someone like me who wants to be liked and accepted. God, through the impartation of knowledge, allowed me to understand these people were so self-absorbed they did not care about the impact of their harmful behaviors. This realization was shocking to me, as I do not see people or life this way. I care about people and the impact my behavior has on them. But not everyone is like this. This life lesson was difficult for me to learn, but necessary. As through this experience God has fine-tuned this gift of discernment and revelation to equip me to an even greater level of understanding. I can use this gift with more power and with increased giftedness in words of wisdom, words of knowledge and words of encouragement. What the enemy meant for harm; God is using for good.

Demonstrating and having love and forgiveness towards people are not necessarily associated with being able to trust them again. Trust requires repentance and reconciliation by both people involved. Instead, forgiving people means we can let go of the pain and the hurt and to hand it over to God. True forgiveness is asking God to see them through the eyes of His love. All truth is found in the Bible, and Jesus tells us, *"I am sending you out like sheep among wolves. Therefore, be as shrewd as snakes and as innocent as doves"* (Matthew 10:16 NIV). Through this profound teaching Christ is making us aware there are people in this world we are not to trust. Yet we are to be wise and loving.

Moreover, forgiveness is not associated with continuing to be victimized. There are people in this world who will never change, and God knows this. But we are commanded to forgive them, and to clothe ourselves with humility when dealing with them. However, trusting is not always a part of the equation connected with forgiveness. People must earn trust through their actions. If people who betrayed us in the past continue to victimize us, this is not healthy. God does not want us to remain in situations that victimize us. Seek godly counsel if this is your situation to determine what you are to do. Forgiveness is a gift to us from God. Refusing to forgive others only causes us hurt and pain. Whereas trusting someone who is not trustworthy will also continue to hurt us, as they have not repented and realized the errors of their ways. Therefore, they will continue to victimize us. Be wise in this regard.

When we intentionally choose to forgive, we intentionally choose to clothe ourselves with humility. This can be difficult depending on the actions of the person(s) who has hurt us. I must admit, I was not always humble as I interacted with the people who had hurt me so. Developing, practicing and integrating humility into my character came with a big price tag. I am certainly not perfect. But every day I know I am a new creature in Christ, the old has passed away and all things become new (2 Corinthians 5:17). I am transformed by renewing my mind, body and soul (Romans 12:2).

People who clothe themselves in deceit and manipulation are often covering up addictions such as pornography, drinking, adultery, drugs, lying, gossiping and gambling. Remember, people have free will, and they have a choice to work through the hurts and wounds causing their addictions and are causing such devastation in their lives and the of those around them. They have a choice to live a life that is free from deceit, secrets and manipulation, masked by their addictions. It is their choice to rid themselves continually needing to cover up and instead make a wise choice to stop pretending.

God has shown me that *trust and reconciliation* may never happen between myself and others, as relationships consist of two or more people. If the other person(s) is not wanting to be truthful in what they have done, continuing to be clothed in deceit regarding what they've done, trust may never be restored, and reconciliation may never happen. This was difficult for me to accept, as it is my desire to be reconciled with everyone and in right relationship with everyone. To live in perfect unity is God's original design for all humans. God originally designed all relationships to be harmonious.

> *The language and design of God is love and unity. The language and design of Satan is hatred and destruction.*

Forgiveness is an intentional choice. God wants to take on the mess brought about by destruction and make it into something beautiful. But He does not force His WILL on us. Forgiveness is our commitment to hand over control to God in every situation. This takes the responsibility off our shoulders and transfers it to God's shoulders. God wants all of us who are suffering from deep and painful wounds to transfer our problems completely to Him. God wants to take the heavy burden from us caused by unforgiveness and to relieve us from the painful past so we can live an abundant life. We are commissioned in the Bible to pray for our enemies and to bless those who curse us. However, nowhere can it be found in the Bible we are to trust them again or to allow them into our inner circle.

> *People who betray others are clothed in deceit. God calls us to be clothed in Righteousness. We are children of the Most-High God!*

Key 39

Unlovely, Loving

Where are you on this journey of being committed to love and to blessing your enemies? On our QUEST to unlock the mysteries of humanity, all of us need to acknowledge and understand an important key. The key is to acknowledge and accept loving and blessing our enemies are essential so we can freely love God, ourselves, and others. Throughout this book we have circled around this subject repeatedly. However, on our QUEST to find true love, it is easy to love those who love us and to rejoice with those who rejoice with us. However, as I quested to unlock the mysteries of humanity, I knew something was missing. There were still areas of my life not filled with love, areas that needed to be uprooted and replanted in relation to the people who betrayed me.

As I quested for the keys to unlock the mysteries of true unconditional love, I discovered I needed to dig deeper into God's word. To allow it to penetrate my very spiritual being to a level beyond betrayal and self-righteousness. I needed to reach a spiritual depth that allowed me to love and to bless my enemies. Not just loved one or two of my enemies, but ALL of them. Jesus is commissioning you and I to love ALL our enemies. Found in the scriptures, as has been mentioned before in this book. Jesus gives us two commandments found in Mark 12:30-31.

As outlined by Jesus, these two commandments are the most important for us to follow. Yet with all the cares of this world and the pressures and stresses we find ourselves facing, these two commandments, located in the New Testament, are probably the most difficult to fulfill. That is if we are not daily walking and talking with God and allowing Him into the dark secret corners of our lives. Even when we are in a daily relationship with God, loving people who are not lovely is the biggest challenge and most difficult challenge all of us face. To know the true love of Jesus is encouraging. I learned daily that I must repent of not loving others. I must confess the sin of hatred and anger towards others, as some people are difficult to love. Only when I started to choose loving my enemies as a daily intentional decision, did God begin to move in profound ways in my life. I discovered I needed to have a deeper sense of God's love and forgiveness, so I could turn around and freely love others and forgive them. It is a process like peeling the skin off an onion. It is difficult at times to peel and painful as the sting from the onion causes our eyes to tear up. So does the sting of unforgiveness. It causes pain and sadness. Our joy is stolen away by the sting of anger and bitterness.

How are you faring in loving ALL? Do you sometimes love ALL? Do you pretend to love them? However, when you are out of earshot do you begin to gossip and slander them? Do your thoughts and actions betray them? Where are you on the journey of loving the unlovely?

Who are Your Enemies?

Our enemies are sometimes not in the form of human beings. Our enemies are anything that is separating us from the love of God. So, our enemies can be the love of material goods, money, status, power, sports, and self-promotion. Our enemies can also be our addictions to alcohol, drugs, adulterous affairs, overspending, gambling and pornography. If you are out of balance in any area of your life, that is an addiction. *Are you rebellious towards God's voice and not acting in obedience?* If so, then rebellion is your addiction. *Are you half in and half out, by choosing to only listen to certain things God is telling you?* If so, you are double-minded and double-mindedness is your addiction. You are in a dysfunctional codependent relationship with these things. This unhealthy codependent relationship is an enemy. It is blocking you from living your life to its full potential. You might also be in a dysfunctional relationship with another person. Being in any relationship that is out of balance and that is obsessively consuming you, is not living the life you were intended to live.

Anything that is standing in the way of you and God is an idol, and it is an enemy. God has clearly commanded we are to have no other gods before us. These gods are our enemies, as they separate us from the full power found in the true unconditional love of God. These are the enemies we must rid from our lives. We must not love these enemies. In the Bible Jesus is commanding us to love ALL people, not to have the LOVE of money, possessions, power, and status. Instead, to hate what is evil and to cling to what is good. Confusion, double-mindedness, and rebellion are evil enemies of God. God wants the best for us, but if we are loving all these things above God, then they are our enemy. By submitting to these things over submitting our WILL to God, we are placing them ahead of God.

#8: Freedom is Found in Forgiveness

To follow these commandments on how to love and to find true love, even loving our enemies, we need to discover how to trust God implicitly. We need not rely on the stuff in this world that clutters our mind, that clutters our home closets, that clutters our workspace. Instead, we need to draw closer to Him and trust Him at a much deeper level. Some of us are only giving *lip service* to God and saying we trust Him. To trust God in ALL things is a matter of the *heart* and not the *head*. We need to know and experience walking in the fullness of His love depending on loving God completely, regardless of stuff and status. We need to ask God to forgive us for loving these things or people more than we love God. I am not delving into this issue to condemn you and to make you feel bad. Instead, I am discussing this serious issue so you can be aware of it, choose to stop it and ask God to forgive you. Sometimes the very things separating us from God are not at a conscious level. By discussing some of these enemies that may have a stronghold in your life, I am hoping to expose them, so you recognize them as being a part of your life. You can ask God's forgiveness. If your heart is honest with the request, God will forgive you. He then promises to never remember your sins anymore. He will wipe the slate clean.

Is God nudging you to give up your love for the things in this world? If so, God is asking you to give up the obsessive love of these things, not to necessarily completely give them up - just the idolizing of them. If you are relying on these things ahead of relying on God, if your world would crumble tomorrow if they were taken from you, then they are your idols. An idol is anything standing in the way of a right relationship with you and God. It is a barrier affecting your dependence and your relationship with God. If you think of these things more than you do God and His ways and purposes, if they are your lifeline instead of God, then you are obsessed and in love with them. Putting them ahead of the love of God. God wants you to be totally dependent on Him and His love and not to be dependent on these things. God is calling you to store up your treasures in heaven, instead of here on earth.

> *Do not store up for yourselves treasures on earth, where moths and vermin destroy, and where thieves break and steal. But store up for yourselves treasures in heaven, where moths and vermin do not destroy, and where thieves do not break in and steal. For where your treasure is, there your heart will be also (Matthew 6:19-21 NIV).*

Do you sense God prompting you to give up hurt, anger and resentment towards others? Do you worship bitterness and resentment? Worshiping anger, resentment and hurt is also idol worship. An idol is an image, representation, person or thing that is greatly admired and loved. It is anything you love more than you love God. You may think, 'I don't love anger, hatred and bitterness.' Yet, if they are keeping you from thinking clearly, acting clearly, if you are always dwelling on them, then they are an idol. If you are obsessed with being angry, bitter and resentful towards the people who have hurt you. If you are placing these feelings above God's will and way for your life, then these things are hindering you from being totally free. In these past few paragraphs, I asked a lot of questions, hoping you can recognize we all need to ask God what each one of us needs to give up. I am discussing this very critical issue, as in our material world we have many items and many outlets for addictions that stand in the way of a right relationship between ourselves and God. Due to our ability to obtain 'stuff' and to 'maintain' a certain standard of living, we may falsely believe we do not need to humble ourselves and rid ourselves of anger, bitterness and resentment. We may have been quite self-righteous. We may believe we have the right to be right, as we have 'options'. If Plan A doesn't work, then we proceed to Plan B, because we can. This line of thinking is in stark contrast to what the word of God teaches us about ridding ourselves of bitter, anger and resentment.

> *And do not grieve the Holy Spirit of God, with whom you were sealed for the day of redemption. Get rid of all bitterness, rage and anger, brawling and slander, along with every form of malice. Be kind and compassionate to one another, forgiving each other, just as in Christ, God forgave you (Ephesians 3:30-32 NIV).*

I am shedding light on this subject not to condemn but instead to hopefully encourage you. You need to reflect on what you need to rid your life of to live more fully in the presence of God and His purposes for you on this earth. Like I said earlier in this chapter, loving God so we can truly forgive others is like peeling away the layers of an onion. Some of what God prompts us to give up is a slow process, while other things are fast and quick. Rely on God to tell you what you need to start to give up having Him fill you up with His goodness, grace and love. Ask God what you need to seek forgiveness on and what you need to forgive. He will tell you.

> *Is God calling you to forgive others as He has forgiven you? If God is speaking to you about this, are you listening to the voice of God? Are you willing to let go of the love of everything else that is separating you from the true unconditional love of God?* For this love of "stuff" will not bring you satisfaction, as this love manifests itself in the worship of idols and not the worship of God. This obsessive unhealthy love is your enemy. Get rid of the love of

worldly "stuff". If you do, you will no longer face the unhealthy idols of selfishness, bitterness, and lack of self-control.

God wants us to have nice things. God created this world in all its splendor for us to enjoy. God wants us to be prosperous. However, it is the LOVE of prosperity, above the LOVE of God that is an idol. It is also the LOVE of anger, and the LOVE of holding in resentment that trumps your LOVE of God. *If this is you, what do you need to balance in your life so none of these idols exist? What might you need to give up loving so you can love God more?* This does not necessarily mean you give up all your possessions, it just means you give up idolizing them. If God asks you to give up your possessions, you need to be willing to do so. Surrendering to God's will means discovering God's voice and God's WILL for your life. It is being obedient to what God is telling you to do. *Are you listening?*

> *For God is love and He loves you. God is saying to you, "I want you to completely and truly trust me and to know I AM LOVE, I WAS LOVE, and I WILL ALWAYS BE LOVE!"*

Do you want to know and experience this unconditional love that is not at all dependent on your status, what you own or what you feel? This love is not dependent on how much money you make, or how many tasks you complete every day. This unconditional love is solely dependent on the fact God is love and you were created out of His perfect love so you can love Him, love yourself and love others. This unconditional love is calling out to you! Seek forgiveness from everything you are harboring that is separating you from God's fullness. Unforgiveness causes barriers. Hatred, anger and jealousy are obstructions in your life. If you love always feeling angry and bitter, requiring this addictive fix as a part of your life, then you love these feelings and these patterns of behavior more than you love God. Not letting go of unforgiveness is loving unforgiveness more than loving God. The love of anything more than God erects a barricade between us and Him.

I encourage you to read on and discover He is not pressuring you into loving Him is a vital key for you to understand. He loves you so much He is continually saying to you, "I Love You". However, God did not create us to be robots. He has given you the free choice to *Just Say It!* "I love you God!" *Do you trust in God's true unconditional love enough to accept His gift of forgiveness from the people who have betrayed you?*

Dr. Cheryl Bauman

This QUEST for true unconditional love is not an intellectual assignment instead this is an assignment of the heart! Forgiving yourself and others takes courage and strength from God. It does not come from anything or anyone in this world.

Key 40

What Does the Bible Say About the Importance of Forgiveness and Freedom?

The scriptures clearly tell us, "*Do not let the sun go down while you are still angry*" (Ephesians 4:26 NIV). The reason God instructs us in His word about immediately forgiving others is so we can be free to live in His fullness and fulfill our assignments here on this earth with joy and enthusiasm. If we let the sun go down on our anger and go to bed thinking about the people that hurt us, we are continually reliving hurts, sadness and disappointments. This bitterness leads to anger. If we go to bed each night with this bitterness, then we are more than likely to wake up with bitterness and resentment. We are drinking poison and allowing our enemies to consume us.

Living continuously with anger and unforgiveness robs us from the blessings God has in store for us and does not allow us to fulfill our purposes here on this earth. Anger blocks our view. Bitterness and resentment will cause the brightness of the physical sun as well as the Son of God to be shielded from our lives. *Have you ever taken a walk on a sunny day carrying a load of bitterness and anger with you, never seeing the sun, or appreciating its warmth because all you can see, and feel are anger and hatred?* I think many of us could answer yes to that last question. We have all missed a great time of enjoyment due to the weight of unforgiveness. This is not how God intended for us to live. God wants our days and our future to be filled with hope and joy, soaking up the warmth and the brightness from His Son.

If you are suffering by going to bed at night with anger and resentment, how can you change this pattern that is now a habit and instead forgive others? You can begin by intentionally not focusing on hatred and anger. You probably feel justified in festering in the feelings of anger and contempt. They crowded out the open spaces in your heart and mind, allowing no room for love and forgiveness. If this is you, you need to be free to love yourself and to love others. If you want the sun and the Son to shine brightly in your life once again, I suggest before you go to bed pray something like the following. "God, I am letting go of every disappointment and negative thing that happened to me today. I am releasing every worry and hurt into your hands. I am forgiving the people who have done wrong to me. I am forgiving my trespassers as you have forgiven me for my trespasses. Let your will be done in my life as it is written in Heaven. God, thank you for helping me to go to bed in peace and for helping me to wake up tomorrow in peace. God thank you for helping me to love my enemies, as I am not capable of doing this on my own. Thank you for giving me strength, for giving me wisdom, and for giving me a love that only comes from above - Amen".

It is important to not go to bed every night with any kind of resentment or defeat in your mind, as you are what you think. The words that feed your mind are critical, as your thoughts become your words. In my first book, *Just Say It: Four Phrases That Will Change Your Life Forever*, I outlined in more detail how stress and unforgiveness can cause a person to become ill physically, emotionally and spiritually. I challenge you to finish each day without blocking anything so when you wake up the next morning, *you will wake up with the bright sun as well as the wise Son*! You will be able to exclaim, "This is the day the Lord has made, I will rejoice and be glad in it." If you do this, you'll hopefully be excited about the day and about your future, without the heavy burden of anger, bitterness and hatred weighing you down and blocking your view of the sun's rays. You will be aligning yourself with the Son of God and allowing his warmth to penetrate through any dark areas of your life.

Knowing the Depth of God's Love for Your Health & Wholeness

I came to a crossroads in my life where I knew to feel healthy and whole I needed to know and to have a deeper sense of God's love for me. I needed this so I could get to the point of choosing to love my enemies. I was stressed out, and the stress was causing all sorts of physical ailments. I discovered that *want* and *act* are two separate identities. We may *want* something, but to *act* on it takes intentional motivation and commitment. The motivation to alter our mind-set needs to happen, and for some of us, like myself, this can take a long time, as pride, bitterness and self-righteousness hold us back. It is an intentional deep commitment to change the voices we are allowing to enter our minds, as these voices often tell us we are justified not to love our enemies. These voices can convince us of the offences against us and help us legitimize why it is okay not to love those who persecute us.

Or worse yet, these voices might even be telling us what our enemies are saying and doing to us are true. These voices are lying. If you believe in these voices, then they are defining who you are. I challenge you to shut these voices out. Do not give them any more time, as they are wasting your time with lies. Instead let God refine you into who you are to be through the saving power of Christ Jesus. Allow God to refine you with the purifying fire He speaks about in scriptures. *"He will sit as a refiner and a purifier of silver; he will purify the Levites and refine them like gold and silver. Then the Lord will have men who will bring offerings in righteousness"* (Malachi 3:3 NIV). I learned through this QUEST my enemies do not *define* me. Instead, they help to *refine* me by knowing beyond a shadow of a doubt God's love for me molds me and refines me. What my enemies say and do towards me and their opinion of me does not matter. What God says about me does matter.

Do you trust God enough and the promises found in His word your enemies are under your feet? Your enemies are a footstool to you because God has set you apart. You are holy and righteous, a joint heir with Christ. You are a child of God, set apart! God *defines* you through His *refining* fire, people do not. *Going through a fiery trial right now?* God wants to burn off all the undesirable thoughts and behaviors, so as you walk through the fire you will be purified, whole and righteous. *Do you want to be righteous and holy unto God? Will you allow Him to purify you with His refining fire?* Ask yourself, *"What is holding you back from allowing God's love to flood you, so your enemies' words and opinions no longer matter?"* To quote Graham Cooke, "Whatever we focus on, we give power to. Take your eyes off the negative and you will dis-empower it."

Love as an Action – Love is Beyond a Feeling

In the Bible in 1 Corinthians 13, we find one of the most familiar chapters ever written on love. This chapter is typically read at weddings and anniversaries. Yet this was never the original intent of the Apostle Paul who authored it. Paul was writing a rebuke to the dysfunctional Corinthian church. This church was abusing their spiritual gifts and often the original intent of the 1 Corinthians 13 is ignored. In 1 Corinthians 13, Paul is speaking of a love that is an action, not an emotion. This kind of love is to be seen, to be demonstrated and to be experienced. This is contrary to our culture that honors personal feelings above almost everything. This love Paul speaks of is the unconditional *Agape* love that can only come through God's love enveloping us and changing our hearts, minds and souls.

Dr. Cheryl Bauman

We live in a very, ME centred society. For some of us, we do what we want to do because we *feel* like it. If we do not *feel* like it, we often do not do it. However, as I study this passage I am reminded of the complete absence of feelings and the completeness of God's unconditional love towards us and through us. Therefore, if love is an *action* and not an *emotion*, we need to study what God has to say about it. We need to study and know what love is and what it looks like through the lens of God.

As a young child of seven years of age, my father who is a minister, had me read 1 Corinthians 13 in front of the church congregation one Sunday morning. As I stood up at the pulpit, feeling totally inadequate, I was shaking and trembling. I practiced reading these scripture verses out loud at home. Studying the words, ensuring I knew the pronunciation of each one of them, even though the deep meaning of most eluded me as a young child. Yet as I opened my mouth, and my throat felt tight, God in His infinite love and mercy supported me as I read through the scripture verses one-by-one. Gazing out over the congregation that had at times demonstrated God's love and at other times had not demonstrated it towards my father, my mother, my siblings and myself. As I read this scripture, the Holy Spirit provided to me a revelation, I knew in that moment God is, was and will always be LOVE. God enveloped me with such a peace, such a hope, such a faith and with such a joy. I knew His LOVE for me surpassed the thoughts and feelings of the people in attendance that morning. I know God's love is an action, not an emotion. As thoughts and feelings are fickle if not bridled by the Holy Spirit. Jesus tells us to enter God's presence and to present our petitions like a young child, who is vulnerable, trusting and loving. As an adult, at times I most certainly confess I did not enter God's presence like a child by totally trusting and relying completely on His LOVE and mercy. This was my mistake, not God's. God was always there loving me each step of the way. If throughout my life, I would have abided in the revelation of 1 Corinthians 13 as that young, innocent seven-year-old, I probably would have been able to forgive others more easily and more readily. All these years later through the bumps and bruises of life, 1 Corinthians 13 remains my favorite chapter in the entire Bible. It describes the *Agape* love of God, the love that never changes, the love that is steadfast and never leaves us or forsakes us. God's love is a powerful action in our lives.

The Apostle Paul emphasizes for us as to what love is and is not in 1 Corinthians 13.

- Love is greater than any spiritual gift.
- Love is expressed by supernatural responses.
- Love is patient.
- Love is kind.
- Love is not jealous.
- Love does not brag.
- Love is not arrogant.
- Love does not act unbecomingly.
- Love does not seek its own.
- Love is not provoked.
- Love does not take into account a wrong suffered.
- Love does not rejoice in unrighteousness.
- Love rejoices in the truth.
- Love bears all things.
- Love believes all things.
- Love hopes all things.
- Love endures all things.
- Love is an eternal gift.

Paul concludes the chapter in 1 Corinthians 13:13 (NIV) with these words: *"And now these three remain: faith, hope and love. But the greatest of these is love."*

Unlocking Mystery #8

Freedom is Found in Forgiveness

> **Reflect:** Do you harbor bitterness and unforgiveness towards a person or persons? Who are they? I encourage you to name them out loud.
>
> **Relate:** What is holding you back from fully surrendering to forgive them? Why are you keeping them on "your hook", instead of "transferring them to "God's hook". Remember, they are not off "God's hook". God is a just judge, and He will repay you and bring order back into your life. But first you need to fully surrender your Will to His Will.
>
> **Respond:** Daily, I encourage you to pray for the person or persons with whom you need to seek forgiveness.
>
> Ask God to allow you to see these people through His eyes.
>
> Ask God to change your heart towards them so you can genuinely ask God to forgive you for harboring unforgiveness towards them.
>
> Intentionally pray God blesses the people with whom you have been wronged by. Even if in the beginning it is difficult for you to do, Just Say It! "I forgive XXXX and God bless XXXX". Say it and do it, even if you do not want to. Remember, we must let go of feelings and instead latch onto God's principles that are contained in the Bible. I know this is a difficult hurdle to overcome, but without this step, God cannot fully bless you.
>
> Also, I encourage you to approach the throne room of Heaven and to ask for forgiveness for any idols or gods you have had in place of the Almighty God.
>
> *Speak the Truth*
>
> *Just Say It! The Keys to Freedom are Found in Forgiveness.*

The Lord's Prayer

Our Father, which art in heaven,

Hallowed be thy Name.

Thy Kingdom come.

Thy will be done on earth, as it is in heaven.

Give us this day our daily bread.

And forgive us our trespasses,

As we forgive them that trespass against us.

And lead us not into temptation,

But deliver us from evil.

For thine is the kingdom,

The power, and the glory,

Forever and ever. Amen.

(Matthew 6:9-11 KJV)

Dr. Cheryl Bauman

#9

GOD IS LOVE

Let every heartbreak and every scar be a picture to remind you of who has carried you this far – Danny Gokey.

\

Dr. Cheryl Bauman

Key 41

Never-ending Love Story

By unfolding the pages of this book, hopefully the keys required to unlock your QUEST to the mysteries of humanity have been revealed as you realize it is the never-ending love story between you and God. Your love story with God is the Greatest Love Story ever told. For some of you, I am surmising this QUEST has taken you on a rough ride through choppy waters. *Are you able to look yourself in the mirror to speak out from Chapter #1 and say, "I am Lovable?"* Are you able to state, "*I am Lovable, because God first loved me?*"

God promises to take all your scars and make you beautiful through His perfect, transforming power of true unconditional love. God's love is pure, it never changes. It was the same yesterday; it is the same today; and it will be the same tomorrow and forever more. God is the Alpha and the Omega; He is the first and the last; He is the beginning and the end. It is you and I who change. It is you and I who waver in our love relationship with God, our Heavenly Father. God is steadfast, His love endures forever. In our human wanderings, we are the ones who move away from Him. He never moves away from us. He is continually pursuing us with open arms, full of grace and mercy. His love is the unconditional, *Agape* love.

Many of you think you must earn God's love by doing things, and the more you do, the more God loves you. This is distorted thinking in relation to God's true unconditional love. We do not deserve His love, yet He loves us despite our faults. God's unconditional love is freely given to us; it is not dependent on what we do for Him. What a wonderful reassurance you and I have, we are loved no matter what! *Yet why do so many people doubt God's love or do not even give Him an opportunity to work in their lives? Could it be they have never even thought about God's love, or could it be they do not believe they are worthy of God's love because of past and present mistakes?*

Jesus' great-grandmother was Rahab, the Harlot. In the Bible it refers to Rahab this way, as God wants you to know no matter how far you strayed, you can never veer away from His love and from His forgiveness. You cannot *out shock* God. He is in constant pursuit of you because He loves you so much. In His only Son's earthly family tree, God purposefully placed an adulterer and murderer, King David. He also placed a prostitute and a Gentile, Rahab, and Bathsheba a woman who suffered sexual abuse and the murder of her own husband at the hands of King David. God intentionally did this to demonstrate to all of us no one is perfect here on this earth, yet nothing is impossible to God. Nothing separates us from the love of God found in His Son, Christ Jesus. God's love redeems; God's love reconciles. God remembers our sins no more; they are as far as the east is from the west. The proof is in the human family tree of His only Begotten Son, Jesus!

Even in our own genealogies, God weaves His miraculous graces, as He loves to redeem sinners. God loves projects, and He loves to produce something magnificent out of sordid family backgrounds. God loves to make foreigners His children and to reconcile enemies. He loves to make all things work together for good for those who love Him and are called according to His purpose (Romans 8:28). What God has made clean, do not call common (Acts 10:15). That's God's word and promise to us. The amazing news of the Christmas story is Jesus came to make notorious unclean sinners and foreigners like us, people filled with disgraceful pasts, who believe on His name, clean and whole (John 1:12)! What a promise! What a loving God!

Key 42

God's Relentless Pursuit of You

As I reflect on my own love story with God, I am reminded of a narrative from my life as it relates to God's steadfast love and His relentless pursuit of every single one of us. At one point in my career, I worked as a Vice-Principal in a special needs school. To qualify to attend this school, students need to have a severe developmental disability in terms of cognitive functioning. According to the most recent Wechsler Intelligence Scale-Fifth Edition (WISC-V), an IQ between 90 and 109 is considered average. An IQ of 110-119 is a high average, 120-129 is very high and 130 and above is extremely high. Roughly 68% of the population in this world have an IQ between 85 and 115. Whereas 80-89 is a low average, 70-79 is very low and 69 and below is extremely low. All students would have been well below 69 IQ. So, I think you are understanding the students who attend this school are very special. Many of them also suffer from a severe form of autism. As you can imagine this is a unique place to work and I was honored to have been the Vice-Principal at this school.

There was a young girl who would come into the school office every day to ask for me. As she walked through the office doors, the first thing that came out of her mouth was, *"Where is Cheryl?"* I would jump up from my desk and always greet her with open arms, hug her, and laugh with her. She was so happy to see me, and I with her. It was a glorious and joyful meeting, every single time she walked into the office. Due to the behaviors resulting from the developmental disorder of autism, her question remained steadfast, as she would repeatedly ask for me every time she entered the school office. Staff would tell me even years after I moved on and had not worked at the school anymore, she would bound through the office doors and question, *"Where is Cheryl?"* Up until the day she graduated from the school, she never changed her question, she always queried, "Where is Cheryl?" Even though I had left years before, this girl's behavior and tireless pursuit of me remained constant. It was I who changed, not her.

This profound account of a little girl's determination and unwavering search reminds me of our loving Father, God. He is always seeking us out and calling us by name. He never leaves us or forsakes us. It is us who forsake Him; we are the ones who change. We knowingly or unknowingly move farther away from Him by spending less time with Him, or by completely ignoring Him altogether. Yet His love remains. He never moves away; He is always available. He keeps calling us by name. He relentlessly searches to find the one lost sheep, the one who has left the fold, by never giving up, as He calls out to us... "Where is Jim?" ... "Where is Marg?" ..."Where is Will?"

God is questing after you.... He is relentlessly seeking you....
Are you seeking Him?

You may be basing your love story with God on the disappointment of a pastor who moved away, a friend who betrayed you and moved on. Perhaps, a family member who did not demonstrate love towards you. So, you decided to move on and to shut God out, as you associate God with the pain of loss or broken trust. In your flawed thinking you view God through these clouded lenses. You view His love as changing moment by moment, circumstance by circumstance, as if He has left you. Yet it is you who has left Him. Just like I had left the school where I was a Vice-Principal to move on to become a principal at another school, the student did not leave and kept pursuing me. It was I who moved on, not her. Some of you faced the reality of a pastor with whom you enjoyed his or her ministry and they moved to another church. You are finding you are not enjoying your new pastor's ministry as much as the old pastor's. You may also begin to think God moved on with the old pastor. That God is not near to you anymore because you are associating God with your old pastor. This is a false belief. God never moves. If a beloved pastor moves away, God is still with you. If a family member speaks to you sternly and says mean, hurtful, and unkind things to you, you must remember this is not God. God is not a hurtful and unkind God. God is a God of love. His love endures forever. It is without fault, it is without condition, it does not change. You may change, your circumstances may change, the people in your life may change, but God never changes. He is a God of promises and He is a God of love based on the truth found in His word.

The problem is we all suffer from the human condition of sin. We all sin and fall short of the glory of God. However, God is glorious and without fault. No human being is without fault, every single human being at some time or another will disappoint you, will harm you, will hurt you, but God will not. Due to God's relentless love, He continuously chases after us because of His unfailing faithful love that endures forever. He will never stop loving us and wanting us to be in relationship with Him.

Every human being on this earth is significant. We can all be involved in the Greatest Love Story Ever Told, enveloped in a love that never fails and never stops questing after us.

If we believed and lived our lives according to these three words, *God is Love,* I would have never had to write this book as we would all be living in the fullness of God's love. It would be so natural to us. I would not have to type, research, edit or write anymore if we truly captured the essence found in these three words, *God is Love.* All our world's problems would disappear. We would have Heaven on earth, as it was intended before the fall of Adam and Eve. I believe there would be no more divorces, estranged relatives, abuse, addictions, and no more hatred. This happens only if we truly believed and lived by the words and the power contained in, *God is Love.*

The disciple John understood God's love. He continuously writes about it throughout the book of John. He even calls himself the disciple Jesus loved. When John proclaimed he was the disciple with whom Jesus loved, this stirred up jealousy among the other disciples especially Peter. As they questioned Jesus regarding his love for John in comparison to his love for them. The other disciples wanted to know if Jesus loved John more and loved them less. The unfortunate issue surrounding this conversation was they did not comprehend the limitless love of Jesus through the love of his Heavenly Father. But John really "got it". John understood Jesus' love for him and for all of us is endless. John "got it", that this unending love is only made possible through the love of his and our Father in Heaven through accepting Jesus in our lives as Lord and Savior.

I am so grateful John "got it"! He wrote about it in the Bible so all the generations that came after him could more fully understand the love of our Father in Heaven, and the love of His Son Jesus. It is exciting when we can fully fathom this boundless and relentless love of God. *Do you "get it" the QUEST you are on, the longing deep within your inner self can be quenched by the all-consuming love of God?* As King Solomon, the writer of Ecclesiastes so wisely proclaims, *God has also set eternity in the human heart* (Ecclesiastes 3:11 NIV). Therefore, every human being is questing to live eternally with God in Heaven, as it is part of our composition. Eternity is stamped on our DNA. Even if you try to deny it, this eternal QUEST to spend forever in the presence of God and bask in His unconditional love, is indisputable. It is who we are as humans. The

QUEST for an eternal love to satisfy this deep void within all of us is part of our DNA. It can only be filled by the unconditional love of our Creator and Designer. *How exciting is that?!* The Bible states it and the Bible is based on absolute truth.

John writes the profound scripture quoted countless times as it rings out continuously in Heavenly places. F*or God so loved the world that he gave his only begotten son that whosoever believes in me shall not perish, but have everlasting life* (John 3:16 KJV). That is a whole lot of love. To send your only Son down to a dying world, to a world filled with broken human beings who are filled with deadly corruption. To sacrifice your only son so broken human beings like you and I could have a place in Heaven just as His Son Jesus does. That is a whole lot of love. The only man-made thing in Heaven are the scars on Jesus' hands from the nails pierced through them by humans purposed with evil in their hearts, not love. These scars are on the hands of the one who loved us so much he sacrificed it for all of us. These are the only scars that will be found in Heaven.

The only scars in Heaven are man-made scars. They are found on the hands that hold you now!

God's unconditional love is a selfless, sacrificial love. *Do you believe the scripture John 3:16? Or do you not fully have the faith and the belief in this type of love?* John explains further in the 17th chapter of the fullness of God's love for us and how His Son prayed for this love and unity among believers and those who would eventually believe. Jesus prays, *"that all of them may be one, Father, just as you are in me and I am in you. May they also be in us so that the world may believe that you sent me. I have given them the glory that you gave me, that they may be one as we are one. I in them and you in me – so that they may be brought to complete unity. Then the world will know that you sent me and have loved them even as you have loved me"* (John 17:20-23 NIV). I welcome you to take a moment and reflect on these scriptures. *Do you get what Jesus is proclaiming about the love of his Father?* The love of God for us is the same love God has for His Son Jesus, no more and no less. It is an equal love. It is a love that knows no limits, it is a boundless love, a steadfast love.

Through these scriptures, John is explaining to us God does not love Jesus 100% and only loves some of us 80% while others of us 60%. John is clearly outlining for us God loves all of us, including His son Jesus 100%. God's unconditional true love of 100% is for all time and for all people. It does not depend on what we do for a living or how much we measure up, or our status in life, or how much money we make. Nor how much of a mess we made of our lives. God's love is 100% of love 100% of the time for all. I think many of us see God with a measuring stick and a scorecard. I think we figure, "Ok, I did well today, so God loves me 75% today, however, I really messed up yesterday, so He only loved me 15% yesterday."

John confirms in the true living word of God that God loves us the same way yesterday as He does today. He does this with the same amount of love He loves His son Jesus, and that is 100% of love 100% of the time. John wrote the words of Jesus so we today would know God loves us 100% of the time all the time. I know this is difficult for many of us to believe and to accept, as we have been so ruined by human love, or humans attempting to love. So, we see our Heavenly Father through the lens of the hurt and the pain we suffered. Hurt and pain at the hands of an earthly parent, a spouse, relative, friend or stranger. These people abused us because they falsely believed they held power and authority over us to do so. They used their power not for good but for evil.

Key 43

Do You Believe in the Goodness of God's Love?

Some of you see God through the lens of abuse, through the lens of heartache and pain. You may see God as all-powerful, but He sometimes uses His power in a negative, abusive manner. This is not true, and this is not true unconditional love. God wants you to see and know Him through the lens of true unconditional love. That is the love Jesus His Son prayed about in John 17:23b, *Then the world will know that you sent me and have loved them even as you have loved me* (NIV). This is the pure form of *Agape* love God has for all of us, including His Son. God's love is the same for all; the same love God has for His Son He has for you. We are Joint-Heirs with Jesus in the Kingdom of Heaven (Romans 8:17). The word of God says it and so it is. *What does it mean to be Joint-Heirs?* An heir is someone who inherits and continues with the legacy. This is a great spot to be in! By accepting God's love, along with Jesus as your Lord and Savior, we all inherit the riches in Heaven. The riches and the life of abundance in Heaven is ours, we are entitled to it, due to Jesus paying the price on the cross for our sins. Through unconditional love, Jesus paved the way so we can walk on streets paved with pure gold. Yet, to receive our inheritance, we need to accept Jesus as our Savior and Lord and God's living word as absolute truth.

God's word is eternal, and it is truth (Revelation 21:5). Found in Revelation Chapter 21:18-21 (NIV), it describes what the Holy City looks like.

> *The wall was made of jasper, and the city of pure gold, as pure as glass. The foundations of the city walls were decorated with every kind of precious stone. The first foundation was jasper, the second sapphire, the third agate, then emerald, then onyx, ruby, chrysolite, beryl, topaz, turquoise, jacinth, finally the twelfth amethyst.*

> *The twelve gates were twelve peals; each gate made of a single pear. The great street of the city was of gold, as pure as transparent glass.*

Wow, the beauty of this new Holy City is difficult to imagine. It seems so surreal. We will be inhabitants one day of the Holy City. How exciting that we will inherit this, if we continue the legacy of Jesus Christ here on earth, and accept God's true unconditional love by confessing with our mouth Jesus is Lord. God promises, "*I am the Alpha and the Omega, the Beginning and the End. To the thirsty I will give water without cost from the spring of the water of life. Those who are victorious will inherit all of this, and I will be their God, and they will be my children*" (Revelation 21:6-7 NIV).

If you are a parent or grandparent, think about the love you have for your children and grandchildren. Think about the riches you are trying to store up on earth so you can pass along blessings to your children and grandchildren when you leave this earth. Think about the legacy you are trying to leave. This is what God instructs us as parents and grandparents to do. God wants us to live a life of spiritual, financial, physical, social and emotional prosperity on earth, so we can pass it along to our children and grandchildren. This prosperity on earth will bless them for generations so they can bless others and live out the lives they were created to live here on earth by furthering the Kingdom of God. God is training us in His image to leave an inheritance of speaking love, showing love, thinking love in all we do and say to those entrusted to us. God has an abundance of riches for us to inherit in Heaven. The riches we are to inherit in Heaven are endless and are so much more than any of us could ever comprehend or store up here on earth. God is our Heavenly Father and He has stored up our inheritance in Heaven for all of eternity. Our desire to leave our children good things is part of our DNA as it reflects the goodness of our Creator.

God's Love is for ALL…it is everything…this great QUEST that all of humanity find themselves on will define where you spend eternity. *Will you embrace God's Agape love?* It is your choice. There are three absolute truths in relation to human life and the mysteries of the QUEST. Two truths I know the answer to for all of humanity. The first truth is you have free will and choice to choose God's love or to reject it. The second truth is you will eventually die and leave planet earth. *The third truth that I do not know the answer to is, where will you spend eternity?* Only you and God can answer this third truth. One day, whether you believe it or not, you will have an eternal home, and it will be in either Heaven or Hell (Matthew 25:46; John 14:1-3). Your belief or unbelief does not change this reality. God's word promises that you will spend eternity in either Heaven or Hell (Matthew 25:41; Mark 9:48; Revelation 20:11-15). God's word is truth. It does not lie (Revelation 20:10).

God sent His Son to die on the cross to take on the sins of the world, because He loved the world so much, and did not want any of us to perish. *Ever wonder why we do not feel totally comfortable on this earth?* It is because this is just our temporary home. We all have eternity etched on our hearts. We are spirit beings housed in human bodies. Our souls are eternal; they cannot be destroyed. They will live forever. That is how we were created, even if you try, you cannot undo this reality. It does not matter how full of unbelief you are; the fact is, earth is only your temporary home. *"For here we do not have an enduring city, but we are looking for the city that is to come"* (Hebrews 13:14 NIV). Ever wonder why you have that "homesick feeling". Carrie Underwood's song, *Temporary Home*, creatively explains why this is. I encourage you to listen to the song and reflect on how this song relates to your life and your QUEST for true unconditional love. *"But our citizenship is in heaven. And we eagerly await a savior from there, the Lord Jesus Christ"* (Philippians 3:20 NIV).

God is true unconditional love, and He is calling all of us to live with Him forever. Your QUEST for true unconditional love can be quenched by accepting the love relationship God has for you through His Son Jesus. This QUEST can be over, and it can be a lasting love relationship that will endure forever! Our Heavenly Father is a good, good Father! His Love endures forever! I encourage you to read Psalm 136 (NIV) aloud:

> *Give thanks to the Lord, for he is good. His love endures forever.*
> *Give thanks to the God of gods. His love endures forever.*
> *Give thanks to the Lord of lords: His love endures forever.*
> *to him who alone does great wonders, His love endures forever.*
> *who by his understanding made the heavens, His love endures forever.*
> *who spread out the earth upon the waters, His love endures forever.*
> *who made the great lights – His love endures forever.*
> *the sun to govern the day, His love endures forever.*
> *the moon and stars to govern the night. His love endures forever.*
> *To him who struck down the firstborn of Egypt His love endures forever.*
> *and brought Israel out from among them His love endures forever.*
> *with a mighty hand and outstretched arm. His love endures forever.*

To him who divided the Red Sea asunder His love endures forever.
and brought Israel through the midst of It, His love endures forever.
but swept Pharaoh and his army into the Red Sea. His love endures forever.
To him who led his people through the wilderness. His love endures forever.
To him who struck down great kings, His love endures forever.
and killed mighty kings – His love endures forever.
Sihon king of the Amorites His love endures forever.
and Og king of Bashan – His love endures forever.
and gave their land as an inheritance, His love endures forever.
an inheritance to his servant Israel. His love endures forever.
He remembered us in our low estate His love endures forever.
and freed us from our enemies. His love endures forever.
He gives food to every creature. His love endures forever.
Give thanks to the God of heaven. His love endures forever.

I encourage you to make a habit each day of declaring as to what God has done in your life and then to repeat at the end of each declaration, "*His love endures forever*". Do this with a boldness and a confidence. Ask the Holy Spirit to guide and direct you. I encourage you to make these declarations knowing and believing that God's love does not fail. God's love goes on and goes on and goes on. *How can you ever doubt God's love?* To doubt is to be unwise. By never wanting to understand and never wanting to unlock the mysteries of humanity, which is ultimately God's unconditional love for you, would be an eternal tragedy for you.

Do you want to die, facing an eternity in Hell, by never surrendering and accepting God's unconditional love? Is pride, and believing you are better than your Creator holding you back from living forever in a place of peace, joy and love?

I encourage you to surrender to the great mystery of humanity, which is God's LOVE. I encourage you to delve deeper into the scriptures to find answers that will unlock further questions you are confronting. Hopefully by questing after the truth your search will end when you discover that there is only one God that will meet all of your needs. Psalm 138:1 (NIV) states, "*I will praise you Lord, with all my heart; before the "gods" I will sing your praise*". Then in verse 3 (NIV) it goes on to say, "*When I called, you answered me; you greatly emboldened me.*"

According to Merriam-Webster's (2019) Dictionary, the definition of "emboldened" means, "to give (someone) the courage or the confidence to do something or to behave in a certain way". Another definition is "to make brave or to encourage". God is telling us through His written word He provides us with great confidence and courage when we call upon Him. We can be confident and brave what is declared in His word is accurate and true. God is encouraging us through His word. We need to be confident and brave in Him and call upon Him. Just as in the first chapter of Joshua, God encouraged Joshua, "*Be strong and courageous*". Then came the promise, "*because you will lead these people to inherit the land I swore to their ancestors*" (Joshua 1:6 NIV).

Thus, when you are declaring scriptures such as Psalm 136:23-24 (NIV),

> *He remembered us in our low estate His love endures forever.*
> *and freed us from our enemies. His love endures forever.*

You can be confident God will encourage you and provide you with courage and strength when you are feeling low and doubting your eternity. But it does not stop there. He promises He will free you from your enemies because *His love endures forever*. That is a lot of love. Therefore, put your trust in God's unending love when you face your enemies and problems arise. No one has the depth nor the capacity to state their love endures forever, as we are all imperfect. Our love for one another even though we try to have an unconditional love is still flawed. So, we have the perfect love of God to encourage and provide us with confidence and strength. Therefore, when we are let down on this earth by people, we can be confident in God's steadfast love, as *His love endures forever*. God's love also provides us with the confidence and courage to love others unconditionally. God allows us to see people and their circumstances through His eyes, so we have the strength we can embrace them with open, loving arms, because God first loved us!

Key 44

God is the Lover of Your Soul

God is the lover of your soul, and the devil is the hater of your soul. God wants you to live forever in His love with Him in heaven. The devil wants you to be condemned for eternity and live-in hatred, being forever tortured in the pits of hell. The devil's objective is to kill, rob, and destroy. *God's love endures forever.* The word of God is truth and light. In God's word it states His love knows no limit. In God's word it states the enemy roams this earth seeking whom he may devour. If you were to choose right now whose side you want to be on, would it be on God's side or the devil's side. Think of who is in your favor and who is against you.

Choosing to be on God's side or the devil's side is the most important decision you will make; it determines your destiny for eternity. It determines something you have no control over after you die. If you proclaim you are "sitting on the fence", half in and half out, then you made the choice to be on the devil's side; as there are only two choices, not three. As to be on God's side you need to be ALL in. You may think you have a lot of time to make a choice but think about it for a moment. *Do you know anyone that died suddenly from a heart attack or a tragic car accident?* This person might have left the comforts of his or her home in the morning never to return to their earthly residence again. They did not have extra moments on this earth to make a choice; their time was up, and they could do nothing within their control to stop the fact they died. This will also happen to you one day. Whether you die more slowly from a disease, from old age or very fast from a heart attack or an unexpected accident, it is a definite you will eventually die. *Why would you leave this important decision up to chance, when you could live forever and forever in Heaven? Why would you gamble with the most important decision you will ever make?*

You may say, "that's all good and great to live forever with God, but I have been slighted by the church, I have been condemned by people that called themselves Christians. I have been hurt worse from a Christian person than from people who do not profess to be Christians". If this is true, I am sorry this happened to you. These circumstances happened to many people, and this is very tragic. However, we were all born flawed. We all suffer from the human condition of imperfection. The only right, true and just beings are God who made Heaven and Earth, His son Jesus whom He sent to die on the cross for our sins and the Holy Spirit who is our comforter (Trinity). Jesus came to die on the cross so we could live forever, and so the Holy Spirit can dwell on the inside of every Christian.

If you ever felt unloved, if you want to know true love know the God of the universe loves you more than you could ever love Him. People will let you down, but God will not let you down. He continually chases after you with a relentless, undying love, because He is the true lover of your soul. Even if you do not admit or believe there is a God, there is a God. This is a fact, and someday all will know there is one true living God. Look around you... *how are the stars held in space? How did the stars even appear in the first place? Walk through a world-class aquarium and look at the magnificent beauty of the tropical fish with their bright colours and perfectly designed colourful stripes, spots and fins. How did all of this happen? Was it by chance?* To believe it was by chance takes more faith than to believe a Higher Being designed and created everything for us to enjoy. I encourage you on your QUEST to seek and find, knock and the door will be opened by the Great Lover of your soul...God, the Maker of Heaven and Earth.

> *Here I am! I stand at the door and knock. If anyone hears my voice and opens the door, I will come in and eat with that person, and they with me. (Revelation 3:20 NIV).*

#9: *God Is Love*

Key 45

The Bible Says Your QUEST Can Be Over

The final key to unlock the mysteries of *The QUEST* is to know God's love and to experience it. This is by having a close relationship with God. *Think about a spouse, or someone close to you, how do you develop an intimate, close relationship with them?* On a regular basis, you choose to spend time with them, you listen to them, you talk with them, they listen to you, and they talk with you. You have fun together, you laugh together, you share good moments and some not so good moments together. If you are committed to a love relationship with another person, you will want to build them up, encourage them and take time to continue to develop a positive and wholesome relationship with them. You do this by the things you say and do. It is a choice, and it is an intentional commitment to continuing to develop an intimate relationship with them. This is the same with God; you need to commit to regularly developing a daily intimate relationship with Him. As you are waking up in the morning you need to invite Him to spend the day with you, just as you would invite a loved one to spend time with you. God is waiting for an invitation. He is open and willing to accept. *Are you open and willing to ask Him to spend the day with you by guiding and directing your thoughts, words, and actions?*

I challenge you to call on the name of God, to accept His invitation of unconditional love. He will not let you down. He is always there. He will answer you when you call on Him. Listen, He is speaking to you all the time. He speaks through people, through situations and through His word. He speaks to your inner being. Your assignment is to accept His love that He has freely given to us through His Son Jesus.

> *If anyone acknowledges Jesus is the Son of God, God lives in them and they in God. And so, we know and rely on the love God has for us. God is love. Whoever lives in love lives in God, and God in them. This is how love is made complete among us so we will have confidence on the day of judgment: In this world we are like Jesus. There*

is no fear in love. But perfect love drives out fear, because fear has to do with punishment. The one who fears is not made perfect in love. We love because he first loved us (1 John 4:15-19 NIV).

God wants us to love and accept His perfect, selfless, unfailing love for us. This form of love is pure. It is free from all selfishness. Selfishness leads to lust, it leads to immorality, it leads to contempt, it leads to destruction. Instead, God wants us to be totally free from selfishness, and He wants us to be selfless towards Him and towards others. *"Whoever claims to love God yet hates a brother or sister is a liar. For whoever does not love their brother or sister, whom they have seen, cannot love God, whom they have not seen. And he has given us this command: Anyone who loves God must also love their brother and sister"* (1 John 4:20-21 NIV).

Just as His Son was selfless by coming down to earth to sacrifice his life for our sins. Jesus came down from the magnificence of Heaven with no sin and bore all our sins, as we all sin and fall short of the glory of God. Jesus could have said, "Sorry, dad (God), but this world I am looking down on is so out of control! Sin is rampant and if I look into the future, it is only getting worse. Sorry, but these crazy humans are on their own…I do not want to leave the comfort of Heaven. I have done nothing wrong, why should I bear all their sins? Let them figure it out for themselves."

This love is a selfish love.

But instead, Jesus looked down on us with grace, mercy, compassion and a sacrificial *Agape* love and said to his Heavenly Father, "Yes, dad (God), I will die for these people. For if I do not take on the sins of the world, they will be eternally dammed, never to live in freedom or experience the true love you and I have for them. They will never experience the original LOVE story that was set out for them before the beginning of time. I must go, I must do it, so all can have the choice to experience eternal life."

This love is a selfless love.

This selfless love Jesus demonstrated for all of us is a love beyond our human cognition. This love has no limits. This is a relentless, faithful, and enduring love. God and His Son Jesus are committed and are in love with you forever and forever. *Are you committed and in love with them?* If you answer yes, then discover the freeing power to unlock the mysteries of humanity and *Just Say It!* "I love you, Jesus, and I love you, God!" If you do this, your QUEST for true unconditional love is over, you found it!

For God so loved the world that he gave his only begotten son, that whosoever believes on him should not perish but have everlasting life (John 3:16 KJV).

You are the Whosoever!

If you want to be born again into a new family with a Heavenly Father that always offers unconditional love, then wherever you are, I encourage you to repeat this prayer:

Thank you, Lord Jesus, for dying on the cross for all my sins. I admit I am a sinner. I ask you to come into my heart, forgive me of my sins and live in my life forever. From this day forward I make you my Lord and Savior. Amen.

If you prayed this prayer and believed it in your heart, then you are born again, and you have been given the gift of eternal life with Christ Jesus in Heaven. You have become a child of the Most-High God. You are now Joint-Heirs with Jesus in the greatest love story ever told! This love story continues to unfold, as you can now share the love of God and Jesus with others!

Here I am! I stand at the door and knock. If anyone hears my voice and opens the door, I will come in and eat with that person, and they with me. (Revelation 3:20 NIV).

Unlocking Mystery #9

GOD IS LOVE

Reflect: Being honest, can you now look at yourself in the mirror and say: "I am Lovable". Remember this was the challenge from Chapter #1. If you can state this with confidence and genuine belief about yourself, this is wonderful. If you're still not able to do this, I challenge you to continue standing in front of the mirror every morning, looking at your beautiful face, smiling and saying the absolute truth, "I am Loveable".

I then challenge you to add this next phrase, "God Loves Me". If you do this for 21 days, you will begin to create a habit of saying and believing this profound truth.

Relate: On your QUEST to unlock the mysteries of humanity, have you come to a point of reconciliation with the Creator of the Universe and of every human being born or ever to be born on the planet? The deep void, the deep loneliness, the deep longing to love and to be loved can only be filled by God, His Son and the Holy Spirit - our Comforter. Being honest with yourself, where are you at in terms of reconciling this truth? Are you willing to accept the truth and follow the voice of Truth, or are you rejecting the truth and the voice of Truth that is ALL Love? Are you fully committed or only half in and half out?

If you were to die tomorrow, could you be certain as to where you would end up? There are only two places you can go after death – Heaven or Hell. You may think you can control your destiny by not believing. Unbelief does not provide you with control in death as to where you will end up for eternity. Instead, unbelief leads to deception, and it only provides you with one option – an eternal death sentence in Hell.

Respond: I challenge you today to take a leap of faith. I challenge you to walk in freedom and in the true conditional love that only comes from God our Father. If you are ready to take and accept God's unconditional love in all its glory and splendor, then pray this simple prayer:

#9: God Is Love

Lord Jesus, I accept you into my heart. I commit today you are my Lord and Savior and my Redeemer. Thank you for coming into my heart and for flooding me with a love that knows no limits. I now know and believe I will never be alone, as you promised to never leave me or forsake me. Amen. (John 3:16).

If you prayed this prayer and believed it in your heart, then you are born again. You will live in Heaven for all of eternity with God your Father, Jesus His Son, and the Holy Spirit who is your comforter.

Speak the Truth.

Just Say It! GOD IS LOVE - GOD LOVES YOU!

Dr. Cheryl Bauman

Afterword

My hope is by reading this book you have been able to unlock the mysteries to discovering real true love that only can be found in and through God. If there remain issues holding you back from experiencing God's true unconditional love, I encourage you to begin to work out the issues. This is vital as it will determine where you will spend eternity as well as how you can live a life of abundance, filled with God's unconditional love. Your QUEST can be over. Do not try to work out these issues on your own. I urge you to find a reliable counselor who believes in the true living word of God. Next, find a good Bible-based church. In addition, and most importantly, go to God! He is your healing source and the well spring of life produced through His eternal living water. You may need to pass through a season of change as you begin to alter the engrained patterns of how you think, speak, and act. Practice the new habits that have been encouraged within the contents of this book. The people closest to you may have difficulty adjusting to the new person you are becoming. It may take them some time to believe and trust the change in you is genuine.

Do not give up! I encourage you to be determined and to persevere in your QUEST to unlock the mysteries of humanity by finding true unconditional love. I guarantee your life will change forever! If you choose to walk and talk in *Agape* love, you also can change the lives of those around you forever, to leave a legacy of love! I urge you to be brave and courageous as you intentionally make the choice to alter your patterns of interactions with others. Allow God's relentless love to fill you from the top of your head to the tips of your toes. If you do, I can guarantee your QUEST will be over!

I encourage you to find a Bible-based church. A Bible-based church is a church that believes and teaches on the Good News of Jesus Christ that can only be found in the Bible.

> *You, my brothers and sisters, were called to be free. But do not use your freedom to indulge in sinful nature, rather serve one another in love. (Galatians 5:13 NIV)*

Dr. Cheryl Bauman

Bibliography

Adler, A. (1964). The individual psychology of Alfred Adler. In H.L. Ansbacher & R.R. Ansbacher (Eds.). Harper Torchbooks.

Adler, A. (1979). Superiority and social interest: A collection of later writings. In H.L. Ansbacher & R.R. Ansbacher (Eds.). W.W. Norton.

Cahn, J. (2016). The book of mysteries. Charisma Media/Charisma House Book Group.

Cahn, J. (2023). The Josiah manifesto: The ancient mystery & guide for the end times. Charisma Media.

Dobson, J.C. (2007). Love must be tough: New hope for marriages in crisis. Word Publishing.

Dweck, C.S. (2006). Mind-set: The new psychology of success. How we can learn to fulfill our potential. Random House.

Emerto, M. (2004). The hidden messages in water. Atria Books.

Graham, R. (2019). Forgiving myself, forgiving my father: An invitation to the miracle of forgiveness. Baker Books.

Kendall, R.T. (2001). Total forgiveness: Achieving God's greatest challenge. Charisma House.

Kendall, R.T. (2022). Fear: The good, the bad, and the ugly. Charisma House.

Krauss Whitbourne, S. (2010). The search for fulfillment: Revolutionary new research that reveals the secret to long-term happiness. Ballantine Books.

Leaf, C. (2015). Switch on your brain: The key to peak happiness, thinking and health. Baker Books.

Liddell, H.G., & Scott, R. (1940). A Greek English lexicon. Clarendon Press.

Loyola University Health System. (2014, February 6). What falling in love does to your heart and brain. ScienceDaily. https://www.sciencedaily.com/releases/2014/02/140206155244.htm

Mehler, J., Lambertz, G., Juszyk, P.W., & Amiel-Tison, C. (1986). Discrimination de la langue maternelle par le nouveau- né [Discrimination of the mother tongue by the newborn]. Comptes rendus de l'Académie es sciences. Série 3, Sciences de la Vie, 303(15), 637-640.

Merriam-Webster. (2019). Merriam-Webster's collegiate dictionary (11th ed.). Merriam-Webster, Inc.

Meyer, J. (2012). Change your words, change your life: Understanding the power of every word you speak. FaithWords.

Meyer, J. (2018). Living a life you love: Embracing the adventure of being led by the Holy Spirit. FaithWords.

Meyer, J. (2022). Loving people who are hard to love: Transforming your world by learning to love unconditionally. Hachette Book Group, Inc.

Moon, C., Lagercrantz, H., & Kuhl, P.K. (2013). Language experienced in utero affects vowel perception after birth: A two-country study. Acta Pediatrica, 102(2), 156-160.

Newberg, A., & Waldman, M.R. (2012). Words can change your brain: 12 conversation strategies to build trust, resolve conflict, and increase intimacy. Hudson Street Press.Osteen, J. (2007). Become a better you: 7 keys to improving your life every day. Free Press.

Osteen, J. (2015). The power of I am: Two words that will change your life today. FaithWords.

Osteen, J. (2018). Next level thinking: 10 Powerful thoughts for a successful and abundant life. FaithWords.
Ray, R., & Dash, A. (2019). 96 words for love. Jimmy Patterson Books.

Walsh, S. (2017). In the middle of the mess: Strength for this beautiful, broken life. Thomas Nelson.

Walsh, S. (2018). It's okay not to be okay: How to move forward one day at a time. Baker Books.

Walsh, S. (2019). Praying women: How to pray when you don't know what to say. Baker Books.

Warburg, O. H. (1928). The chemical constitution of respiration ferment. Science, 68, 437-443.

Wilkins, R., & Gareis, E. (2005). Emotion expression and the locution "I love you": A cross-cultural study. International Journal of Intercultural Relations, 30, 51-75. http://www.elsevier.com/locate/ijintrel

Dr. Cheryl Bauman

Dr. Cheryl Bauman is available for author appearances or interviews. For more information, contact us at info@advbooks.com

For additional copies of this book, visit advbookstore.com

advbookstore.com
we bring dreams to life ™

www.ingramcontent.com/pod-product-compliance
Lightning Source LLC
Chambersburg PA
CBHW070640160426
43194CB00009B/1526